GREAT WHOLE GRAIN
B·R·E·A·D·S

Also by Beatrice Ojakangas

GREAT WHOLE GRAIN
B·R·E·A·D·S

BEATRICE OJAKANGAS

Illustrations by Susan Gaber

University of Minnesota Press
Minneapolis / London

First published by E. P. Dutton in 1984
First University of Minnesota Press edition, 2002

Published by the University of Minnesota Press
111 Third Avenue South, Suite 290
Minneapolis, MN 55401-2520
http://www.upress.umn.edu

Library of Congress Cataloging-in-Publication Data

Ojakangas, Beatrice A.
    Great whole grain breads / Beatrice Ojakangas.— 1st University of Minnesota Press ed.
        p. cm.
    Originally published: New York : Dutton, 1984.
    Includes index.
    ISBN 0-8166-4150-1 (pbk. : alk. paper)
        1. Bread. I. Title.

    TX769.O384 2002
    641.8'15—dc21   2002072664

Printed in the United States of America on acid-free paper

The University of Minnesota is an equal-opportunity educator and employer.

17 16 15 14 13 12 11 10   10 9 8 7 6 5 4 3 2

To

Theodore Luoma,

my father, who is lovingly called "Isä" ("Father" in Finnish)

and who has always been a devotee of rye bread,

and

Esther Luoma,

my mother, whose hands have kneaded thousands of loaves

which fed not only the family but anybody who appeared

at the farmhouse door.

CONTENTS

ACKNOWLEDGMENTS

A portion of this work originally appeared in *Gourmet* magazine, February 1976, as well as in *Bon Appetit,* Spring 1983.

I would like to acknowledge the home economists at the North Dakota State Wheat Commission, the Kansas Wheat Flour Institute, Red Star Yeast, and Pillsbury Mills for valuable information.

A big thank you to hundreds of friends, relatives, and fellow home economists, writers and bread bakers (too many to name) who have encouraged me over the years. Thanks to the editors at *Sunset* magazine, and to Carol Peterson, who first introduced me to California sourdough.

Thanks to the home economists in Finland at the Finnish Institute of Bread, enthusiasts of the "Whole Grain."

Special thanks to my own husband Richard, who tasted almost every bread in this book, and to my editor Diane Harris, who encouraged the writing of this book, and who patiently clipped and pasted and edited the manuscript.

FOREWORD

My mother tells me I was a hungry baby. Before I was one year old, I would wake in the middle of the night and eat a snack of rye bread she had placed beside the bed each evening—one hundred percent stone-ground rye bread. Why rye bread? Well, my family is of Finnish extraction, and to the Finns, bread isn't bread unless it's rye. What's more, the loaf had to be round and crusty, with fork holes lacing the top. It was always made from rye *meal*, a coarse form of rye flour. It had no sweetening in it or seeds, or orange peel, or other fancy ingredients.

All through my years of childhood and adolescence, it was this hearty bread that my mother baked for our family at least twice a week. I remember that the rich aroma of freshly baked rye bread greeted us as we alighted from the big yellow school bus a full quarter of a mile away. We would race madly toward the white farmhouse, and sure enough, on the kitchen table were sixteen or twenty plump loaves of Finnish rye. The loaves would still be warm and moist with the butter glaze glistening on the top.

As soon as I turned twelve, I joined the 4-H Club, enamored with foods and cooking and enticed by the prize of a trip to the Minnesota State Fair. Carried along by enthusiasm and hard work, I won trips to the fair in St. Paul, with a chiffon cake demonstration and then with a cheese soufflé presentation. The following year, Isä (Finnish for "Father"), insisted that I compete with some "real food."

"Like what?" I asked.

"Like good rye bread!" was his reply. The bread-making part was a breeze, but I had to brace up for the "grilling" by the judges and audience on topics such as yeast, flour milling, dough handling, dough temperatures, even the history of bread baking. The project turned out to be worthwhile. This time I won the trip to the state fair *and* a National Grand Championship!

During those years of learning I discovered that the bread we ate at home, with its sandy-colored crumb and rich honey-hued crust, was not the only rye bread that existed. Sometimes my mother would experiment with other grains and flavors, though never so seriously as to exclude our old favorite. Often I would discover a delicious new loaf. I loved the idea of new whole grain breads, and enjoyed my explorations. In our community there were Poles, Bohemians, Germans, Russians, Czechs, as well as Norwegians, Swedes, and Danes. They all made their own style of whole grain bread. Through their breads I came to learn more about the fascinating diversity of the people around me whom I knew and loved.

Some years later, as a bride on a U.S. Air Force base in England, I found it difficult to duplicate my favorite breads because whole grains were hard to find. As a compromise, I purchased cornmeal at the PX and made anadama bread. Because of the molasses it looked like dark bread and was satisfying. Then one day I noticed some entry blanks for the annual Pillsbury Bake-Off pinned on a bulletin board at the Officers' Club. Naturally I took one home. After discussing possible entries with my husband, I came upon the idea of making a layered cheese sandwich with my anadama bread. The bread was delicious and since the postmark deadline was the next day, I simply guessed at a few minor changes I wanted to make and popped the recipe in the mail.

Back home in the United States, I was no sooner settled than I got a phone call from the local Pillsbury representative. "Congratulations! You're one of the one hundred finalists in the Bake-Off!" Could

I go to the Bake-Off in Los Angeles? Well, this was Big News in Floodwood, Minnesota! At my family's urging I went off to Los Angeles and to the Second Grand Prize of $5,000. The winning recipe, "Cheesy Picnic Loaf," as I made it, is on page 257. This was the beginning. Now, many hundreds and thousands of loaves later, I've gathered them into this volume. I hope you will enjoy them just as much as we have.

INTRODUCTION

Bread, whether whole grain or not, has two basic ingredients: flour and water. Indeed, the simplest unleavened breads, such as the tortillas of Mexico, are merely mixtures of these two ingredients—sometimes with salt added—that are baked on a griddle. But when most of us think of bread, what we're thinking of are yeast-leavened loaves. Leavening not only gives the bread more lightness and shape, it also adds an interesting taste. Breads can also be raised by means of sourdough starter, eggs, or baking powder. All have their distinct qualities, and all can produce delectable loaves. I have included a variety of every kind in this collection.

My search for whole grain breads for this book began by gathering up ideas, notes, and recipes I had collected over the years. Many of these recipes came from old church cookbooks, notes written at bake sales, yellowed tearsheets from newspaper and magazine articles, friends, relatives, and ethnic books from many parts of the country. Almost every one of these recipes needed "work" in one way or another. Often old recipes are incomplete, listing only ingredients and a baking temperature. Others were in such large quantities that only a farmer with a dozen helping hands could have eaten all that bread!

WHOLE GRAINS FOR WHOLESOME EATING

Bake bread and you've got a meal! Just the mention of whole grain breads to most people creates an image of wholesome, healthy eating.

Golden brown loaves of hearty wheat or rye or oats not only taste good, they're good for you. Home-baked breads with whole grain flours add the fiber lacking in many of our diets. This fiber comes in the form of bran contained in whole grains, and the bran adds bulk to the diet without adding calories.

Nutritionists are the first to admit that there is much more to human nourishment than the vitamins and minerals known today. Those that we do know about are important, but there are so many others, such as trace elements and other naturally occurring nutritional factors which scientists have not yet studied. It is not enough to say that flour has been "enriched." Enrichment is by itself a good thing, but all that has been added back to enriched flour are those elements which have been identified as "lost" in the milling and processing of the grain. This means that it is nutritionally wise to consume whole grains when there is a choice.

Freshly baked whole grain breads can be the focus and theme of an economical but marvelous party menu. Serve loaves on boards along with butter, cheese, lettuce, tomatoes, onions, avocados, pickles, sprouts, and other raw vegetables. Have guests slice their own bread and spread and top the slices themselves. Provide hot or chilled beverages depending on the season.

STAYING FIT WITH WHOLE GRAIN BREADS

Even though many of us think of bread as fattening, it also represents to us all that is warm, healthful, homey, good, and nutritious. Just a few years ago people actually felt a bit guilty eating a slice of bread, a crusty roll, or a hearty sandwich. But recent nutritional studies have laid that guilt to rest. We now know that this is one instance in which what we like likes us. It's not necessary to sneak a piece of cinnamon-raisin bread as a midnight snack or to relegate a rye bread sandwich to a once-a-week treat.

The recent craze for fitness and sound nutrition has sparked a new awareness of what we are eating. But did you know that whole grain breads fit right in? A slice of whole grain bread ranges in calories from 70 for whole wheat or cracked wheat to 140 for Swedish limpa. Usually it is what you spread on the bread that triples or even quadruples the calorie count. We would do well to learn to eat our bread the European way—without any spread at all. The French, for example, eat their wonderful breads without butter.

New revised dietary standards call for less protein and fat. In the United States, we have consumed quantities of fat and protein way beyond even the older, higher recommendations. Recent studies have shown that eating too much animal protein (and along with that, the fat that accompanies it), and too many refined carbohydrates in the form of refined sugars and starches can lead to serious health problems. Cancer, heart disease, high blood pressure, diabetes, obesity, and other modern medical problems have been linked with overconsumption of these foods. Not only is human health risked, but processing these foods is ecologically and economically expensive. The answer is to eat more fresh vegetables, fresh fruits, and whole grains. To gain a healthy balance, we can begin by eating rich-tasting, healthy, whole grain breads.

How wonderful to think that we can and should be eating our daily bread! Whole grain breads are not only loaded with complex carbohydrates but also with B vitamins (riboflavin, niacin, thiamin) and iron. Also they are usually low in fat or cholesterol and always high in fiber.

Whole grains also contain protein. (Vegetable protein is less expensive to produce than is animal protein. Combining the two makes the best of both worlds, which translates to a more varied and exciting diet for all of us.) With a new, healthy balance of food we can cut down on protein we once ate in superabundance. Red meats, which constitute a large portion of our dietary protein, are also very high in fat and calories. We do not need to eliminate them entirely (although it wouldn't hurt us), but we should cut down on them. (Whole grain breads can be the basis of a meal rather than just an accompaniment.)

Our biological heritage has developed in us an ability to utilize a variety of foods to keep ourselves at the peak of fitness. If we include a higher proportion of the complex carbohydrates—whole grains, fresh vegetables, and fruits—we will feel better and our bodies will function better. At the same time, we should exclude excess fat, refined sugar, and highly processed foods.

Bulk for bulk, whole grain breads have about half the calories of traditional breads, supply the more preferable plant protein, and offer valuable fiber to the diet. If we also add more vegetable-based dishes such as soups and salads to our menus, our diet will be lighter, we will shed pounds, and we feel healthier.

LEARNING TO BAKE WHOLE GRAIN BREAD

In my youth, bread baking was a huge chore. On our farm we baked fifteen to twenty loaves at a time, two or three times a week. It was part of our household routine. My mother had her "bread pan," a big metal bowl that held about ten gallons. When the dough had risen until huge and mounded, she pinched off loaves and filled pans; fired up the stove and put in the bread; and as the crusty loaves came out of the oven, we brushed them with butter and set them to cool on the counters. Freshly baked bread covered every workspace in the kitchen. But our family was big, and there were hired men to feed. In addition, a large share of our daily nutrition came from whole grain bread.

As families shrank and women went to work outside the home, bread baking fell out of fashion. General cookbooks published from the mid 1940s through the 60s skimped on yeast bread recipes if they included any at all. Quick breads flourished, and many innovative recipes were developed, especially by the test kitchens of food companies who enticed readers to make nut breads, coffeecakes, and muffins with a great variety of their ingredients. But the bread-baking revolution has begun, and bread baking is not a lost art. In fact, it is coming back with imagination and character.

Yeast bread recipes today serve a different purpose from those of two generations ago, when recipes were written with ingredients in such massive quantities that the whole operation was a major production. Today baking a loaf of bread can be as manageable a task as mixing up a batch of cookies. And the results can be even more satisfying. Also you can do it if you have very limited time, because of the great variety of short-cut mixing and dough-handling techniques that have been developed. Recipes now yield one or two loaves of bread rather than a dozen. With the food processor, you can mix up a loaf of bread in seconds (see special instructions on page 18).

Yeast doughs seem to present the greatest challenge to the beginning bread baker, often seeming intimidating at first glance. True, there are basic techniques to be learned, but they are simple and can be mastered with just one or two bakings. Breads made with whole grain flours have properties that white breads do not, however. They tend to rise more slowly and generally do not achieve the lightness white breads do. They may brown more quickly than white loaves baked at the same temperatures. When you use herbs and spices in a whole grain loaf you may need slightly more than you would in a white loaf, because the whole grain flour has a more robust flavor. These differences can be considered problems, but only if you are surprised by them. With the aid of this book, you will be equipped to handle every stage of the whole grain bread baking process, and alerted to those steps where special care must be taken to assure delectable loaves.

WHERE DO YOU BUY WHOLE GRAINS AND WHOLE GRAIN FLOURS?

Just a few years ago it would have been impossible to devote a complete book to whole grain breads without including an extensive list of mail-order sources, so that readers would be able to find the ingredients. Even today, you don't find much of a selection in the baking section of many supermarkets. A supermarket manager is happy to stock new items if he thinks they will sell; today, however in most cities, there are also whole-food co-ops, nutrition centers, and natural foods stores which stock a plentiful supply and variety of whole grain flours. But in case you don't have such a store in your neighborhood, I've included a list of mail-order flour mills and natural foods stores.

Unless I'm planning to do extensive baking, I've found it practical to buy one-pound packages of a variety of whole grain flours, and keep them in the refrigerator. Whole grains contain more of the natural oils and can become rancid at warm temperatures. Unless they are stored in a dry place, these flours or grains will absorb moisture, which can throw off the quantity of flour required in a recipe. When you refrigerate flours, put the entire bag into a covered cannister, container, or plastic bag to prevent absorption.

Any special instructions required for using certain whole grain flours will appear either in the individual recipes (when the information applies only to that particular bread) or in the introductions to the chapters on whole wheat, rye, corn, oat breads, and so forth.

USING WHOLE GRAIN FLOURS IN BREADS

ACTIVATING THE GLUTEN

Of all the grains, wheat has the most gluten, a key protein in flour. Rye has some, but much less than wheat. Other grains may be high in protein, but they don't have gluten. And it is the gluten in bread doughs that forms the elastic meshwork in a well-kneaded dough. This mesh traps the carbon dioxide produced by the action of the yeast and sugar in the flour. This fermentation forms little bubbles in the dough as it rises. In the baked loaf the bubbles are visible as holes, and we call this its texture.

The more thoroughly a dough is kneaded, and the more times it is "punched down" after rising, the more the bubbles are broken down into finer ones. For the finest texture in bread, it is important to thoroughly knead the dough and to let it rise once or twice before the final shaping and rising prior to baking. Batter breads, which may have only one rising, usually have a coarser texture.

COMBINING FLOURS

Unlike white flour, whole wheat flour includes the germ and the bran, and so it has proportionally less gluten. Other whole grain flours have even less gluten. As a result, loaves made completely from whole grain flours have a dense, heavy texture. In fact, without the addition of some white flour, such breads are often *too* heavy and dense. So most of the bread recipes in this book include about 50 percent white flour.

When I shop for flour I usually look for unbleached all-purpose flour and always check the nutrition label for protein content. Because all-purpose flours are a blend of hard and soft wheats, the gluten will vary. All-purpose flour which contains 13 or 14 grams of protein per cup is better for bread baking because it has more gluten. All-purpose flour which contains 14 grams per cup may also be labeled "Bread Flour." All purpose flours that list 11 or 12 grams per cup are better for cakes, cookies and pastries. For ease of use, I keep them in separate containers in my cupboard.

BREAD FLOUR: Bread flour is made from hard wheat which is unique in that it contains a high level of gluten. This type of flour recently reappeared in many supermarkets. Home bakers who make a great deal of bread will find that bread flour will yield a better volume, a tenderer crust and an evenly distributed, finer grain. Bread flour is best suited for yeast breads. A longer kneading time is recommended to fully develop the gluten, and less flour may be necessary for a smooth, elastic dough.

As a general rule, when the flour mixture in a whole grain bread is 50 percent white or whole wheat flour, the gluten content will be sufficient to have a well-risen loaf. For a lighter texture, all or part of the 50 percent should be bread flour or unbleached all-purpose flour. A 50 percent whole wheat flour mixture makes a good bread, too, but expect a denser texture.

You will notice throughout this book that most recipes call for wheat flour in addition to other whole grain flours. The inclusion of wheat flour is for its gluten content, while the other whole grains are used for flavor. The varieties possible are almost endless!

Only one yeast bread in this book is totally without wheat flour—that one is made with 100 percent rye flour. To make this rye bread, you must provide long souring and rising periods to develop both the gluten and the flavor of rye. Rye flour rather quickly produces a pleasantly sour flavor, and 100 percent rye bread has a close, heavy texture, but should not be doughy.

MIXING AND KNEADING WHOLE GRAIN BREAD DOUGHS

After adding the smaller of the two quantities of flour in a recipe (most recipes specify flour amounts such as 4 to 4½ or 5 to 5½ cups), mix the dough thoroughly with a spoon and then with your hands. Expect the dough to feel "tackier" or stickier than white bread doughs, even after you have kneaded for as long as 10 minutes or even for the full length of time specified. If you're used to working with white flour this may make you feel that the dough is not properly kneaded. But when whole grain doughs feel moist they will produce a much lighter loaf than those that feel drier yet actually have too much flour kneaded in. Resist the temptation to keep adding flour until you have a smooth, unsticky dough; if you don't resist, you are very likely to end up with a dry loaf that is just about right as a doorstop.

But how can you tell when the dough has been kneaded enough? In spite of the tackiness, the dough will have a "springiness," and it should feel smooth, well mixed, and without dry lumps. If you are in doubt, simply let the dough rest for 15 minutes. Then when you return to it, if the dough is holding its own shape (rather than spreading out over the countertop), there is enough flour in it, and the kneading has been sufficient. Sometimes I just get tired of working the dough (after 10 minutes), and put it into the greased bowl anyway, remembering the adage my mother always quoted, that "It is better to leave the dough too wet than too dry!"

This is just one example of a fact I've long believed—that whole grain bread doughs are tolerant. It pays to be a relaxed bread baker. Remember you are in control. There is no great urgency to knead the dough quickly. The slower the better! Let it rest a few minutes (most of my recipes recommend 15 minutes). It can actually rest for a couple of hours. Using the "resting" trick, you can actually "force" a 100 percent rye dough to work. (See the recipe for Finnish Sour Rye Bread, page 203, and for 100 Percent Rye Bread, page 85.) If the dough is rather moist, during that resting time the gluten will have a chance to absorb moisture, which will make subsequent kneading easier. Once you have added the recommended amount of flour to the dough, let it rest again if it still feels sticky. Scrape the board clean, rub it lightly with oil, then knead the dough on the oiled surface. You may be surprised at how much better the dough feels when it has a very light coating of oil.

HOW TO KNEAD YEAST DOUGHS

Kneading whole grain bread doughs may seem to take more patience than plain white doughs. If the beginning mixture is very sticky and heavy, I often start out by grasping the mixture in my hands and squeezing it through my fingers to determine when the flour and liquid are pretty evenly mixed. After that, I scrape my hands clean (they clean easily if you rub a bit of flour into them), and let the dough rest a few minutes.

Following the traditional kneading method is still my favorite. Spread a work surface—a clean countertop is just fine—with a dusting of flour. Turn the dough out onto the flour and scrape the bowl clean. *Gather the lumpy dough into a mass.* If it seems that the entire batch is way too dry, sprinkle a little water over and let it be absorbed. Then, using a scraper, *fold one side of the mass of dough over onto the other. Repeat that again from one-fourth the distance around the dough.* It is easiest

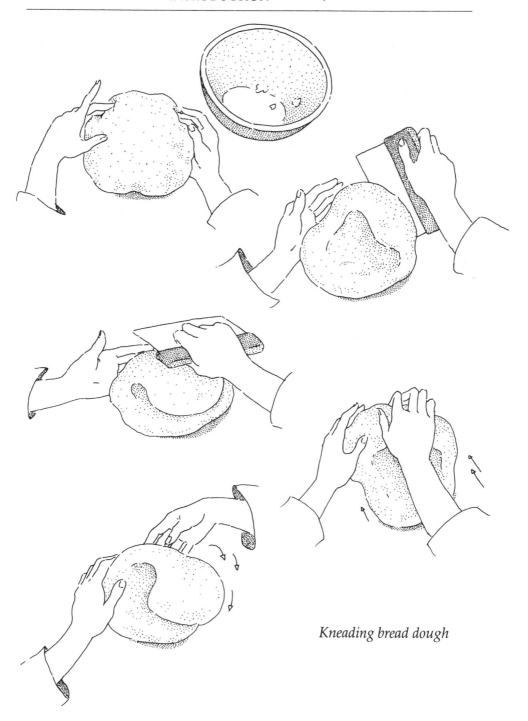

Kneading bread dough

to turn the mass of dough over and fold it over onto itself. By the fourth turn, the dough has taken on a ball-like shape. With dry, floured hands, begin to fold the dough over onto itself, make a quarter turn, fold again. Make a quarter turn, and continue to repeat this, adding just a sprinkle of flour as needed if it is very moist. If the work surface gets a suedelike coating of dough, scrape it up with the dough scraper (my favorite flat-edged tool) and work the scrapings into the dough. Once the dough feels springy, smooth, and well mixed (it will take ten minutes for a batch that makes two loaves of bread), let it rest fifteen minutes while you wash the bowl and grease it. (Although I often do not mention this in the recipes, I like to scrape the counter clean and then lightly oil the surface. Then I give the dough a couple more kneading turns, just to get the satiny feel, with lightly oiled hands.) The dough goes into the bowl, then gets turned over to lightly grease both sides (so its top won't dry while it rises). Cover the bowl with plastic wrap and place it in the sunshine for the quickest rising.

HOW MUCH FLOUR IS ENOUGH?

You may notice a great difference in the quantities of flour a dough will "take" from season to season. In the climate where I live, it's very dry and cold in the wintertime. The flour, too, is very dry. Sometimes, after we have gone through a cold, dry spell, I use as much as a cupful less in a recipe that calls for 5 cups of flour. Summertime humidity, on the other hand, causes flour to absorb moisture, so that along with the flour you are adding an unknown quantity of liquid to the dough. The difference generally isn't enough to alter other ingredients, but you may be surprised at the discrepency in the amount of flour you use. For that reason, all doughs made by the hand-kneaded method always call for a fluctuating quantity of flour.

ABOUT YEAST

Not long ago, I pulled up to a stop sign on a busy street in Duluth and casually glanced over to the car next to me. The woman driver was waving frantically, and I thought she might be in some trouble, so I rolled down my window. She shouted excitedly, "My husband just started making bread and it's been great, but last time it didn't rise. What did he do wrong?"

"He probably killed the yeast," I called out as I pulled away from the intersection.

Because yeast is a living plant, which must grow to produce the carbon dioxide that will be entrapped in the gluten meshwork of well-kneaded dough, it must be treated like a plant. The water or other liquid used with yeast must be neither too hot nor too cold; the correct range is between 105° and 115° F. If you dissolve yeast in water with a temperature lower than 105° F., it does not get an adequate chance to start growing. Consequently, the yeast is "stunted," especially if the remaining ingredients are cold and the temperature of the air in the kitchen is also cold. On the other hand, if the temperature of the water is higher than 115° F., you'll kill the yeast, because high temperatures tend to "scald" the plant. In either extreme, the result is bread that either rises very slowly or doesn't rise at all.

One exception is when yeast has already been mixed with a part of the flour. In this case the temperature of the liquid added can be 120° to 130° F. One problem with these generally quicker methods is that if you are using yeast that is coarser than ordinary packaged yeast (for instance, the bulk yeast sold in natural food stores) the yeast doesn't adequately dissolve, resulting in slow rising.

THE NEW YEAST

Recently the two major yeast companies, Red Star and Fleishmann's, have introduced packaged yeast which rises quickly. This new strain of yeast makes dough rise faster. But there are some cautions! Be sure to read the package directions before using the yeast. One of the brands cannot be rehydrated in warm water, as most of my recipes direct (it can only be used in the method where the yeast is mixed first with part of the flour and hot water added to the mixture). The other can be used either way, but it is recommended that you add a bit of sugar to the water when dissolving the yeast. The water temperature is the same. The recommended water temperature is the same—105° to 115° F. Properly dissolved and mixed into a whole grain bread dough, these products cause the dough to rise faster. Begin to check the dough after half the normal rising time is up.

GETTING WHOLE GRAIN BREAD DOUGH TO RISE

Whole grain bread doughs often take longer to rise simply because of their weight. There are two basic remedies—one lies with the mixing of the dough, the other with the temperature of the room. Some people have trouble getting their bread dough to rise because they have worked too much flour into the dough. Never add significantly more flour to the dough than the top amount within the range suggested. As I've pointed out, whole grain bread doughs feel sticky even after they are, in fact, well kneaded and already have the right amount of flour. It is a consistency you must become accustomed to, especially if you have been a white bread baker all your life. Bread that is too dry will not rise.

If you do have a dough that does not rise, however, you can correct the situation. Use your food processor. Cut the dough into chunks—four chunks if it is a dough that will yield two loaves of bread, two chunks if it will yield one loaf. Tear the chunks apart and put one at a time into the food processor with the steel blade in place. Sprinkle 1 tablespoon of water over it. Turn the processor on and let it go until the dough has absorbed the water. If it still is stiff, repeat, adding another tablespoon of water. But if it seems springy and moist, simply process the remaining chunks of dough. If you do not have a food processor, you can accomplish the same effect by hand. After cutting the dough into chunks, sprinkle each with one tablespoon of water at a time, and with your fingers squeeze the water into the dough. This may be messy at first, but eventually you can get the water worked into the dough. I might add that this is excellent therapy!

The ideal room temperature for bread dough is 80° to 85° F., however, the temperature can be as high as 100° to 110° F.! Nowadays many of us keep our homes quite cool in fall and winter, especially during that time of year when we are most interested in bread baking. If you have trouble with slow-rising bread, it may be because the temperature in your kitchen is too low. Find a cozy, warm place in which to place the bread for both the first and final risings. Where could this be in your home? Purchase a small stand-up thermometer and check several locations. Here are some suggestions:

1. On top of the water heater. Even energy-saver water heaters are warm on the top.

2. A high shelf in the kitchen. Heat rises, and tops of cabinets are often warmer than counters.

3. A sunny window. To enhance the warmth of a sunny location, invert a glass bowl over the bread dough and make a mini greenhouse. This greenhouse could be right on your kitchen countertop. Leave the kneaded dough on an oiled surface, and invert a glass mixing bowl over it.

4. On top of the refrigerator. Most refrigerators are heat producers, and you can take advantage of that if there is enough clearance between the refrigerator and the cupboard above.

USING A MICROWAVE OVEN

1. Place dough in an oiled glass or pottery bowl.
2. Cover dough with a well-dampened terry towel.
3. Place covered dough in a glass pie pan filled with warm water.
4. Microwave on LOW 5 minutes at a time, feeling the dough with your hands between each 5-minute portion. The dough should feel just slightly warmer than body temperature.

USING A REGULAR OVEN (*Pay particular attention to the time so you don't allow the oven to get too hot!*)

1. Turn oven on to 300° F. for 2 minutes. Turn oven off.
2. Wrap bowl of dough in a damp dish towel.
3. Place in oven. Close door; let rise until doubled.

ABOUT RISEN DOUGH

All of the recipes in this book specify dough that has risen until doubled in bulk or until "puffy" looking. If the dough has risen the recommended length of time and does not look doubled or puffy, give it more time; it may take longer—up to twice the allotted time. More likely, it will need only 50 percent more time than originally stated. Rising times are closely related to room temperature and temperatures of the doughs (dough temperature is affected also by the temperature of the ingredients you have mixed together). Be sure to use the recommended temperature for dissolving the yeast, and wait the recommended five minutes for the yeast to foam up. This assures you that the yeast is fresh and properly activated. If yeast does not foam up in five minutes, either the yeast was old, or the water temperature was too cold or too hot. Start again.

SHAPING WHOLE GRAIN BREADS—STANDARD PANS AND FANCY SHAPES

Shaping doughs is one of the most rewarding and enjoyable parts of baking whole grain breads. Although whole grain breads in simple shapes are wonderfully appealing just as they are, when they are handled by a fanciful baker they can take on really festive airs!

I love to shape a dough into a braided wreath, for instance, bake it around a cake pan, and serve it with either a ripe whole brie cheese, a molded cheese spread, or a vegetable or chicken liver pate in the center. A wonderfully rich yeast-risen cornbread shaped as a turtle, in the Mexican style, makes a great accompaniment to a Tex-Mex meal of chili or enchiladas. As much as possible, I have included unusual shaping methods for these breads, but almost any bread can be shaped any of these ways!

The following are standard bread pan sizes and also some unusual pans, plus some alternative ways to shape breads.

1. Standard pans for baking breads are either the large 9 x 5-inch (2-pound loaf pan capacity) or the smaller 8½ x 4½-inch (1½ pounds). My favorite is the smaller because of the slice size and the appearance of the whole loaf. However, I often like to bake little loaves (5½ x 3) especially for gifts.

STANDARD SIZES OF LOAF PANS: 9″ x 5″ (2-pound capacity)
8½″ x 4½″ (1½-pound capacity)
5½″ x 3″ (½-pound capacity)

For the prettiest shape, the pan should be filled about ⅔ full of dough before rising, and the dough should rise to fill the pan. In baking the loaf rises and humps up above the edges of the pan to make an attractive shape.

2. Many whole grain breads are more attractive when baked in a round pan rather than in an oblong one. I use a standard, 8 or 9-inch round cake pan and shape the loaf into a ball, placing it into the greased cake pan. This is an option for any loaf which otherwise

would be baked in an oblong pan. For variety, the tops of the loaves may be slashed or snipped, covered with various toppings, or glazed with egg white and sprinkled with nuts, seeds, or whole grain flour.

3. Fancy tube cake pans of various sizes may be used for breads. They are available in several sizes, but regardless of size, should be filled about ¾ full with dough, which will rise to make an attractive loaf.

4. Commercial cans that fruits, vegetables, sauces and tuna are packed in can also be optional baking pans, used for special effects. I like to bake large muffins in 8-ounce tomato sauce cans or in 7-ounce tuna cans. Coffee cans make attractive breads, and the Finnish Hop-Flavored Easter bread (page 143) is a bread I often bake in a 2-pound coffee can. Crocks and potter's pots are great for baking bread, too, as the crusts tend to bake thick and crunchy. These make nice gifts.

5. Cookie sheets covered with parchment paper can be used for free-form loaves and fancy shapes. In many of the recipes I call for covering baking sheets with parchment paper. The quality of the baked bread is much improved by the paper, as the bottom crust is always more evenly baked. Parchment paper "breathes" and helps to avoid the over-baking of the bottom, plus it avoids a sticking problem when loaves are brushed with a glaze that runs down the sides of the loaves and often sticks to the pan.

BAKING PAN MATERIALS

Pans made of a shiny metal (or new pans) reflect heat, and the baked bread may have a browned top but pale crust on the rest of the loaf. Seasoned bread pans or black pans will create loaves with a uniformly well-browned crust. Sometimes when using black bread pans you may have to reduce the baking time and temperature. Because black pans absorb more heat, they "increase" the baking temperature. This is an advantage when baking crusty loaves such as French bread or popovers. Glass and pottery also absorb and hold heat, so when you bake in pans made of these materials, reduce the oven temperature by 25° F. to insure even baking. Breads that require long, slow baking, such as heavy pumpernickel, do not bake evenly in black, glass, or pottery pans.

OVENS AND OVEN TEMPERATURES

If the temperature of the oven is too hot, the outside of the loaf is done before the interior is completely baked. If this happens, reduce the oven temperature, and cover the loaf with foil (shiny side up), to prevent overbrowning. Bake until the loaf tests done.

If the temperature is too low, the dough dries out. The temperature in the interior of the loaf does not rise quickly enough to set the gluten and caramelize the starch before the water is evaporated. This makes a loaf that collapses and is not browned.

In yeast breads, the first quick rising of the dough in the oven is called "oven spring." This takes place during the first 10 to 12 minutes of baking. This causes the gluten strands to stretch, shred, and break, usually above the edge of a bread pan, giving the loaf its characteristic shape and bulge at the top. Oven heat also kills the yeast and evaporates the alcohol and leavening gasses.

An uneven oven can be the culprit when loaves are browned on top and white on the bottom. Or, when loaves do not bake evenly side to side. Uneven heat in ovens can be a built-in problem with the oven itself, or it can be a result of opening the oven door too often to check the progress of the baking. Whenever you open the oven door, the heat from the front of the oven escapes very quickly, and can lower the oven temperature as much as 50° to 100° F. in the front, leaving that part of the oven cooler than the back. Heat loss can vary depending on the warmth (or coolness) of your kitchen.

TESTING FOR DONENESS

My favorite way to test for doneness with heavy loaves, such as the whole grain breads in this book, is to run a long wooden skewer right through the center of the thickest part of the bread. If there is any "drag" on the skewer as you pull it out, or if there is dough on the skewer, the bread is not done.

If the bread is not done, but looks brown enough already, you can cover the loaf with foil with the shiny side up, to prevent further browning, and continue to bake until a skewer comes out clean.

LOADING THE OVEN

Bread bakes the best when you use just one level at a time, and the rack is placed as near the center as possible. If you must bake on two racks at one time, place the oven racks before preheating the oven so that all the loaves you plan to bake at once will fit between the racks. When you place the risen loaves into the oven, stagger them to allow for heat circulation. It helps to switch the upper loaves to the lower rack, and vice versa, halfway through baking to insure even top and bottom browning.

Keep in mind that a clean oven will maintain temperature and reflect heat more accurately than a dirty one.

BAKING AT HIGH ALTITUDES

Yeast doughs rise more rapidly at high altitudes; therefore, less yeast may be used. Because water boils at a lower temperature at high altitudes, baking times and temperatures must be increased to bake bread properly. Information about how much to increase baking times and temperatures can be obtained at no or low cost from the University of Wyoming Agricultural Experiment Station, Laramie, Wyoming, from the Colorado Agricultural Experiment Station, Fort Collins, Colorado, or from the U.S. Department of Agriculture in Washington, D.C.

TROUBLESHOOTING BREAD BAKING PROBLEMS

When baking whole grain breads, problems sometimes arise that are not the same as in baking white breads.

LOAF HAS POOR SHAPE: Too much dough for the pan; improper or uneven shaping, or insufficient rising time.

LOAF IS TOO SMALL: Too much salt; not enough yeast; too cool dough mixture to allow for yeast development; insufficient rising; oven temperature too high.

LOAF DID NOT RISE: Yeast killed in too hot liquid when mixing loaf; dough mixture had insufficient gluten (too much low gluten flour in proportion to wheat flour in recipe).

LOAF IS PALE: Little or no sugar; dough temperature during mixing and rising was too high (the yeast consumed the sugar and starches, not allowing enough for caramelization in the baking process); oven temperature too low.

CRUMB IS TOO TOUGH: Insufficient kneading; insufficient rising time; overbaking.

BIG AIR BUBBLE UNDER TOP CRUST: Dough too stiff; insufficient rising time; crusting of dough during rising.

CRUST TOO THICK: Overbaked; oven temperature too low; rising time too long (it formed crust before baking).

TEXTURE STREAKED: Improper mixing of ingredients; not enough kneading; too much flour used in shaping loaf.

COARSE TEXTURE: Dough too soft; temperature of dough during mixing and rising too high; rising time too long; baking temperature too low.

YEASTY FLAVOR: Rising time too long; temperature of dough during mixing and kneading too high; too much yeast.

FOOD PROCESSOR METHOD OF MIXING
AND KNEADING DOUGHS

You can convert almost any recipe to be made with a food processor if you understand the limitations of the machine and the procedures it will perform to make the process simpler.

Look at the recipe. A recipe that calls for 2½ cups of flour and about 1 cup of liquid is the right quantity for a standard food processor. If you have a special dough-mixing blade, you may increase the amount of flour in the mixture by 1 cup. If your food processor is a large model and you have the dough-mixing blade, you may successfully use recipes that call for 5 to 5½ cups flour.

Here's how to convert a standard bread recipe for the food processor:

1. In a small cup, dissolve yeast in the small quantity of water called for in the recipe. If desired, add a bit of sugar to the mixture to make the yeast foam more readily.

2. Place the dry ingredients, including the flour, along with the seasonings and fat, into the work bowl of the food processor. (Note that this is the opposite of the standard procedure, in which you combine all the liquids in a mixing bowl, then add the dry ingredients.)

3. Process 10 seconds until ingredients are mixed.

4. Open cover. Pour yeast mixture over. Cover and turn processor on. Process 10 seconds.

5. Mix liquid ingredients. Turn processor on and slowly add the liquids through the feed tube, processing until dough forms a ball that spins around the bowl about 30 to 50 times. Let dough rest 2 to 3 minutes. Check dough. If it is very stiff and has the consistency of "play dough," cut it into pieces, return it to the bowl, and add 1 tablespoon water. Process again and check again. Add more water if necessary. Dough should be soft and smooth (though whole grain bread doughs are stickier). It should have the same springiness as dough kneaded by hand.

6. You may leave the dough to rise in the processor bowl, unless you want to use the processor for something else. Let rise until doubled; shape and bake according to recipe instructions.

FITTING BREAD BAKING INTO YOUR SCHEDULE

In this book, there are a variety of ways for you to make simple whole grain breads even if your schedule is overcrowded. For example, we offer stir-and-pour batter-type breads in the first chapter that can be made in about an hour from start to finish.

Suppose you are interrupted after you begin preparing yeast bread? What should you do? At any point prior to baking you can "retard" the dough by covering it so it won't dry, and refrigerating it. You can keep it refrigerated this way for several hours or overnight.

At what point is it safe to do this?

1. Before kneading, after you have added most of the flour. Cover and refrigerate as long as overnight; next day, remove from refrigerator and proceed with the kneading.

2. After kneading, before the dough rises in the bowl. Just cover and refrigerate as long as overnight; next day, remove from refrigerator and proceed by shaping into loaves.

3. After shaping into loaves, before the final rising. Cover and

refrigerate as long as overnight; next day, remove from the refrigerator and allow the dough to come to room temperature (about 30 to 45 minutes), then proceed with baking.

4. After shaping the loaves, and after they have risen. Refrigerate loaves immediately, but as soon as you can, reshape the loaves and put them back into the pans, let rise, and bake.

FREEZING AND REHEATING BREADS

Certain bread doughs—those which have double the yeast and contain milk solids—can be frozen before baking. It is better, however, to wrap bread well and freeze it after baking. Baked bread keeps well up to three months. Let frozen bread thaw in its wrapper, and if you want to serve it hot, simply place into a 350° F. oven for 14 to 30 minutes before serving.

STIR-AND-POUR
BREADS

Here is a collection of the simplest of all yeast-raised whole grain breads. They are easy to assemble, quick to mix and bake, and delightful to eat. They go from bowl to oven to table in just about one hour. If you've never baked bread before, this might be the perfect place to start. And if you're a seasoned baker, you'll find these eleven fast breads great quick-to-make treats for busy times.

I got the idea for these stir-and-pour breads from a combination of past experiences. From my childhood days on the farm, I remember my mother and my grandmother making "emergency" bread—*hätäleipä*, in Finnish. If we ran short of bread and had company coming, one or the other of them would stir up quick rye bread. But another source of inspiration was pizza and some of the other breads with toppings from Italy and France.

TIPS AND TECHNIQUES

These stir-and-pour breads are a perfect entrée into the wonderful world of whole grain bread baking. Four basic tips and techniques are important:

1. Yeast, because it is a plant, must be dissolved in liquid, preferably plain water at a temperature no less than 105° F. and no higher than 115° F. Just as seeds do not germinate quickly in the springtime, when the ground temperature is still cold, yeast will also get a slow start in water that is too cold (less than 105° F.). And as plants can be scalded by hot water, so yeast can be scalded by water higher than 115° F. Check the water temperature with a thermometer; you can use warm water right from the tap, but be certain it isn't too hot or cold. My recipes almost always have you wait 5 minutes for the yeast to "foam." This indicates to you that your yeast is active—not old, or dead, or stunted by cold water, or killed by water that's too hot. If nothing happens (the yeast does not foam), either start again or check the water temperature and add more yeast. This procedure is sometimes called "proving" or "proofing" the yeast.

2. Flour, when added to a yeast mixture at first makes a batter. It is important to beat the batter well, until the mixture is satiny and smooth. This begins the development of the gluten in the flour, which will create the necessary meshwork to trap the bubbles given off by the yeast, which makes the bread rise.

3. In order to achieve a bread with a texture that is not hard, doughy, overly chewy, or dry, these whole grain breads contain some all-purpose or bread flour. All-purpose and bread flours blend well in a proportion of about one-to-one with most whole grain flours. A higher proportion of whole grain flour will produce a heavier, chewier texture. Whole wheat flour is one exception: this bread will be successful with a larger quantity of whole wheat flour than all-purpose flour because whole wheat flour has more gluten then most other whole grain flours.

4. If you decide to "wing it" and want to improvise stir-and-pour bread toppings, be sure that the basic bread flavor is compatible with the topping you decide to use. A basically sweet or nutty bread goes well with a cheese or fruit or nut topping. A bread that has little sweetening in it, such as the basic Wheat Germ and Sunflower Bread, can take a spicy pizzalike topping. (Omit the wheat germ–sunflower nut topping if you decide to make pizza.) Look for inspired combinations among your favorite sandwich mixtures. For instance, the Pumpernickel for Impatient Bakers might be excellent with corned beef and Swiss cheese pressed into it before baking.

HÄTÄLEIPÄ

Emergency Bread

Hätä means "emergency" in Finnish, and *leipä* translates to "bread." It's quick to make and delicious to eat. Finns make it when they have run out of ordinary rye bread, because it is so easy to prepare. With just a hint of molasses, the bread has a grainy flavor of coarse rye flour. To serve it, cut the loaf into wedges, then split the wedges. It is wonderful for open-faced sandwiches!

MAKES 1 LOAF, ABOUT 9″ IN DIAMETER

1 package active dry yeast
1 cup warm water,
    105° F.–115° F.
2 tablespoons light or dark
    molasses
1 tablespoon oil, melted lard,
    bacon drippings, or
    melted butter

1 teaspoon salt
½ cup dark or light rye flour
1½ cups bread flour or
    unbleached all-purpose
    flour
Melted butter to brush top of
    loaf

In mixing bowl, dissolve yeast in warm water; add molasses, let stand 3 to 5 minutes until yeast foams. Stir in oil, salt, and rye flour. Stir in bread flour, then beat 50 times. Cover a baking sheet with parchment paper or grease generously. Turn dough out onto the sheet, spreading it into a circle about 8 inches in diameter. Let rise 30 minutes. Preheat over to 400° F. Bake for 20 minutes or until center of loaf springs back when touched. Brush top with melted butter. Serve hot, cut into wedges and split horizontally.

HÄTÄLEIPÄ BAKED WITH HAM AND CHEESE

The topping turns this quick-to-bake bread into a meal. This dish is perfect for casual entertaining when you want something new and delicious to serve. To round out the meal, combine this with a crisp green salad and beer or wine. Or you might serve it along with a hearty split pea or yankee bean soup. The amounts of ham and cheese are variable according to what you have on hand. Of course the more topping you use, the more satisfying the dish, but if you're short on one or the other, don't let that stop you! In fact, you might subtitute summer sausage, thuringer, or another pre-cooked meat.

MAKES 8 SERVINGS

1 recipe Hätäleipä
1 to 2 cups cubed cooked ham

1 to 2 cups shredded or cubed
    Swiss, Monterey Jack, or
    Cheddar cheese

Prepare the bread dough and spread it out onto the prepared baking sheet, shaping the dough into a circle 10 inches in diameter. Let dough rise 30 minutes. Press ham into dough. Preheat oven to 400° F. Bake for 15 minutes, remove from oven, and top with the cheese. Return bread to the oven for 5 to 10 minutes, until bread is browned and cheese is melted. Cool 5 minutes, then cut into wedges to serve.

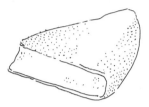

MASA BREAD

Masa harina is a fine-ground cornmeal which is used mainly to make tortillas and other Mexican recipes. Used in this stir-and-pour bread, it is an interesting twist on the standard cornbread, and in the recipe that follows makes a base for a main dish, Nacho Bread.

MAKES 1 LOAF

1 package active dry yeast	1 cup bread flour or
1 cup warm water,	unbleached all-purpose
105° F.–115° F.	flour
2 tablespoons sugar	1 tablespoon softened butter
1 teaspoon salt	for the top of the loaf
2 tablespoons butter, melted	1½ tablespoons additional
1 cup masa harina	masa harina for top

In mixing bowl, dissolve yeast in the warm water; add 1 teaspoon of the sugar and let stand until yeast foams, about 5 minutes. Stir in remaining sugar, salt, melted butter, masa harina, and flour; beat mixture 50 strokes. Cover a baking sheet with parchment paper or grease it generously. Spread dough onto the pan in an 8-inch circle. Smooth top with fingers moistened with water. Let rise 40 minutes. Preheat oven to 400° F. Brush top of loaf with softened butter and slash with knife or razor blade to make 1-inch squares. Sprinkle with the additional masa harina. Bake 20 to 25 minutes or until loaf springs back when touched in the center. Serve hot, cut in wedges.

NACHO BREAD

Embellish this basic bread as much as your imagination (and refrigerator) allows! Add black olives, green peppers or green onions, sausage cubes. . . .

MAKES 10 TO 12 APPETIZERS, OR 5 TO 6 LUNCH OR SUPPER SERVINGS

1 recipe Masa Bread
1 cup diced chorizo or
    pepperoni sausage
2 tablespoons drained and
    chopped canned green
    chilies

2 cups shredded Monterey
    Jack or white Cheddar
    cheese

Make the Masa Bread dough and spread to the edges of a well-greased 12-inch pizza pan. Let rise 30 minutes. Do not spread with butter and masa harina; rather, press diced sausage into the dough, then top with green chilies and cheese. Preheat oven to 400° F. Bake for 25 to 35 minutes or until bread is browned and toppings are bubbling.

NO-TIME-TO-BAKE WHEAT LOAF

When you're pressed for time, or even when you are not, this flat loaf is light, tender, and an excellent accompaniment for any meal. To convert it to a quick brunch coffee bread top it with an almond "crust" as in the next recipe.

MAKES ONE 8-INCH ROUND LOAF

1 package active dry yeast
¼ cup warm water,
    105° F.–115° F.
⅛ teaspoon ground ginger
3 tablespoons sugar
1 cup evaporated milk or
    scalded and cooled whole
    milk

½ teaspoon salt
1 cup whole wheat flour
1¼ cups bread flour or
    unbleached all-purpose
    flour
Melted butter

In large mixing bowl, dissolve yeast in warm water. Add ginger and 1 teaspoon of the sugar; let stand 5 minutes, until yeast foams. Add remaining ingredients except butter. Beat 50 strokes. Cover a baking sheet with parchment paper or grease it generously. Turn dough out onto prepared sheet. Spread to make an 8-inch circle and let rise 30 minutes. Preheat oven to 400° F. Bake loaf 20 to 30 minutes, or until golden and center springs back when touched. Brush top with melted butter. To serve, cut into wedges and split wedges.

ALMOND-CRUSTED STIR-AND-POUR WHEAT BREAD

Munchy, chewy, and delicious! With the almond paste and icing, this is a festive holiday coffee bread. You can purchase almond paste in well-stocked supermarkets or in specialty food stores. To make your own, see directions below.

MAKES ABOUT 8 SERVINGS

*1 recipe No-Time-to-Bake
    Wheat Loaf
1 tablespoon grated orange
    peel
2 teaspoons aniseed
½ cup golden raisins
½ cup diced candied orange
    peel*

*1 egg white mixed with 1
    tablespoon water
½ cup (about 4 ounces)
    almond paste, or ¼ cup
    cinnamon sugar (see
    below)
½ cup sliced almonds
Powdered sugar icing (see
    below)*

Prepare the No-Time-to-Bake Wheat Loaf dough adding the orange peel, aniseed, raisins, and candied orange peel. Cover a baking sheet with parchment paper or grease it generously. Turn dough out onto sheet, making a 10-inch circle. Smooth top and edges with hands that have been dipped in water. Let rise 30 minutes, until puffy. Carefully brush with the egg white mixture. Crumble the almond paste into little chunks no larger than ½ inch and sprinkle over the dough, or sprinkle with cinnamon sugar. Top with the sliced almonds. Bake in a preheated 375° F. oven for about 25 minutes or until golden brown. Before serving, drizzle with powdered sugar icing.

CINNAMON SUGAR: Mix ¼ cup sugar with 1 tablespoon powdered cinnamon.

POWDERED SUGAR ICING: Mix 1 cup powdered sugar with 2 to 3 tablespoons hot coffee or milk; add 1 teaspoon softened butter and 1 teaspoon vanilla extract. Stir until smooth.

YOUR OWN ALMOND PASTE: Place 1 cup blanched almonds into a food processor with the steel blade in place, or use a blender. Process until almonds are pulverized; this may take several minutes. Scrape down several times. Add ½ cup powdered sugar and process until blended. Scrape down sides. With processor or blender running, drop in 2 tablespoons unsalted butter and process several minutes until mixture begins to appear oily. Add 1 teaspoon almond extract and 1 teaspoon vanilla extract, and process until mixture is pastelike. This makes about ⅞ cup almond paste.

OAT-WHEAT TREAT BREAD

Split wedges of this bread and fill it with sprouts, ham, cheese, and chopped green onion to make a great, fresh-tasting sandwich. Or, simply use this as a dinner accompaniment. The variation that follows is based on a favorite sidewalk-snack in Italy, called *focaccia*.

MAKES 1 LOAF

1 package active dry yeast	½ cup whole wheat flour
1 cup warm water,	1 cup bread flour or
105° F.–115° F.	unbleached all-purpose
1 teaspoon sugar	flour
1 tablespoon butter, softened	1 egg white beaten with 2
1 teaspoon salt	tablespoons water
¾ cup rolled oats	

In large mixing bowl, dissolve yeast in warm water; add sugar, butter, and salt. Stir in ½ cup of the rolled oats and all the whole wheat flour and bread flour. Beat 50 strokes. Cover a baking sheet with parchment paper or generously grease it. Sprinkle a 9-inch circle with 2 table-spoons of the remaining rolled oats. Turn dough out onto rolled oats and spread to cover the circle. Let rise 30 minutes. Brush with the egg white mixture and sprinkle with the remaining 2 tablespoons rolled oats. Preheat oven to 400° F. and bake for 20 to 25 minutes or until golden. Serve cut in wedges.

OAT-WHEAT FOCACCIA

In Italy, *focaccia* is made with white flour. The dough is spread out flat and, when risen, is poked with dents to hold the olive oil, garlic, and cheese. It's wonderful freshly baked, cut into wedges or squares. We enjoyed *focaccia* with a variety of toppings in different train station snack bars in Italy. Sometimes *focaccia* took on a pizzalike quality, when topped with a tomato sauce.

MAKES 8 TO 10 SERVINGS

1 recipe Oat-Wheat Treat Bread	*1 clove garlic, pressed*
	¼ cup olive oil
1 teaspoon salt	*⅓ cup grated Romano cheese*

Prepare the Oat-Wheat Treat Bread dough. Cover a baking pan with parchment paper or grease it generously. Spread dough out to make a 12-inch circle. With hands that have been dipped in water, smooth the top out. Let rise 30 minutes. Combine salt, garlic, and olive oil. Poke holes with your finger all over the dough and drizzle the seasoned oil over the bread. Sprinkle with cheese. Preheat oven to 400° F. Bake for 20 to 25 minutes. Serve hot.

WHEAT GERM AND SUNFLOWER BREAD

Whole wheat pastry flour gives this bread a tenderness that you don't get with regular whole wheat flour. Combined with the flavors of wheat germ and sunflower seeds, it is irresistible eaten just as is ... even without butter!

MAKES 1 LOAF

1 package active dry yeast
1 cup warm water,
    105° F.–115° F.
1 tablespoon sugar
1 tablespoon olive oil

½ teaspoon salt
1 cup unbleached all-purpose
    flour
1½ cups whole wheat pastry
    flour

GLAZE:

1 egg white mixed with 1
    tablespoon water
1 tablespoon plain wheat germ
    or wheat germ with
    brown sugar and honey

1 tablespoon sunflower seeds,
    plain or salted

In bowl, dissolve yeast in warm water; add the sugar, olive oil, and salt. Let stand 5 minutes until yeast foams. Stir in the flours and beat 50 strokes. Cover a baking sheet with parchment paper or grease it generously. Turn dough out onto prepared pan and spread to make a 9-inch circle. Moisten hands with water and smooth top of loaf. Let rise 30 minutes until puffy. Brush top with egg white glaze and sprinkle with wheat germ and sunflower seeds. Preheat oven to 400° F. Bake for 20 to 25 minutes, until center springs back when touched with finger. Cool on rack 10 minutes before cutting. To serve, cut into wedges and split wedges.

QUICK WHEAT PIZZA BREAD

This is a soft and chewy pizza. Kids love it, and it's good for them!

MAKES 8 WEDGES OR SERVINGS

1 recipe Wheat Germ and
    Sunflower Bread, minus
    toppings
1 can (8 ounces) tomato sauce
    with mushrooms and
    onions
1 teaspoon chopped basil
    leaves
1 teaspoon chopped oregano
    leaves

½ pound pepperoni, diced or
    sliced
3 tablespoons olive oil
2½ cups freshly shredded
    Mozzarella cheese
1½ cups freshly grated
    Romano or Parmesan
    cheese

Prepare the bread dough. Cover a baking sheet with parchment paper or generously grease it, or generously grease a 12- to 14-inch pizza pan. Turn dough out onto prepared pan and spread to make a 10- to 12-inch round. Mix tomato sauce, basil, and oregano. Pour over the dough. Top with the pepperoni and drizzle with olive oil. Sprinkle Mozzarella, Romano, or Parmesan over all. Bake in a preheated 425° F. oven for 25 to 30 minutes, or until crust is golden and cheese is bubbly and slightly browned. Serve hot. Cut into 8 wedges.

PUMPERNICKEL FOR IMPATIENT BAKERS

You won't believe you can do it in so little time! As you begin stirring up this wonderful, dark, grainy bread, send someone out for a nice round of Brie, or take the Brie out of the refrigerator to "season" to room temperature. Both will be ready to serve at the same time.

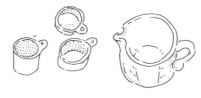

MAKES ONE **10**-INCH ROUND

2 squares (2 ounces) unsweetened chocolate	1 teaspoon salt
2 tablespoons butter	1 cup whole wheat flour
2 packages active dry yeast	1 cup dark rye flour
1 cup warm water, 105° F.–115° F.	1½ cups unbleached all-purpose flour
½ cup milk, warmed to 105° F.–115° F.	1 egg white mixed with 2 tablespoons water
¼ cup dark or light molasses	2 teaspoons coarse salt
	2 teaspoons caraway seeds

Put the chocolate and butter into a small glass dish and set over hot water to melt, or microwave on HIGH for 1 minute at a time until both are melted. In large mixing bowl, dissolve the yeast in the warm water, add milk and molasses, and let stand 5 minutes until yeast foams. Add the salt, melted chocolate and butter mixture, and whole wheat flour; beat well. Beat in the rye flour, then the all-purpose flour. Beat 50 strokes. Cover a baking pan with parchment paper or grease it generously. Turn dough out onto prepared sheet, smoothing it out using fingers moistened with water to make a 10-inch round. Let rise 30 minutes or until bread looks puffy. Brush with egg white mixture and sprinkle with the coarse salt and caraway seeds. Preheat oven to 375° F. Bake for 30 to 35 minutes, or until loaf sounds hollow when tapped.

NO-KNEAD CASSEROLE BREADS

Casserole breads are for the baker who is short of time. They offer an easy way to old-fashioned breads that require no kneading. Some are batter breads that are simply beaten until smooth (and are similar to my Stir-and-Pour Breads), but others are fairly stiff and appear ready to knead but you don't have to knead them. All, however have a higher proportion of liquid to flour, and most of them require just one rise, right in the casserole in which you plan to bake them. If you have the time, let these doughs rise once in their mixing bowls and then again in their baking pans/casseroles; they will achieve a finer texture and crumb. You can use this two-step method for a finer texture with any of the recipes in this chapter.

Bake these breads in handsome ovenproof dishes—antique crockery casseroles, colorful enameled cast-iron, rustic crocks, and ovenproof pottery bowls. As gifts, you can present these breads right in their casseroles. Cover the top with plastic wrap or cellophane and tie a ribbon around the casserole. Presented this way, these breads also make great items for bake sales and bazaars.

The moister dough results in a lighter bread without the long rising time that may be required with more traditional techniques.

Because a casserole bread dough is almost a batter, the bread usually has a rough, uneven surface, unlike the smooth, stretched surface of a bread that has been kneaded. But casserole breads make good eating, despite their somewhat "lumpy" appearance. The casserole bread, with its moist batter, is especially good when made with whole grain flours. The whole grain flavors are intensified by the moistness of the dough, and the addition of cheeses, seeds, herbs, and spices adds interesting flavor notes.

HONEY WHEAT CASSEROLE BREAD

This hearty bread looks pretty with its coating of wheat germ, which toasts on top of the loaf as it bakes.

MAKES 1 LOAF

1½ cups bread flour or unbleached all-purpose flour

1 cup whole wheat flour
3 tablespoons nonfat dry milk
1 package active dry yeast

1 teaspoon salt	1 cup hot water,
2 tablespoons honey	120° F.–130° F.
2 tablespoons oil	1 tablespoon wheat germ

In large mixer bowl, mix ½ cup of the bread flour, all the whole wheat flour, and the dry milk, yeast, salt, honey, and oil. With mixer on low speed, mix until blended. With mixer still going, add the hot water and continue mixing for 3 minutes until smooth. Add remaining flour gradually, mixing at high speed until dough is smooth. Turn batter into a greased 1½-quart casserole. Sprinkle wheat germ over top. Let rise in a warm place until almost doubled, about 45 minutes. Preheat oven to 375° F. Bake for 25 to 30 minutes, until wooden skewer inserted in the center comes out clean. Cool 10 minutes and remove bread from dish; cool on wire rack.

WHEAT GERM CASSEROLE BREAD

If you're in a hurry and if a nutty-flavored yeast bread rich in wheat germ and grainy with whole wheat flour appeals to you, try this quick family favorite.

MAKES 2 LOAVES

2 packages active dry yeast	1 tablespoon salt
½ cup warm water,	1½ cups wheat germ (regular,
105° F.–115° F.	toasted, or with sugar
2 cups buttermilk	and honey)
¼ cup light (unsulphured)	2½ cups whole wheat flour
molasses	2½ cups bread flour or
¼ cup honey	unbleached all-purpose
¼ cup butter	flour
2 eggs	Oil to brush tops of loaves

In large mixer bowl, dissolve yeast in warm water. Let stand 5 minutes until yeast foams. Meanwhile, heat buttermilk, molasses, honey, and butter just until butter melts; cool to 105° F.–115° F. Blend eggs and salt with warm liquid. Add mixture to the yeast, then stir in the wheat germ and whole wheat flour; beat on high speed with electric mixer until smooth. Stir in the bread flour using a wooden spoon; beat until blended and smooth. Cover and let rise in a warm place 1 hour or until doubled. Beat down. Grease two 1½-quart casseroles. Divide batter between the casseroles and brush top of dough with oil. Let rise 45 minutes or until doubled. Preheat oven to 350° F. Bake 35 to 40 minutes or until loaves sound hollow when tapped. Remove from pans immediately. Cool on rack.

THREE-WHEAT CASSEROLE BREAD

Just reading the ingredients of this wheaty loaf makes me hungry. Nutty-flavored, it has a rich taste and a pleasing, crunchy texture.

MAKES 1 LARGE LOAF

1 package active dry yeast
½ cup warm water,
    105° F.–115° F.
⅛ teaspoon ground ginger
3 tablespoons honey
1 large can (13 ounces)
    evaporated milk
1 teaspoon salt
2 tablespoons butter, melted,
    or vegetable oil

¼ cup cracked wheat
½ cup wheat germ
1¼ cups whole wheat flour
2½ cups bread flour or
    unbleached all-purpose
    flour
2 tablespoons sesame seeds

In large bowl, dissolve yeast in warm water; add ginger and 1 tablespoon of the honey; stir and let stand 5 minutes until yeast foams. Add remaining honey, evaporated milk, salt, butter, cracked wheat, and wheat germ; beat well. Let stand 10 minutes. Stir in the whole wheat flour and bread flour, beating to keep batter smooth. Turn batter into a well-greased 2½-quart casserole. Sprinkle top with sesame seeds. Let rise in a warm place (about 45 minutes) until dough fills dish. Preheat oven to 350° F. Bake 45 to 55 minutes, or until a wooden skewer inserted in the center comes out clean. Let cool 10 minutes in pan, then remove and cool on rack.

MOROCCAN ANISE BREAD

This is a free-form whole wheat bread perfumed with aniseeds. During Moroccan meals, chunks of this bread are used to scoop up food in place of using a utensil. This dough does not require kneading.

MAKES 1 LARGE LOAF, ABOUT 2 POUNDS

1 package active dry yeast	2 teaspoons salt
1 cup warm water,	1 tablespoon aniseed
105° F.–115° F.	2 cups whole wheat flour
1 tablespoon sugar	2 cups bread flour or
1 cup milk, scalded and cooled	all-purpose flour.
to 105° F.–115° F.	Cornmeal for dusting

In large bowl, soften yeast in warm water; add the sugar, stir, and set aside for 5 minutes until yeast foams. Add the milk, salt, and aniseeds. Add the whole wheat flour and then the bread flour, 1 cup at a time, beating for 50 strokes until a smooth, soft dough forms. Scrape sides of bowl with spatula. Cover and let rise until doubled, about 1 hour. Lightly grease a baking sheet and sprinkle with cornmeal. Turn dough out onto prepared baking sheet and flatten (use oiled fingers) to 1-inch thickness. Let rise until doubled, about 1 hour. Prick loaf all over with fork. Preheat oven to 375° F. Bake for 30 to 35 minutes, or until loaf sounds hollow when tapped. Baked loaf will have a free form, and be no more than 1¼ inches thick. Tear into chunks or cut into squares to serve.

POTTER'S ONION WHEAT BREAD

This bread looks pretty and bakes well in a rustic pottery casserole, the kind you get from a potter. Moist, with a chewy crust, this old favorite is quick to make, too.

MAKES 1 LARGE LOAF OR 2 SMALL LOAVES

2 packages active dry yeast
¼ cup warm water,
        105° F.–115° F.
1 cup cottage cheese, at room
        temperature
2 tablespoons sugar
1 tablespoon minced dried or
        fresh onion
1 tablespoon butter, softened

2 tablespoons dill seed
2 teaspoons dill weed
1 teaspoon salt
¼ teaspoon baking soda
1 egg
1 cup whole wheat flour
1 to 1¼ cups bread flour or
        unbleached all-purpose
        flour

GLAZE:

1 egg white beaten with
    2 tablespoons water

In large mixing bowl, dissolve the yeast in warm water. Add the cottage cheese, sugar, onion, butter, dill seed, dill weed, salt, baking soda, and egg. Beat well. Beat in whole wheat flour and bread flour to make a smooth, soft dough. Cover and let rise until doubled in bulk, about 1 hour. Stir down and turn into a well-buttered 1½-quart casserole or two 3-cup casseroles. Let rise again 45 minutes to 1 hour until dough looks puffy and about fills the casserole. Brush with glaze; with razor blade or knife, slash a ½-inch-deep X across top of the loaf. Preheat oven to 350° F. and bake for 45 to 50 minutes or until golden for the large loaf, 35 to 45 minutes for the small loaves. Let cool 5 minutes in pan, turn out, and cool on rack.

CARAWAY-RYE LOAF

You can just imagine the aroma of this caraway-rye batter bread coming from the oven in grandma's wood stove. This bread is quick to prepare and has real old-time goodness—a crunchy crust, a soft texture, and a caraway, onion, and whole grain rye flavor.

MAKES 1 LARGE LOAF OR 2 SMALL LOAVES

2 packages active dry yeast	*1 tablespoon butter, softened*
¼ cup warm water,	*2 teaspoons caraway seed*
105° F.–115° F.	*1 teaspoon salt*
1 cup cottage cheese, at room	*1 egg*
temperature	*1 cup dark rye flour*
2 tablespoons dark molasses	*1¼ to 1½ cups bread flour or*
1 tablespoon minced dried or	*unbleached all-purpose*
fresh onion	*flour*

GLAZE:

1 egg white beaten with
2 tablespoons water

In large mixing bowl, dissolve the yeast in warm water. Add the cottage cheese, molasses, onion, butter, caraway seed, salt, and egg. Beat well. Beat in rye flour to make a smooth, soft mixture. Gradually beat in the bread flour to make a smooth, soft dough. Cover and let rise until double in bulk, about 1 hour. Stir down and turn into a well-buttered 1½-quart pottery casserole or 2 well-buttered 3-cup casseroles. Let rise again about 45 minutes to 1 hour until dough looks puffy and fills the casserole. Brush with glaze; with razor blade or knife, slash a ½-inch-deep X across top of the loaf. Preheat oven to 350° F. and bake for 45 to 50 minutes or until golden for the large loaf, or 35 to 45 minutes for small loaves. Let cool 5 minutes in pan, turn out, and cool on rack.

BEER-BATTER RYE LOAF

Beer and caraway seeds flavor this rye casserole bread. Good with ham or roasted meats, it's great for making sandwiches!

MAKES 1 LOAF

2 cups bread flour or
    unbleached all-purpose
    flour
¾ cup dark rye flour
1 package active dry yeast
1 tablespoon caraway seeds

1 teaspoon salt
1 can (12 ounces) beer, or 1½
    cups water
2 tablespoons vegetable oil
2 tablespoons molasses

Measure 1 cup of the bread flour, all the rye flour, and the yeast, caraway seeds, and salt into large bowl of electric mixer. In saucepan, heat beer, oil, and molasses to 120° F.–130° F. Pour liquids over dry ingredients in bowl and beat on high speed until smooth, about 3 minutes, scraping bowl. Add remaining bread flour and stir until flour is evenly blended into mixture. Turn batter into greased 1½-quart casserole dish. Let rise in warm place until almost doubled, about 45 minutes. Heat oven to 350° F. Bake until wooden skewer inserted in the center comes out clean, about 30 minutes. Cool 10 minutes, then remove bread from baking dish and cool on wire rack.

ORANGE-RYE CASSEROLE BREAD

This quick-to-make yeast bread has typical Scandinavian flavors.

MAKES 1 LARGE LOAF

1 package active dry yeast
½ cup warm water,
    105° F.–115° F.
⅛ teaspoon ground ginger
1 tablespoon sugar
3 tablespoons dark molasses
1 teaspoon caraway seeds
1 teaspoon salt
1 tablespoon grated orange
    peel

2 tablespoons salad oil
1 large can (13 ounces)
    evaporated milk
1½ cups light or dark rye
    flour
2½ cups bread flour or
    unbleached all-purpose
    flour
Dark molasses to glaze loaf

In large bowl, dissolve yeast in warm water; blend in ginger and sugar. Let stand until yeast foams, about 5 minutes. Add molasses, caraway seeds, salt, orange peel, oil, and evaporated milk. Add rye flour and beat until batter is smooth. Gradually beat in the bread flour, keeping batter smooth and satiny looking. Turn into a well-buttered 2½-quart casserole. Let rise in a warm place about 1 hour until dough just fills the dish. Bake in a 350° F. oven for 55 to 60 minutes, or until a skewer inserted into the center comes out clean. Brush top with molasses while hot. Let cool 10 minutes in dish, then remove and cool on wire rack.

PEPPERED POTATO-RYE LOAF

Coarse black pepper and potatoes add unusual touches to this casserole bread, which is quick to stir up and ideal to serve with a bowl of hearty vegetable soup.

MAKES 1 LARGE LOAF OR 2 SMALL LOAVES

1 package active dry yeast	1½ cups scalded milk (milk
¼ cup warm water,	brought just to boiling
105° F.–115° F.	point)
½ cup instant potato flakes	2 eggs
1 tablespoon sugar	1 cup dark rye flour
2 teaspoons coarse-ground	2½ cups bread flour or
black pepper	unbleached all-purpose
2 teaspoons salt	flour
2 tablespoons shortening or	Softened butter to brush top of
butter	loaf
	Coarse salt

In small bowl, dissolve yeast in warm water; let stand 5 minutes until yeast foams. Meanwhile, in large mixer bowl, combine potato flakes, sugar, pepper, salt, shortening, and boiling milk. Add eggs, then cool to 105° F.–115° F. Add yeast mixture. Blend in the rye flour and 1 cup of the bread flour; with mixer on medium speed, beat for 2 minutes.

Stir in remaining bread flour to form a stiff batter. Cover; let rise in warm place until light and doubled in size, about 45 minutes. Stir batter down. Spoon into a well-greased 2-quart casserole or two well-greased 1-quart casserole dishes. Cover; let rise in warm place until dough fills the pan. Preheat oven to 350° F. Bake for 55 to 60 minutes or until deep golden brown for large loaf, or 45 to 50 minutes for small loaves, or until a wooden skewer inserted through the center comes out clean. Remove from pan and cool on wire rack. Brush while still hot with softened butter and sprinkle with the salt.

CHEESE-OAT CASSEROLE BREAD

The cheese in this loaf adds a wonderful aroma to the kitchen as it bakes—and a great taste when you bite into it! Serve it with a hearty vegetable soup when the weather turns chilly.

MAKES 1 LARGE CASSEROLE BREAD OR 2 MEDIUM LOAVES

2 packages active dry yeast
1½ cups warm water,
    105° F.–115° F.
¼ cup sugar
1½ teaspoons salt
2 eggs
1 cup rolled oats, quick or
    old-fashioned

3½ cups unbleached
    all-purpose flour
2 cups shredded Cheddar
    cheese
3 tablespoons caraway seeds
Melted butter

In large mixer bowl, dissolve yeast in warm water. Stir in the sugar, salt, eggs, and oats. Add half the flour and beat for 2 to 3 minutes with electric mixer until dough is very smooth and satiny. Add cheese and caraway seeds, then 1 cup more of the flour. Beat until blended. Work in the remaining ¾ cup flour until it can no longer be seen in the dough. Cover and let rise in a warm place until doubled, about 30 minutes. Stir down and turn into a greased 3-quart casserole dish or into two 8½ x 4½-inch loaf pans. Let rise 45 minutes to 1 hour, until batter reaches top of the pan. Preheat oven to 350° F. Bake for 45 minutes to 1 hour for the casserole loaf, or 35 to 40 minutes for the standard loaves. Remove from pans and cool on rack; brush with melted butter.

CORNMEAL-OAT ENGLISH MUFFIN BREAD

Basically a batter bread, this can be baked in a casserole. However, because the texture of the bread is open and it is ideal for slicing and toasting, 1-pound cans or 2-cup charlotte molds are ideal. Or use three 5 x 3-inch loaf pans.

MAKES 3 LOAVES

> 2 packages active dry yeast
> 2 cups warm water,
>   105° F.–115° F.
> ½ cup shortening or lard,
>   softened
> 1 tablespoon sugar
> 2 teaspoons salt
>
> ½ cup yellow cornmeal,
>   preferably stone ground
> 1 cup rolled oats
> 4 cups bread flour or
>   unbleached all-purpose
>   flour
> Additional rolled oats to coat
>   loaves

In a large bowl, dissolve yeast in warm water. Let stand 5 minutes until yeast foams. Add shortening, sugar, salt, cornmeal, oats, and 1 cup of the bread flour; beat until smooth. Gradually add remaining flour to make a stiff dough, beating well after each addition. Lightly oil a working surface (bread board or clean countertop), and turn dough out onto it. Divide dough into 3 portions. Shape each into a smooth, round ball, then roll each in additional oats to coat evenly. Place into 3 well-greased baking pans or cans. Let rise in a warm place for 50 to 60 minutes or until doubled. Preheat oven to 350° F. Bake for 40 to 45 minutes, or until golden. Remove from pans immediately, and cool on rack. To serve, cut into slices crosswise and toast.

CORNMEAL-RAISIN CASSEROLE BREAD

The crunchiness of cornmeal, rich flavor of molasses, and chewiness of golden raisins are an irresistible combination in a yeast bread. This bread has a crusty coarseness and is excellent sliced while still warm. You can serve it plain or slathered with butter and a dollop of homemade fruit jelly or jam.

MAKES 2 LOAVES

1 cup milk
1 cup water
1 cup yellow cornmeal
3 tablespoons butter
½ cup light (unsulphured)
    molasses
½ cup warm water,
    105° F.–115° F.

2 packages active dry yeast
1 teaspoon sugar
2 teaspoons salt
5½ to 6 cups bread flour or
    unbleached all-purpose
    flour
1 cup golden raisins

In large saucepan, bring milk and water to a boil. Remove from heat and add the cornmeal, stirring with a whisk until smooth. Add butter and molasses and stir until no lumps remain. Cool to lukewarm. In large mixer bowl, mix the warm water and yeast. Add sugar. Let stand 5 minutes until yeast foams. Add cornmeal mixture, salt, and about half the flour. Batter should be thick, but still soft enough to beat. Beat 5 minutes with electric mixer. With spoon, stir in the raisins and gradually add more flour, stirring until batter is very stiff. When flour is moistened, cover and let rise until doubled, about 1 hour. Stir down. Divide dough between 2 buttered 9-inch round pans or casseroles, or two buttered 9 x 5-inch loaf pans. Smooth tops of loaves. Cover and let rise in a warm place 45 minutes to 1 hour, until batter reaches tops of the pans. Preheat oven to 350° F. Bake for 40 to 50 minutes, until loaves sound hollow when tapped. Remove from pans and cool on wire rack.

WHOLE WHEAT BREADS

Wheat is the backbone of bread baking, because it is the grain that contains the most gluten, which gives bread doughs the elasticity to capture and hold the carbon dioxide given off by yeast or other leavening agents. The most common way we use wheat in bread is as white flours designated as "bread flour" or "all-purpose flour." Usually a recipe calls for about half or more of white flour so that the dough will have enough gluten to make it easy to handle and give it a lighter texture. One hundred percent whole wheat bread is a close textured, heavy loaf, and may be a bit harder to handle than loaves which include some white flour.

SHOPPING FOR WHOLE WHEAT BREAD INGREDIENTS

These are the forms of wheat flour generally available. Some are available only in natural foods stores, whole-food cooperatives, or nutrition centers.

ALL-PURPOSE FLOUR

All-purpose flour is a blend of wheats and was developed so the home baker could buy one type of flour and still get satisfactory baking results in everything from bread to cakes and pastry. White flour of any type is milled from the endosperm of the wheat kernel. Different brands vary in performance and nutrient content. When purchasing all-purpose flour, check the nutrition label. Some brands will list 11 grams protein per cup, others will list up to 13 grams per cup. All-purpose flour rated at 13 grams per cup makes a better bread flour than flour rated at 11 grams per cup, which is better for cakes, cookies, and pastries. When they are placed next to one another, unbleached flour will appear creamier in color than bleached flour.

BREAD FLOUR

This is a refined wheat flour similar to all-purpose flour, but with a higher gluten content, and thus it absorbs more liquid in a dough mixture. When making bread with this flour, you will usually need less flour. It is very important to knead well any doughs made with bread flour so as to adequately develop the gluten. Bread flour makes a very compatible mix with whole grain flours because of its high gluten content (14 grams per cup). Bread flour is available in well-stocked supermarkets.

GLUTEN FLOUR

Gluten flour is white flour with additional gluten, creamier in color than unbleached all-purpose flour. Gluten is removed from high-protein wheat flour by rinsing off the starch; then this gluten is dried, ground, and added to regular white flour. You can use gluten flour in combination with low-gluten flours to produce a bread dough that will handle well and rise to a lighter finished product. Gluten flour by itself produces a bread that has a texture so tough it resembles chewing gum and cannot be broken down! You can purchase gluten flour in whole-foods cooperatives and nutrition stores. Check the percentage of gluten, and the recommended usage. The protein content may vary but it ranges from 25 to 75 percent gluten.

WHOLE WHEAT PASTRY FLOUR

This flour is ground from soft wheat and is comparable to white cake flour. It usually has both the bran and the germ of the wheat, which give it its speckled whole wheat appearance. However, this pastry flour has less gluten, which makes it perfect for quick breads, pie crusts, muffins, and cakes. It cannot be used alone in baking yeast breads because of its low gluten content, but added to a yeast dough, whole wheat pastry flour renders a sweeter flavor and more tender texture to the final product. Whole wheat pastry flour is not usually available in supermarkets, but is available in whole-foods cooperatives and nutrition stores.

WHOLE WHEAT FLOUR

Ground from hard winter wheat, this flour varies in protein content depending upon the manufacturer, the miller, and the wheat variety. Whole wheat flour is milled from the whole kernel. Nutrient content is not affected by the method of grinding. Because of the bran, whole wheat flour has proportionally less gluten and therefore 100 percent whole wheat bread may be heavier and more coarse than breads in which half of the flour is white. Bran also absorbs moisture, so allowance should be made for this by adding less flour to the dough. Whole wheat flour contains fiber and naturally existing vitamins. Because of the fat contained in the germ, it should be refrigerated. Whole wheat flour technically should be labeled "light," "medium," or "coarse" grind. Most of what we find on the market is "medium" grind. "Stone ground" whole wheat flour is generally considered a "coarse" grind and, when labeled as such, must be ground between stones. Otherwise the grinding is done with metal blades. "Graham" flour also is considered a "coarse-ground" whole wheat flour. Whole wheat flours, regardless of the grind, can be used interchangeably in recipes. If you have a favorite recipe which calls for "graham" flour, you may use whole wheat flour, and vice-versa.

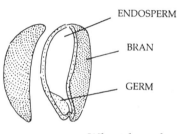

ENDOSPERM

BRAN

GERM

Wheat kernel

WHOLE UNPROCESSED BRAN

Bran is the husk or cover of the wheat kernel. It is not to be confused with bran cereals, available in supermarkets. We add bran to bread dough for interesting appearance, texture, flavor, and extra fiber. Unprocessed bran flakes are usually available in bulk from whole-foods cooperatives and nutrition stores.

WHEAT GERM

This is the embryo of the wheat kernel, delicious both raw or toasted. Wheat germ adds a nutty flavor to yeast bread doughs, and makes a nutlike ingredient for fillings. Wheat germ is available in both untreated and in toasted, sweetened forms, and these can be used interchangeably in most recipes. When used as a crust topping, wheat germ toasts as the bread bakes and gives the loaf additional flavor and texture. Because wheat germ contains oils that can become rancid at room temperature, it should be refrigerated after opening. This is one reason why wheat germ is removed from white flour—to increase the shelf life of the flour. Buy wheat germ in supermarkets, often in the cereal section, or purchase it in bulk from whole-foods cooperatives and nutrition stores.

WHOLE WHEAT BERRIES

These are the whole wheat kernels themselves. You may be able to buy whole wheat berries in bulk from a farmer if you are lucky, but be sure that the wheat is clean and free of sprays. The berries can be ground, using a stone or steel grinder, or you can soak them until they are soft, and even cook them before adding to bread doughs. If you sprout the grains, they take on a wonderful crunchy texture and a sweet flavor. Added to a bread dough, the sprouts add both flavor and texture to a loaf.

CRACKED WHOLE WHEAT

These are whole wheat berries that have been "broken" into rather large pieces. To use in whole grain breads, soak them in boiling water for 45–60 minutes until they are soft enough to add to the dough. Without soaking, the wheat has an unpleasant sandy texture. Cracked whole wheat can be purchased in 5-pound bags in well-stocked supermarkets; however, it is also available from whole-foods cooperatives, natural foods stores, and nutrition stores.

BULGUR

To prepare bulgur, whole wheat is first cooked, then dried and cracked. The texture of bulgur is much like that of cracked whole wheat. Bulgur will absorb liquids more quickly than cracked whole wheat, and sometimes it is added to a bread dough in the beginning of the mixture so that it can absorb the liquid ingredients before the remaining flour is added. Bulgur is often used as a cereal or for making pilaf, a side dish, and is available in well-stocked supermarkets as well as specialty food shops, natural foods stores, nutrition stores, and whole-foods cooperatives.

WHOLE WHEAT FLAKES OR ROLLED WHEAT

This is whole wheat that has been heated and pressed, and looks much like rolled oats. The flakes cook quickly and can be added without prior soaking to a bread dough. Whole wheat flakes give an interesting texture and flavor to a loaf of bread. They are sold as a breakfast cereal ready for cooking in supermarkets, but are available in bulk in whole-foods cooperatives and nutrition stores.

WHOLE WHEAT TOASTING BREAD

Cut this bread into ¼- to ⅓-inch slices and toast it for a marvelous, nutty wheat flavor. Then top it with thin shavings of sharp Cheddar cheese and chopped walnuts; broil until the cheese is melted. This makes an excellent but simple-to-make appetizer!

MAKES 1 LOAF

1 package active dry yeast	2 tablespoons vegetable
¼ cup warm water,	shortening or butter,
105° F.–115° F.	melted
1 tablespoon sugar	1 egg
1 cup milk, scalded and cooled	1 teaspoon salt
to 105° F.–115° F.	3 to 3½ cups whole wheat
	flour

In large mixer bowl, dissolve yeast in warm water; add the sugar and set aside for 5 minutes or until yeast foams. Add the milk, shortening, egg, salt, and 1 cup of the flour; beat until smooth using electric mixer or wooden spoon. Slowly add the remaining flour to make a stiff dough. Cover and let rest for 30 minutes. Turn out onto lightly floured board and knead until smooth, about 10 minutes. Wash bowl, grease it, and place ball of dough into bowl; turn over to grease top. Cover and let rise in warm place until doubled, about 1 hour. Punch down. Shape into a loaf and place in greased 8½ x 4½-inch loaf pan. Cover and let rise until doubled, about 45 minutes to 1 hour. Preheat oven to 375° F. Bake for 25 to 35 minutes, or until loaf sounds hollow when tapped. Cool on rack.

HONEY WHOLE WHEAT HEALTH BREAD

This is a bread that is ideal if you're interested in good taste and also want a low-fat loaf. It's good just as it is and it's delicious toasted.

MAKES 2 MEDIUM LOAVES

1 package active dry yeast
2 cups warm water,
  105° F.–115° F.
1 cup nonfat dry milk
¼ cup honey
2 teaspoons salt

2 tablespoons vegetable oil
2 cups bread flour or
  all-purpose flour
3 to 3½ cups whole wheat or
  graham flour

In large mixing bowl, dissolve yeast in the warm water; add milk and honey and stir until yeast is dissolved. Let stand 5 minutes until yeast begins to foam. Add salt, butter, and bread flour; beat until smooth. Add graham or whole wheat flour 1 cup at a time, beating well between each addition until dough is stiff. Let rest 15 minutes. Turn out onto board lightly sprinkled with some of the remaining flour. Knead until smooth and springy, about 10 minutes. Wash bowl, grease, and add dough to bowl, turn over, and cover. Let rise until doubled, about 1 hour. Punch down and divide into 2 parts. Cover baking sheet or sheets with parchment or lightly grease. Shape loaves into ovals about 10 inches long that are fat in the middle and pointed on the ends. Place loaves smooth side up on baking sheet. Let rise until about doubled, about 45 minutes. Brush with water and then slash lengthwise on top of loaf, making the cut almost horizontal (as if you were going to slice a little cap off the top of the loaf, only cut just one side). The cut should be about ½ inch deep. Bake at 375° F. for 25 to 30 minutes or until loaves sound hollow when tapped. Remove from pan and cool on wire rack.

HONEY WHOLE WHEAT BREAD

The flavor of honey blended with the wholesomeness of whole wheat gives this bread character. The eggs give the bread tenderness.

MAKES 2 LOAVES

1 package active dry yeast
1½ cups warm water,
    105° F.–115° F.
2 eggs, at room temperature
¼ cup honey
2 teaspoons salt

¼ cup butter, margarine, or
    lard, melted and cooled
3 cups whole wheat flour
2 cups bread flour or
    unbleached all-purpose
    flour

In large bowl, dissolve yeast in warm water; let stand 5 minutes until yeast begins to foam. Add eggs, honey, salt, lard, and whole wheat flour; beat until smooth. Let stand covered for 30 minutes or until mixture looks puffy. Beat in the bread flour, ½ cup at a time, until dough is stiff. Let stand 15 minutes. Turn out onto floured board and knead until smooth, about 10 minutes. Wash bowl, grease lightly; add dough to bowl, turn over to grease top. Cover and let rise in a warm place until doubled, about 1 hour; punch down. Divide into 2 loaves. Place into two 8½ x 4½-inch lightly greased loaf pans. Let rise until doubled, 45 minutes to 1 hour; bake in a preheated 375° F. oven for 30 to 35 minutes, or until loaves sound hollow when tapped. Remove from pans and cool on racks.

100 PERCENT WHOLE WHEAT BREAD

The extra nonfat dry milk in this recipe allows you to make this bread ahead and freeze it before baking; simply shape it right after kneading, wrap, and freeze. Shaped into a 3-stranded braid, this makes a great party bread. To greet your guests with bread-baking aromas, remove the frozen dough 4 hours ahead, and simply let it thaw and rise before baking. If you live in a cold climate or your house is kept at a minimal temperature, let the bread thaw and rise for 6 hours.

MAKES 2 LOAVES OR 1 BRAID ABOUT 18 INCHES LONG

2 packages active dry yeast
2 cups warm water,
    105° F.–115° F.
⅓ cup honey
1 cup nonfat dry milk

¼ cup butter, softened
2 teaspoons salt
5 to 5½ cups whole wheat
    flour

In large mixing bowl, dissolve yeast in the warm water; add the honey, dry milk, butter, and salt. Let stand 5 minutes until yeast foams. Stir in 2 cups of the flour and mix until dough is very smooth. Cover and let rest for 30 minutes. Stir in enough additional flour to make a stiff dough. Let rest 15 minutes. Turn out onto board sprinkled with remaining flour and knead until dough is smooth, about 10 minutes. (For frozen loaves, shape and freeze at this point). Wash bowl, lightly grease it, then place ball of dough into bowl, turn over to grease top of dough, and cover. Let rise in a warm place 1 to 1½ hours or until doubled.

Grease two 8½ x 4½-inch loaf pans. Divide dough in half. Shape into loaves and place into pans. For braided bread, divide dough into 3 parts and roll each into a strand about 24 inches long. Braid strands, and then place bread on lightly greased or parchment-covered baking sheet. Let rise until doubled, about 45 minutes to 1 hour. Preheat oven to 375° F. and bake for 35 to 40 minutes, until loaf sounds hollow when tapped. Remove from pans and cool on racks.

ENGLISH GRANARY BREAD

Wonderfully grainy in texture, English golden syrup blends naturally with the flavor of whole wheat. The topping of wheat germ and sesame seed echo and emphasize the whole grain taste. This is a "natural" with Stilton cheese and apples!

MAKES 2 ROUND LOAVES

2 packages active dry yeast
½ cup warm water,
    105° F.–115° F.
½ cup golden syrup or light
    corn syrup
4 cups whole wheat flour

¼ cup butter or margarine,
    softened
1 tablespoon salt
2 cups hot water,
    120° F.–130° F.
1½ to 2 cups bread flour

GLAZE:

1 egg mixed with   *2 tablespoons each wheat germ*
   2 tablespoons water   *and sesame seeds*

In large mixer bowl, combine yeast, warm water, and 1 tablespoon of the syrup; let stand 5 minutes until yeast foams. Stir in the remaining syrup, 2 cups of the whole wheat flour, the butter, and the salt; beat with electric mixer until very smooth. Let stand 30 minutes until dough becomes puffy. Add the hot water. Beat for 2 minutes and slowly add remaining whole wheat flour and the bread flour to make a stiff dough.

Turn out onto lightly floured board and knead until smooth and satiny, about 10 minutes. Wash bowl, lightly grease it; add ball of dough and turn over to grease top. Cover and let rise until doubled, about 1 hour. Punch dough down and divide in half. Shape each into a round loaf and place on lightly greased baking sheets. Let rise until doubled again, about 45 minutes to 1 hour (or brush with oil or melted butter and refrigerate for 8 to 24 hours for baking later). Preheat oven to 375° F. Brush tops of loaves with egg mixed with water. Sprinkle with wheat germ and sesame seeds. Slash loaves with sharp serrated knife or razor, making cuts so that they start and end at the same point on the loaf, but widen out on the top. When baked, slashes open up to make a pretty design on top of the loaf. Bake 35 to 40 minutes, or until loaves sound hollow when tapped. Cool on rack.

COUNTRY HEARTH BREAD

In the old days, bread such as this was baked in quantity on flat stones in an open fire or in a wood-fired brick oven. Although our baking methods today are more streamlined and bread baking is as easy as mixing up a cake, the goodness of this earthy bread remains the same. This bread has no white flour in it at all.

MAKES 1 LOAF

1 package active dry yeast
1 cup warm water,
    105° F.–115° F.
2 tablespoons light
    (unsulphured) molasses
1 tablespoon melted butter or
    vegetable oil
1 teaspoon salt

¼ cup nonfat dry milk
2 tablespoons wheat germ
2 to 2½ cups whole wheat
    flour
Milk to brush over top
Rolled oats to sprinkle over
    top

In large mixing bowl, dissolve yeast in warm water; add honey and let rest 5 minutes until yeast foams. Stir in butter, salt, dry milk, wheat germ, and half the flour. Add remaining flour slowly to keep dough smooth. Let rest 15 minutes. Turn dough out onto lightly floured board and knead for 5 minutes until smooth and elastic. Wash bowl, grease it; add dough to bowl, turn over to grease top, cover, and let rise until doubled, about 1 hour. Cover a baking sheet with parchment or lightly grease it. Punch dough down and shape into a ball. Place ball on prepared sheet and roll or pat into a circle about 8 inches in diameter. Let rise in a warm place until doubled, about 45 minutes. Brush top of loaf with milk and sprinkle generously with oats. Preheat oven to 375° F. Bake for 25 to 30 minutes, or until loaf sounds hollow when tapped. Remove from oven and cool on wire rack.

GRANDMA'S BUTTERMILK WHEAT BREAD

Grandma used to use up the extra buttermilk in light whole wheat loaves that had just a touch of sour flavor.

MAKES 2 LOAVES

1 package active dry yeast
¼ cup warm water,
    105° F.–115° F.
2 tablespoons sugar
6 tablespoons butter or
    margarine, softened
2 teaspoons salt

1½ cups warm buttermilk,
    105° F.–115° F.
2½ cups whole wheat flour
2 to 2½ cups unbleached
    all-purpose flour
Melted butter

In large mixing bowl, dissolve yeast in warm water; add sugar and let stand 5 minutes until yeast foams. Stir in the butter, salt, and buttermilk. Add whole wheat flour and beat well. Slowly add the all-purpose flour and beat until a smooth but stiff dough forms. Let stand 15 minutes. Turn out onto lightly floured board and knead until smooth and springy, about 10 minutes. Wash bowl, grease it, add dough to bowl, and turn over to grease top. Cover and let rise until doubled, about 1 hour. Punch dough down and divide in half. Shape each half into a round loaf. Grease two 8- or 9-inch round cake pans. Place loaves in pans with seam side down. Let rise until almost doubled, 45 minutes to 1 hour. Preheat oven to 375° F. Bake 25 to 30 minutes, or until loaf is golden and sounds hollow when tapped. Brush with melted butter. Remove from pans and cool on racks.

ENGLISH FARMHOUSE LOAF

A hearty, simple country bread with a firm texture and a "dusty" floured crust, this loaf has true whole grain flavor. Shaped into a round loaf and slashed with a cross on the top, it rises high as it bakes.

MAKES 1 LARGE LOAF

1 package active dry yeast
1 tablespoon sugar
½ cup warm water,
    105° F.–115° F.

2 cups milk, scalded
    and cooled to
    105° F.–115° F.

2 tablespoons butter,
    margarine, or lard,
    melted
2 teaspoons salt
3 cups whole wheat flour

3 to 3½ cups bread flour or
    plain or unbleached
    all-purpose flour
Additional whole wheat flour
    to sprinkle on top

In large bowl, dissolve yeast and sugar in warm water. Let stand 5 minutes or until yeast foams. Add milk, butter, salt, and whole wheat flour; beat until mixture is smooth and free of lumps. Add bread flour 1 cup at a time until a stiff dough forms. Cover and let rise for 15 minutes. Turn out onto lightly floured board and knead 10 minutes or until dough is smooth and springy to the touch. Wash bowl, lightly grease it, add dough to bowl, and turn over to grease top. Cover and let rise until doubled, about 1 to 1½ hours. Cover a baking sheet with parchment paper or lightly grease it. Punch dough down. Shape into a smooth ball and place with the smoothest side up on prepared baking sheet. Brush with water and sprinkle with flour. With sharp knife, slash top of the loaf in 3 places, making the cut ¼ inch deep and cutting all the way across the loaf. Let rise 45 minutes to 1 hour, or until loaf is about doubled. Preheat oven to 375° F. Bake 35 to 40 minutes, or until loaf sounds hollow when tapped. Cool on rack.

GRANDMOTHER'S COTTAGE LOAVES

These round, 100 percent whole wheat breads are shaped a little like a grandmother's hairdo, with a topknot. The method of preparation is a little unusual, too.

MAKES 2 LARGE, ROUND TOPKNOTTED LOAVES

2 packages active dry yeast   *1 tablespoon salt*
¼ cup warm water,   *4 to 5 cups warm water,*
 * 105° F.–115° F.*   * 105° F.–115° F.*
⅛ teaspoon ground ginger   *¼ cup butter, melted*
1 tablespoon sugar   *Milk to brush on loaves*
10 cups whole wheat flour

In a small bowl, dissolve the yeast in warm water; add the ginger and
sugar, and stir; set aside 5 minutes until yeast foams. Measure the
flour into a large, wide mixing bowl and make a hole in the center. Put
the yeast mixture into the hole, and sprinkle the salt over the flour.
Pour 4 cups of the water into the hole and add the melted butter. Stir
until flour is moistened and a rather lumpy dough is formed. If necessary, sprinkle with additional water. Turn out onto lightly floured
board and knead until dough is shiny, elastic, and smooth—about 15
minutes. Wash bowl, lightly grease it, and add dough to bowl. Turn
over to grease top. Cover with a damp cloth and let rise in a warm

place until doubled, 1 to 1½ hours. Cut dough in half and remove ⅓
off each portion. Roll the 2 larger pieces into balls. Grease 2 baking
sheets or cover with parchment paper. Place large balls of dough on
prepared sheets. Roll the 2 smaller pieces into balls and place one on
top of each of the larger pieces. With a floured finger, poke a hole
right down the middle of each loaf through both the small and the
large balls of dough. Let rise again in a warm place until doubled,
about 45 minutes to 1 hour. Preheat oven to 375° F. and bake 35 to 40
minutes, or until loaves sound hollow when tapped. About 10 minutes before the end of the baking time, brush loaves with milk to give
a shiny finish. Cool on wire rack.

WHEAT GERM AND SESAME SIX-STRAND BRAID

European bakeries display 6-strand braids to boast their bread-baking expertise. This voluptuous loaf is made with whole wheat flour, and the strands of the braid are rolled in toasted wheat germ and sesame seeds to give it a beautiful crunch and texture.

MAKES 1 BRAID

1 package active dry yeast	1 teaspoon salt
1 cup warm water,	1 egg
105° F. – 115° F.	1 cup whole wheat flour
1 tablespoon sugar	2 to 2½ cups unbleached
1 tablespoon butter, melted	all-purpose flour

GLAZE:

1 egg yolk beaten with
    2 tablespoons cold water
¼ cup toasted wheat germ
2 tablespoons sesame seeds

In large mixing bowl, dissolve yeast in warm water; add sugar. Stir and let stand for 5 minutes until yeast foams. Add butter, salt, and egg; beat well. Beat in the whole wheat flour and add all-purpose flour gradually to make a stiff dough. Cover and let stand 15 minutes. Turn out onto lightly floured board and knead until smooth and springy, about 5 minutes. Wash bowl, lightly grease, and add dough to bowl. Cover and let rise until doubled, about 1 hour. Cover baking sheet with parchment paper or lightly grease it. Turn dough out onto lightly oiled surface. Divide into 6 parts. Shape each into a strand about 12 inches long by rolling between palms of hands and board. Brush strands with mixture of egg yolk and water. Sprinkle wheat germ and sesame seeds on board and roll strands in the combination. Braid and pinch ends to seal. (See directions which follow (page 64) for making a 6-stranded braid). Lift braid onto prepared baking sheet and let rise until doubled, about 45 minutes to 1 hour. Preheat oven to 375° F. Bake for 25 to 30 minutes or until golden. Cool on wire rack.

BURGUNDIAN WHEAT AND WALNUT LOAVES

These wonderfully coarse and chewy breads owe their texture to a lot of chopped walnuts worked into the wheaty yeast dough.

MAKES 3 LOAVES

2 packages active dry yeast
2 cups warm water,
    105° F.–115° F.
1 tablespoon light or dark
    molasses
½ cup nonfat dry milk
2 tablespoons butter, at room
    temperature

2 teaspoons salt
1 cup unprocessed bran
3½ to 4 cups whole wheat
    flour
2½ cups coarsely chopped
    walnuts

GLAZE:

1 egg mixed with
    1 tablespoon milk

In large bowl, dissolve yeast in warm water; add molasses, stir, and set aside for 5 minutes until yeast foams. Stir in the dry milk, butter, salt, and bran. Beat in 3½ cups of the whole wheat flour, ½ cup at a time, until a stiff dough forms. Let rest 30 minutes. During this resting period the stickiness will have disappeared enough so that you may need to add only 1 to 2 tablespoons more of flour when you knead the dough. Turn dough out onto lightly floured board and knead until smooth, about 10 minutes. Wash bowl, and lightly oil it. Put kneaded dough into the bowl. Top dough with the chopped walnuts in an even layer. Cover with plastic wrap and let rise in a warm place until about doubled in bulk, 1 to 1½ hours. Turn out onto oiled work surface and knead walnuts into the dough until evenly dispersed. Add flour if necessary to keep dough from being sticky, but do not add more than 1 to 2 tablespoons. Keep pushing nuts back into dough until they stay in place. Divide dough into 3 parts. Shape each into a ball. Flatten slightly and place on baking sheet covered with parchment paper. Brush with egg-milk glaze and make 4 parallel slashes in the top of

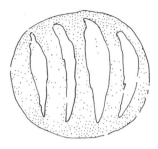

each loaf about ½ inch deep. Let rise until loaves are doubled and slashes have opened up, 45 minutes to 1 hour. Preheat oven to 375 ° F. Bake loaves for 35 minutes, or until they are evenly browned and sound hollow when tapped. Cool on rack.

CRACKED WHEAT CRUSTY LOAVES

These are crusty, long, slender loaves with the grainy texture of cracked wheat.

MAKES 4 LOAVES

1 cup cracked wheat	1 package active dry yeast
2 teaspoons salt	1½ cups whole wheat flour
1½ cups boiling water	2 to 2¼ cups bread flour or
1 tablespoon dark molasses	all-purpose flour
¾ cup warm water,	Cornmeal to cover baking
105° F.–115° F.	sheets

Put cracked wheat into large bowl, add salt and boiling water; stir. Cool to 105° F.–115° F. In small bowl, combine molasses, warm water, and yeast; stir and set aside for 5 minutes or until yeast foams. When cracked wheat mixture has cooled, stir in yeast mixture, then add whole wheat flour. Beat well. Stir in 2 cups of the bread flour and mix until mixture is stiff. Cover, and let rest for 15 minutes. Turn out onto lightly floured board and knead until smooth, about 10 minutes. Wash bowl, lightly grease, place dough into bowl, turn over once,

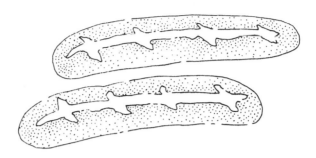

cover, and let rise until doubled. Divide into 4 parts. Shape into 4 long, slender loaves, as long as you can make them and still have them fit diagonally across your baking sheets.

Sprinkle 4 baking sheets with cornmeal. Place loaves diagonally on the sheets. Let rise until doubled, about 45 minutes. Preheat oven to 400° F. Using a sharp knife or razor blade and cutting to a depth of about ½ inch, slash lengthwise, then make 4 equally spaced crosswise cuts. Brush with water and bake loaves for 30 minutes or until crusty. If you can't fit all the loaves in your oven at once, bake 2 at a time. Cool on rack. To retard the rising of remaining loaves during baking, place in refrigerator or in a cold place (in the winter that can be outdoors), or if necessary, do not shape all 4 loaves at one time; stagger the shaping and rising steps so that loaves will not be over-risen when ready to bake.

WHOLE WHEAT BAGUETTES

The baguette of France is a long slender loaf that is usually made from white dough. Here the slender, crusty loaves are made from whole wheat dough and the flavor is a rich and robust one.

MAKES 2 BAGUETTES

1 package active dry yeast	*Pinch of ground ginger*
2 tablespoons light or dark	*1¼ cups warm water,*
brown sugar	*105° F.–115° F.*

1½ teaspoons salt
1½ cups bread flour
1½ cups whole wheat flour

Cornmeal for dusting baking
    sheet

In large bowl, dissolve yeast, brown sugar, and ginger in warm water. Let stand 5 minutes until yeast foams. Add salt and bread flour; beat well. Stir in whole wheat flour to make a stiff dough. Turn out onto lightly floured board and knead 10 minutes or until dough is springy, smooth, and satiny. Wash bowl, grease it, and add dough to bowl; turn over to grease top. Let rise in a warm place until doubled in bulk, about 1 hour. Lightly oil or grease a 14 x 17-inch baking sheet and sprinkle with cornmeal; set aside. Punch down the dough. Divide in half and, on a lightly floured surface, shape into long loaves, rolling each piece first into a 5 x 12-inch rectangle, then rolling each up along the long side to make a long, narrow loaf. Pinch ends to seal. Place loaves, seam side down, on prepared baking sheet. Make 4 to 5 slashes across each loaf with sharp knife or razor blade. Let rise until doubled, about 45 minutes. Brush each loaf with water and sprinkle with whole wheat flour. Bake in a preheated 400° F. oven for 15 to 20 minutes, until loaves are browned and crisp; remove to a wire rack to cool completely.

CRUSTY WHOLE WHEAT WREATH

MAKES 1 WREATH

Whole Wheat Baguette
    dough

1 egg white mixed with
    1 teaspoon salt

Shape the Whole Weat Baguette dough into 1 narrow loaf 36 inches long. Grease or cover baking sheet with parchment paper. Place loaf onto baking sheet. With scissors make snips almost all the way through the loaf every 2 inches, and turn the loaf into a circle, with the cuts on the outside of the circle and the connected part on the inside. Brush with egg white mixture. Let rise until puffy. Preheat oven to 400° F. Bake for 15 to 20 minutes, or until golden and crusty.

WHOLE WHEAT EGG BRAID

This is a big, beautiful 6-stranded braid that's encrusted with an appealing combination of sesame and poppy seeds. Although this is not a sweet bread, it has an intriguing hint of maple flavor.

MAKES 1 LARGE BRAID OR 2 LOAVES

2 packages active dry yeast
2 cups warm water,
   105° F.–115° F.
1 cup nonfat dry milk
⅓ cup maple syrup
5 eggs
3 cups whole wheat flour

2 to 3 cups bread flour or
   plain or unbleached
   all-purpose flour
1 tablespoon salt
⅓ cup butter, melted and
   cooled
½ cup unprocessed bran

GLAZE:

1 egg plus 2 tablespoons water

1 tablespoon each sesame seeds
and poppy seeds

In a large mixer bowl, combine yeast with warm water, dry milk, and maple syrup. Let stand 5 minutes until yeast is foamy. Whisk in the eggs; add half the whole wheat flour and half the bread flour; beat until smooth using electric mixer or wooden spoon. Cover and let rise 1 hour, until puffy. Stir down and add the salt, butter, and unprocessed bran. Add remaining whole wheat flour and beat until smooth. Slowly add the bread flour until dough is stiff. Let rest 15 minutes. Turn out onto lightly floured board and knead until dough is smooth, about 10 minutes. Wash bowl, lightly grease it, add dough to bowl, and turn over to grease top. Cover and let rise until doubled, about 1 hour.

    To shape, turn dough out onto lightly oiled board. Divide into 6 equal pieces. Roll each piece of dough into a strand about 20 inches long. Place strands side by side. To shape this six-stranded bread, start with the right outer strand, picking up the strand and weaving it over and under each of the other strands until it is at the far left of the braid. Repeat, always starting with the outside right strand, weaving it first under then over each successive strand until it is at the far left side of the braid. Continue until the braid is complete. Pinch ends together and compress the braid lengthwise with both hands to make a long, narrow loaf.

Place on lightly greased baking sheet. Let rise for 45 minutes to 1 hour, or until about doubled. Brush with egg-water glaze and sprinkle with sesame seeds and poppy seeds. Preheat oven to 375° F. and bake bread 40 to 45 minutes, or until loaf sounds hollow when tapped and appears golden brown. Cool on rack.

WALNUT WHEAT BERRY BREAD

Whole wheat kernels or "berries" soften after soaking and give this bread a doubly rich flavor and chewy texture. Walnuts have a natural affinity to whole wheat. This is simply wonderful served with good aged Cheddar cheese, apples, and pears.

MAKES 2 ROUND LOAVES

⅓ cup whole wheat berries
1 package active dry yeast
2½ cups warm water,
   105° F.–115° F.
¼ cup honey
2 tablespoons butter, softened
2 teaspoons salt
¼ cup wheat germ

5 cups whole wheat flour
½ to 1 cup bread flour or
   unbleached all-purpose
   flour
2 cups coarsely chopped
   walnuts
Melted butter for brushing
   loaves

The night before, put whole wheat berries into a small bowl and cover with warm water; let stand overnight, then drain. In large bowl, stir yeast into warm water; add honey, butter, salt, wheat germ, and drained whole wheat berries. Add 2 cups of the whole wheat flour; let stand 15 minutes or until yeast foams. Slowly stir in remaining whole wheat flour until stiff dough forms. Cover and let stand again for 30 minutes. Stir in enough bread flour to make dough no longer sticky. Turn out onto floured board and knead until smooth, about 10 minutes. Meanwhile, wash bowl and lightly oil it. Shape dough into a ball and place into bowl; turn over to grease top. Cover and let rise in a warm place until doubled, about 1 to 1½ hours. Punch dough down. On lightly floured surface, pat into a 10-inch circle. Press nuts into dough and knead until they are completely incorporated. Divide in half and shape into two round balls. Place on parchment-covered or lightly greased baking sheet. Let rise 1 hour or until loaves have doubled. Heat oven to 375° F. Brush loaves with melted butter and slash a ½-inch-deep X using a razor blade or a sharp knife. Bake 30 to 40 minutes, or until loaves sound hollow when tapped. Remove from baking sheets and cool on rack. Brush with butter.

WHOLE WHEAT BRIOCHE

My favorite brioches are shaped with the classic French topknots, but you can shape this dough into small oval loaves or individual breads as well. When you start this dough the day before, you'll discover that the chilled dough is very easy to shape; this version also requires no kneading.

MAKES 24 BRIOCHES OR 1 LARGE LOAF

2 packages active dry yeast	1 teaspoon salt
½ cup sugar	3 eggs, at room temperature
½ cup warm water,	2 cups whole wheat flour
105° F.–115° F.	2 cups bread flour or
½ cup milk, scalded	all-purpose flour
½ cup butter, softened	

GLAZE:

1 egg white	1 tablespoon sugar

In small bowl, dissolve yeast and 1 tablespoon of the sugar in the warm water. Let stand 5 minutes until yeast is foamy. In large bowl, mix the milk and butter; stir until butter is melted. Add salt, eggs, and whole wheat flour, mixing until smooth. Stir in the yeast mixture. Beat

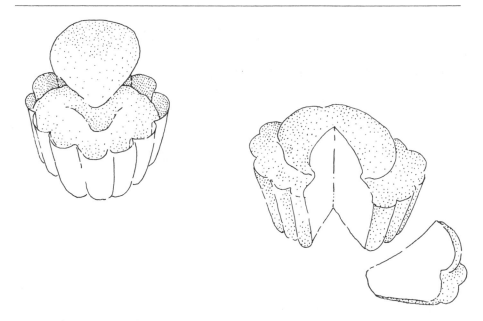

well. Beat in the bread flour to make a stiff dough. Cover with plastic wrap; let rise in refrigerator overnight. Stir down batter.

To shape 1 large brioche, cut off about 1 cup of the dough and set aside. Shape the remaining portion into a smooth, round ball. Place into well-greased large brioche tin. Make a deep indentation in the center of the ball of dough (your finger should touch the bottom of the pan). Shape the remaining dough into a teardrop with a smooth top. Insert pointed end into the center of the indentation. Let rise until doubled. Preheat oven to 350° F. Bake for 35 to 45 minutes, or until loaf sounds hollow when tapped. Cool on rack.

For smaller individual brioches, divide half the dough (return second half of dough to refrigerator) into 16 parts (divide into quarters, then divide each of the quarters into 4 parts). Shape 12 of the parts into balls and place in greased muffin or brioche cups. Flatten balls and make deep indentations in the centers. Divide remaining parts into 3 parts each. Roll each into little tear-shaped balls and place pointed side down into the indentations on the larger buns. Repeat shaping procedure for second half of the dough. Cover and let rise in a warm place until doubled, about 45 minutes. Beat egg white and 1 tablespoon sugar, then brush each brioche with the mixture. Bake in preheated oven at 350° F. for 20 minutes or until golden. Cool on rack.

CRACKED WHEAT MINILOAVES

These little pull-apart loaves have cracked wheat for texture and flavor blended with the aromatic sweetness of honey.

MAKES 6 SMALL LOAVES, 3 SERVINGS EACH

3 cups boiling water
1½ cups cracked wheat
⅓ cup plus 1 teaspoon honey
1 teaspoon salt
2 tablespoons oil
2 packages active dry yeast

⅔ cup warm water,
   105° F.–115° F.
2 cups gluten flour
2 to 3 cups whole wheat flour

In large mixing bowl, pour boiling water over the cracked wheat. Stir in the ⅓ cup honey, salt, and oil. Let stand 30 to 45 minutes, or until cooled to room temperature.

In small bowl, combine the yeast, warm water, and remaining honey. Let stand 5 minutes or until yeast foams. Blend into cracked wheat mixture, then stir in the gluten flour; beat well. Add 2 cups of the whole wheat flour and mix with hands, squeezing and pushing dough between fingers until dough feels evenly blended without any hard lumps. Cover and let rise for 1 hour. Punch down, then knead for 10 minutes or until dough is very smooth and springy, adding more whole wheat flour as needed.

Divide dough into 18 equal portions. Shape each into a ball. Place 3 at a time into 6 greased 5½ x 3-inch loaf pans. Let rise until doubled, 45 minutes to 1 hour. Preheat oven to 350° F. and bake 30 to 35 minutes or until golden. Cool on rack.

HIGH-PROTEIN DIETER'S BREAD

This is a dense, substantial bread that blends the flavors of high-protein soy flour with 3 forms of wheat! A thin slice (about 85 calories) is satisfying!

MAKES 2 LOAVES

> 3 cups warm water,
>   105° F.–115° F.
> 2 packages active dry yeast
> ¼ cup honey
> 3 cups whole wheat flour
> ¼ cup wheat germ
>
> ½ cup soy flour
> ¾ cup nonfat dry milk
> 2 teaspoons salt
> 2 tablespoons oil
> 3 to 4 cups bread flour or
>   all-purpose flour

In large mixing bowl, combine warm water, yeast, and honey. Stir and let stand 5 minutes until yeast foams. Mix in the whole wheat flour; beat well. Stir in the wheat germ, soy flour, dry milk, salt, and oil. Beat well. Add bread flour 1 cup at a time, beating well after each addition. When dough is stiff, turn out onto lightly floured board and knead until smooth and elastic. Wash bowl. Oil bowl and add dough; turn over and cover. Let rise in warm place until doubled, about 1 hour. Punch down, divide in half. Shape each into a loaf and place into greased 8½ x 4½-inch loaf pans. Let rise until doubled, about 45 minutes. Preheat oven to 350° F. Bake for 45 to 50 minutes, or until loaves pull away from sides of pan and sound hollow when tapped. Remove from pans and cool on racks.

SPROUTED WHEAT BREAD

You can buy wheat kernels for sprouting from almost any natural foods store that carries a good supply of natural grains. Plan to start this bread 3 days in advance! Wheat sprouts are especially sweet and chewy in this moist bread.

MAKES 3 LOAVES

> 1 cup whole wheat berries
> 2 packages active dry yeast
> 2 cups warm water,
>   105° F.–115° F.
> 1 cup nonfat dry milk
> ½ cup honey
>
> 1 tablespoon salt
> ⅓ cup lard, melted and cooled
> 2 cups whole wheat flour
> 4 to 4½ cups bread flour or
>   all-purpose flour

Three days in advance, cover whole wheat berries with warm water in glass bowl or jar. Replace water every 12 hours, adding warm, not hot, water each time. When berries have sprouts as long as the kernels themselves, they are ready. Drain well. They should measure about 4 cups. In large bowl, dissolve yeast in warm water; add the dry milk and honey, and set aside for 5 minutes until yeast foams. Add salt, sprouts, lard, and whole wheat flour. Beat until smooth. Add bread flour, 1 cup at a time, until a stiff dough forms. Let stand for 15 minutes. Turn out onto floured board and knead until dough is springy and smooth, about 10 minutes. Wash bowl, grease lightly, and add dough to bowl; turn over, cover, and let rise in a warm place until doubled. Punch dough down, divide into 3 parts. Grease three 8½ x 4½-inch loaf pans or three 9-inch round cake pans. Shape 3 loaves and place in pans. Cover and let rise until doubled, 1 hour and 15 minutes. Bake at 375° F. for 35 to 40 minutes, or until loaves sound hollow when tapped. Cool on rack.

FOUR-WHEAT BREAD

Ideal for sandwiches and toast, this bread has wheat in 4 different forms: all-purpose flour, whole wheat flour, whole wheat berries, and wheat germ. Make it as a 'snipped wreath' for a party!

MAKES 2 LOAVES

½ cup whole wheat berries
2½ cups water
1 package active dry yeast
2 tablespoons sugar
2 cups warm water,
    105° F.–115° F.
2 teaspoons salt
¼ cup butter, margarine, or
    oil, melted

1 cup nonfat dry milk
½ cup wheat germ
1 cup whole wheat flour
4 to 4½ cups bread flour or
    unbleached all-purpose
    flour

The day before you plan to make the bread, put the whole wheat berries and 2 cups of the water into a saucepan; heat just to lukewarm, cover, and set aside overnight or longer. Drain well. In large mixing bowl, dissolve yeast and sugar in warm water. Let stand 5 minutes until yeast foams. Add salt, butter, dry milk, whole wheat berries, wheat germ, and whole wheat flour. Gradually add bread flour until dough is stiff. Let rest 15 minutes. Turn out onto board sprinkled with some of the remaining flour and knead until smooth and elastic, about 10 minutes. Wash bowl, grease it, turn dough over to grease top, and cover. Let rise in a warm place until doubled, about 1 hour. Punch dough down. Divide in half. Grease two 8½ x 4½-inch loaf pans or two 9-inch round cake pans and shape loaves for the pans. Let rise until doubled, about 45 minutes. Preheat oven to 375° F. Bake for 25 to 30 minutes, until loaves sound hollow when tapped. Cool on rack.

SNIPPED WREATH: Shape the dough into 1 strand about 20 inches long and 3 inches in diameter. Place in a circle on parchment-covered baking sheet. Seal ends to form a big donut. With scissors, snip "leaves" over the entire top of the circle of dough. Spread leaves out. Let rise until doubled. Brush with water before baking. Bake as directed above.

MOLASSES WHOLE WHEAT BREAD

Whole wheat has a special affinity to molasses. Combined with oats, the whole wheat in this recipe makes a loaf with a close texture and wholesome flavor. It slices best the next day; be sure to slice it thinly. Gluten flour is combined with the whole wheat for extra-easy handling. Be sure to knead the loaf thoroughly!

MAKES 2 LOAVES

½ cup molasses, light or dark	2 teaspoons salt
2 packages active dry yeast	½ cup quick-cooking rolled
1¾ cups warm water,	oats
105° F.–115° F.	½ cup wheat germ
⅔ cup nonfat dry milk	½ cup unprocessed bran
2 eggs, beaten	1 cup gluten flour
2 teaspoons salad oil	2 to 3 cups whole wheat flour

In large mixing bowl, combine molasses, yeast, and warm water. Stir until blended; set aside for 5 minutes until yeast is foamy. Add the dry milk, eggs, oil, salt, rolled oats, wheat germ, bran, and gluten flour; beat well. Stir in enough whole wheat flour to make a stiff dough. Let stand 30 minutes. Turn out onto floured board and knead until smooth and satiny, 10 to 15 minutes.

Wash bowl. Grease bowl, add dough ball, turn over to grease top, and let rise, covered, until doubled—about 2 hours. Punch down; divide in half. Grease two 9-inch round cake pans, then shape dough to fit pans and place loaves into pans. With knife, slash tops of loaves to make 1-inch squares. Brush with water. Cover and let rise again until puffy, about 1 to 1½ hours. Bake in a preheated 350° F. oven for 35 to 45 minutes. Cool on racks.

PARSLIED MONKEY BREAD WREATH

This is the best kind of bread to have handy for a holiday dinner. You can make it 2 days in advance, then shape the bread and refrigerate it again for 8 hours before allowing it to rise and bake. Monkey bread traditionally is made of small puffs of dough, which after baking can be easily torn apart, rather than cut, while being served. This is easy for either a buffet or sit-down dinner.

MAKES ONE 10- TO 12-INCH RING

2 packages active dry yeast
1 cup warm water,
    105° F.–115° F.
1 cup butter, melted
½ cup sugar
3 eggs, at room temperature

1 teaspoon salt
1 cup whole wheat flour
3½ to 4 cups unbleached
    all-purpose flour
½ cup finely chopped fresh
    parsley

In large mixing bowl, soften yeast in warm water; stir and let stand until yeast foams, about 5 minutes. Add ½ cup melted butter, plus the sugar, eggs, and salt; beat well. Beat in the whole wheat flour and add the all-purpose flour 1 cup at a time until dough is stiff. Cover with plastic wrap and refrigerate 2 hours to 2 days. Heavily grease one 11-cup or two 5- to 6-cup ring molds. Turn dough out onto lightly floured board and divide into quarters. Divide quarters again into quarters, making 16 pieces, then divide each of those pieces into quarters. You should have 64 little pieces of dough. Dip each of the dough pieces into the remaining melted butter and the chopped parsley. Place dough dipped side down into the prepared ring mold or molds. Layer the dough balls evenly. When all are dipped, cover and let rise for 45 minutes or until almost doubled. Preheat oven to 375° F. and bake for 20 to 30 minutes, until golden. Invert onto serving tray and serve warm.

ROSEMARY WHOLE WHEAT BREAD

A hint of rosemary blended with the flavor of whole wheat makes this bread perfect to serve with antipasto or cheese, sliced meats, or Italian-style foods.

MAKES 1 FLAT ROUND LOAF

1 package active dry yeast
1 cup warm water,
105° F.–115° F.
3 teaspoons dried rosemary
leaves
1 tablespoon sugar
1 teaspoon salt

1 cup whole wheat flour
1½ to 2 cups unbleached
all-purpose flour
2 tablespoons olive oil
2 teaspoons grated Parmesan
cheese

In large mixing bowl, dissolve yeast in warm water; add 2 teaspoons of the rosemary and all the sugar; let stand 5 minutes until yeast foams. Stir in salt, whole wheat flour, and 1½ cups of the all-purpose flour to make a stiff dough. Let stand 15 minutes. Sprinkle board with remaining flour and turn dough out onto it. Knead until smooth and satiny, about 5 to 8 minutes. Wash bowl, grease it, place dough in bowl, turn over to grease top. Cover and let rise in warm place until doubled, about 1 hour. Cover baking sheet with parchment paper or lightly grease it. Punch dough down and shape into a flat round about 9 inches in diameter; place on prepared baking sheet. Let rise until doubled, 45 minutes to 1 hour. With fork, punch holes into the loaf and sprinkle with olive oil, remaining rosemary, and Parmesan cheese. Preheat oven to 375° F. and bake until loaf sounds hollow when tapped, 25 to 30 minutes. Remove from pan and cool on wire rack.

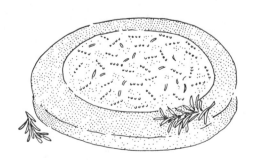

SHAKER GRAHAM BREAD

The Shakers, whose origins can be traced to France, believed in respect for basic foods, the use of herbs, and wholesome bread, which was intended as a true staff of life, not just a crutch. "Bread is to be eaten and enjoyed three times a day" was one saying in their communities.

MAKES 2 LARGE LOAVES

1 cup milk
¼ cup sugar
2 teaspoons salt
4 tablespoons butter
1 cup warm water,
*   105° F.–115° F.*

1 package active dry yeast
2 cups whole wheat flour
3 to 3½ cups bread flour or
*   unbleached all-purpose*
*   flour*
Melted butter

In saucepan, combine milk, sugar, salt, and butter; heat to just a simmer. Remove from heat and cool to 105° F.–115° F. In a large mixing bowl, mix warm water and yeast; let stand until yeast foams, about 5 minutes, and when first mixture has cooled, add it to the yeast mixture. Stir in the whole wheat flour; beat until smooth. Add bread flour slowly, beating to keep batter smooth until it makes a stiff dough. Let rest 15 minutes. Turn dough out onto lightly floured board and knead 10 minutes, or until smooth and springy. Add more flour as needed to keep dough from sticking. Wash bowl, grease it, and add dough to bowl; turn over to grease top and cover. Let rise in a warm place until doubled, about 1 hour. Punch dough down and divide in half. Shape into 2 loaves. Place into 2 greased 8½ x 4½ inch loaf pans. Brush with melted butter. Let rise until dough is rounded above the pans, about 1 hour. Preheat oven to 350° F. Bake for 35 minutes. Brush again with melted butter. Remove from pans and cool on racks.

SHAKER ONION PAN ROLLS: Add ½ cup instant minced onion to the milk before heating with remaining ingredients and increase milk by ¼ cup. Proceed as directed above, but divide dough into 18 equal pieces. Shape each into a ball and arrange in 2 greased 8- or 9-inch round cake pans. Let rise until almost doubled. Preheat oven to 350° F. Bake for 25 minutes, until browned.

NORWEGIAN WHEAT BUN BREAD

Great for a crowd or a church supper! You shape these loaves as if you were making baguettes (French bread). With scissors, snip each loaf into 6 segments, and then turn alternate pieces of dough over so that all 6 buns are "hinged" together. The bread is sweetened slightly with honey and has a healthy touch of soy.

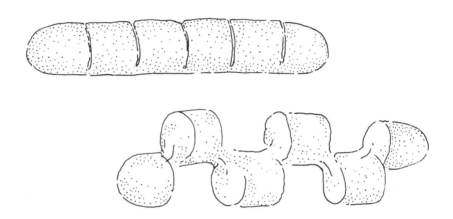

MAKES **3** LOAVES, **6** SEGMENTS EACH

1 package active dry yeast
¼ cup warm water,
　　105° F.–115° F.
1 tablespoon sugar
2 cups buttermilk, scalded
　　and cooled to
　　105° F.–115° F.
2 tablespoons shortening or
　　butter, softened

¼ cup honey
2 teaspoons salt
2 eggs
½ cup soy flour
2 cups whole wheat flour
5 to 5½ cups bread flour or
　　unbleached all-purpose
　　flour

In large bowl, dissolve yeast in warm water; add sugar, then let stand 5 minutes until yeast foams. Add buttermilk, shortening, honey, salt, eggs, and soy flour; beat well. Beat in whole wheat flour, then add bread flour 1 cup at a time, beating well after each addition and keeping the mixture smooth. When dough is stiff, cover and let rest 15 minutes. Turn out onto lightly floured board and knead for 10 minutes or until smooth and elastic. Wash bowl, grease it, add dough to bowl, turn over, and let rise until doubled—1 to 1½ hours. Punch dough down and divide into 3 parts. Shape into loaves each about 16 inches long and evenly thick. Place on parchment-covered or lightly greased baking sheets. With scissors, snip dough almost all the way through to make 6 equal-sized pieces, leaving the pieces attached (see diagram). Lift every second piece up and roll over, topside down. Let rise until doubled. Brush tops of loaves with water. Preheat oven to 400° F. Bake for 25 to 30 minutes or until loaves are crusty. To serve, separate the "buns."

ROLLED WHEAT-FLAKE BREAD

Rolled wheat flakes look a lot like old-fashioned rolled oats, and are available as a cereal in natural foods stores. Rolled wheat flakes give a flavor and texture to a yeast bread that is unlike any other.

MAKES 2 LOAVES

> 1 cup rolled wheat flakes
> 2 cups boiling water
> ¼ cup lard or vegetable oil
> 2 packages active dry yeast
> ½ cup warm water,
>   105° F.–115° F.
>
> ¼ cup honey
> 1½ teaspoons salt
> 2 cups whole wheat flour
> 3 to 3½ cups bread flour or
>   unbleached all-purpose
>   flour

In large mixing bowl combine rolled wheat flakes and boiling water; add lard. Let stand 30 minutes, or until cooled to 105° F.–115° F. In small bowl, dissolve yeast in warm water; add honey and let stand 5 minutes until yeast foams. Add yeast to cooled wheat mixture along with salt and wheat flour. Beat well. Add bread flour 1 cup at a time, beating well after each addition, until dough is soft but stiff enough to knead. Let rest 15 minutes. Turn out onto lightly floured board and knead for 10 minutes or until springy and well mixed. Dough may be slightly tacky to the touch, but should hold its shape on the board. Wash bowl, grease it, and add dough to bowl; turn over to grease top. Cover and let rise in a warm place until doubled, about 1 to 1½ hours. Grease two 8½ x 4½-inch loaf pans. Punch dough down and shape into 2 loaves. Place into pans. Let rise until doubled. Preheat oven to 375° F. Bake for 30 to 35 minutes, or until loaves sound hollow when tapped. Remove from pans and cool on wire rack.

HERBED HEARTH BREAD

Fragrant and moist, these thick warm slices are best served with hearty bean soup.

MAKES 1 LARGE LOAF

2 packages active dry yeast
1½ cups warm water,
        105° F.–115° F.
3 tablespoons tightly packed
        light or dark brown
        sugar
1 cup nonfat dry milk
3 tablespoons vegetable oil
½ cup chopped fresh onion
½ cup chopped fresh parsley

1 teaspoon salt
1 teaspoon dill weed
½ teaspoon thyme leaves
⅓ cup yellow cornmeal
½ cup gluten flour
3 to 3½ cups whole wheat
        flour
Sesame seeds to sprinkle over
        loaf

In large mixing bowl, dissolve yeast in warm water; add brown sugar and dry milk. Let stand 5 minutes until yeast foams. In sauté pan, heat oil and add onion; sauté until onion is soft, about 5 minutes. Add the onion, parsley, salt, dill weed, and thyme to milk mixture. Beat in the cornmeal and gluten flour. Add 3 cups of the whole wheat flour, 1 cup at a time, beating well after each addition, until dough is stiff. Let stand 15 minutes. Sprinkle board with remaining flour, turn dough out onto board, and knead until smooth and satiny, about 10 minutes. Wash bowl, grease it, and place dough into bowl; turn over and cover. Let rise until doubled, about 1 hour. Cover baking sheet with parchment paper or lightly grease it. Punch dough down, and shape into

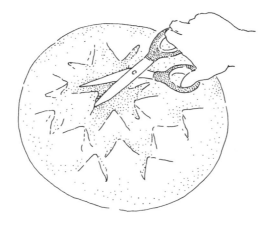

one large, round loaf. Place on prepared baking sheet. Let rise until doubled, about 45 minutes to 1 hour. If desired, use a scissors to snip 2-inch cuts in a concentric circle starting at the outside edge of the loaf and make petal-shaped dough points. The loaf, when entirely snipped, will look like a stylized rose. Brush with water and sprinkle with sesame seeds. Preheat oven to 375° F. Bake for 30 to 40 minutes, or until loaf sounds hollow when tapped.

WALNUT-CRUSTED WHEAT LOAVES

Slashed with a cross on top, these grainy three-wheat loaves are both studded and topped with walnuts. Excellent with sharp Cheddar cheese shaved in thin slices.

MAKES 2 LOAVES

1½ cups boiling water
½ cup honey
⅓ cup vegetable shortening
2 teaspoons salt
2 packages active dry yeast
½ cup warm water,
    105° F.–115° F.
2 eggs

½ cup wheat germ
½ cup gluten flour
1½ to 2 cups bread flour or
    unbleached all-purpose
    flour
3 cups whole wheat flour
1 cup coarsely chopped
    walnuts

GLAZE:

¼ *cup water*   ¼ *cup sugar*

TOPPING:

¼ *cup coarsely chopped*
  walnuts

In large bowl of electric mixer, combine boiling water, honey, short-ening, and salt. Stir until shortening melts, then cool to lukewarm. In small bowl, dissolve the yeast in warm water. Add to honey mixture along with eggs, wheat germ, gluten flour, and 1½ cups bread flour. Beat with mixer for 2 minutes at medium speed. Stir in whole wheat flour and walnuts. Mixture will be sticky. Let rest 15 minutes. Sprin-kle work surface with remaining bread flour, turn dough out onto flour, and knead until dough feels smooth and springy and well mixed. Wash bowl, grease it, and add dough to bowl. Cover and let rise in a warm place until doubled, about 45 minutes to 1 hour. Divide in half and shape into 2 round loaves. Place into well-greased 9-inch round cake or pie pans. Let rise until doubled. Meanwhile in a sauce-pan, combine the ¼ cup water and ¼ cup sugar for the glaze. Bring to a boil and boil until syrupy, about 2 minutes. Brush tops of loaves with the syrup and sprinkle evenly with the walnuts. With sharp knife or razor blade, slash a cross into the top of each loaf about ½ inch deep. Preheat oven to 375° F. Bake for 30 to 35 minutes. Remove from pans; cool on wire racks.

RYE BREADS

As a child, I lived on dark, wholesome, homemade rye bread. Even the bread that we bought at the baker's in our little northern Minnesota town had full-bodied character to it. Most of it was rye or whole wheat in big, fat, round loaves with crackly tops. You needed a really hefty knife to cut it. I have recently enjoyed hefty rye bread in the Scandinavian countries, especially in Finland.

Rye is one of the important cereal grains of the world and grows in more "difficult" conditions than wheat—on poorer soil and in colder climates. In the United States, rye is grown in the high plateaus of Colorado as a winter crop. It is planted in the fall and harvested in the early summer.

Rye breads are often associated with true peasant breads. A rye bread made with 100 percent rye flour is called black bread in many European countries and in the Soviet Union. Today, rye is mixed most commonly with wheat flour to make a bread with a texture that is less dense and with a crisper crust.

Rye flour produces a sour-tasting dough rather easily. (Could that be why it is so useful in the distilling industry?) Rye flour does have the ability to transform itself into a self-rising dough if it is given time to ferment. The peasanty sour rye bread of the Soviet Union, of the German backwoods, and of the Finnish countryside have flavors so compelling that a native forced to live "without black bread" soon craves it!

Caraway seed is the most common flavoring seed added to rye breads. In Scandinavia, a combination of caraway, anise and fennel seeds ground together in a mortar and pestle and combined with the grated rind of an orange makes a typical limpa bread. Molasses or dark corn syrup often is part of the flavor, and in some parts of Scandinavia this bread must also begin with a sourdough starter.

The most common forms of rye flour that are available in the markets today are "light," "medium," and "dark."

LIGHT AND MEDIUM RYE FLOUR

These pale, grayish-tan flours are ground from the endosperm of the rye grain, meaning that the bran and germ are lost. Both light and medium rye flours are fine in texture. These are usually available in supermarkets in 5-pound bags. Side by side, it is difficult to distinguish between the light and medium flours, especially because they tend to vary depending upon the manufacturer. Light and medium rye flours usually are used in breads that include more spices and flavorings, especially those which are "finer" or designated for holidays.

DARK RYE FLOUR

This flour is entirely different from light or medium rye flours. The dark rye flour has a coarser look to it because it also includes the bran and the germ of the grain, and it adds a darker color to the bread. Even though this flour includes more of the grain, and seems to be the more logical choice for all rye breads, it generally is used in pumpernickels and certain peasant breads. Dark rye flour is sold under many names; sometimes it is called "dark rye flour," sometimes "pumpernickel rye flour," sometimes "rye meal," and sometimes "stone-ground rye flour."

CRACKED WHOLE RYE

This is sometimes called rye "groats" because the appearance is much like buckwheat groats. To use it in whole grain breads, the cracked rye—like cracked wheat—needs to be softened in hot water. It adds a delicious flavor and interesting texture to bread.

WHOLE RYE FLAKES

These look like rolled oats, only they are the whole rye grain heated and pressed, as are the oats. They are delicious as a cooked cereal or cooked and added to bread doughs.

WHOLE GRAIN RYE BERRIES

Available in whole foods and nutrition stores, usually by the pound, whole grain rye appears much like whole wheat berries. It can be soaked to soften and added to bread, or it may be sprouted.

HANDLING RYE BREADS

Sometimes, especially when the kitchen is warm, rye doughs will tend to feel "stickier" after rising than they were just after kneading. There is a tendency for rye flours to "break down" during rising at high temperatures, and if this happens to you, resist the temptation to add more flour. Rather, put the dough into the refrigerator and chill it as long as overnight before shaping and baking. If you really want to shape and bake it immediately, dust the work table with rye flour and turn dough out onto it. Dust the ball of dough all over with flour and cut into loaf-sized portions. With well-floured hands, shape the dough into rounded balls, enclosing the stickiest portions of the dough on the inside. Oil the work table and knead each loaf lightly to express the air bubbles. Place on baking sheets and proceed as in the directions.

WHERE TO BUY RYE FLOURS

As mentioned earlier, well-stocked supermarkets often have light, medium, and pumpernickel rye flours, especially in Northern states where people bake more rye breads. If you cannot locate the flour, check natural foods shops and nutrition stores. While you are there, look for whole grain rye (for soaking or sprouting), and cracked whole rye, which can be soaked and added to bread doughs for texture.

BLACK BREAD COLORING OR CARAMEL COLORING

Several years ago, I was in a local bakery trying to decide among light, medium, and dark rye bread, all beautifully displayed inside a glass case. When I asked the baker behind the counter the difference among the three breads, he shrugged his shoulders, fixed his eyes on the ceiling, and said, "Different amounts of black bread coloring." I was taken back. A few years later, when I was teaching at the local Vocational Technical Institute, I asked the bakery instructor about "black bread coloring." "Oh, yes!" he exclaimed, "we use it all the time."

"But what is it made of?" I asked, expecting an answer that would turn me forever from black bread.

"Oh, it's just caramel coloring—made from burnt sugar."

It was an early practice to actually burn bread crumbs to make a coloring for bread; an easier method now is to burn sugar. To make such a coloring, burn a small amount of sugar in a frying pan and add enough water to dissolve it. Then simply boil down the resulting liquid to make a syrupy coloring for bread. (See also the recipe for Heidelberg Rye Bread)

A simpler solution is to locate a local bakery supply or ask your baker if you may purchase a small amount of the coloring. The caramel coloring that is prepared for the bakery industry is very concentrated, and a little goes a long way. Half a teaspoon is sufficient to darkly color a two-loaf batch of bread. I purchased a gallon of coloring about fifteen years ago, and I still have about ½ cup left!

COMBINING RYE WITH OTHER GRAINS

A 100 percent rye-flour bread is possible, and is traditional in many countries of the world. It is a very dense and heavy peasant bread. We include a recipe for it; however, don't expect it to be really easy to handle! Also, don't expect it to be high and light!

For a loaf of bread that rises well, rye flour should be combined with wheat flour, ideally in a 50-50 proportion (or no more than 50 percent rye flour) so that the dough has sufficient gluten to rise properly. But rye flour blends well with whole wheat, oat, barley, and other grains to achieve special flavor effects. If you experiment with these combinations, be sure that half the flour is wheat flour, and use any combination of whole grains for the other half, including rye flour. However, if the bread is to be called a rye bread, then you should use more rye than any other whole grain.

100 PERCENT RYE BREAD

Because rye flour is a low-gluten flour, breads made purely from rye flour require special handling. The long rising period develops a somewhat sour flavor and also serves to encourage the small amount of gluten in the rye flour. Extra yeast is also necessary for rising. This bread bakes into a compact, rather heavy, but delicious loaf that is excellent when sliced extra thin. Bake it a day before slicing it.

MAKES 1 LARGE LOAF

½ cup whole grain rye
2 cups water
2 packages active dry yeast
1 cup warm water,
    105° F.–115° F.

⅓ cup dark corn syrup
5 to 5½ cups dark rye flour
2 teaspoons salt

Wash and pick over the whole grain rye. Put into blender and whirl until grain is coarsely cracked. Place in saucepan and add water; bring to a boil, then simmer 45 minutes or until grain is tender to the bite. Drain, cool to 105° F.–115° F. In large mixing bowl, dissolve yeast in warm water. Add corn syrup; let stand 5 minutes until yeast foams. Stir in the cooled, cooked rye. Add 2 cups of the rye flour; beat until smooth; cover and let rise 30 minutes. Sprinkle salt over mixture and stir in 3 cups more flour until mixure is stiff. Cover and let rise in a warm place for 2½ to 3 hours. Sprinkle board with additional flour and turn dough out onto it. Dough will be sticky. With well-floured hands, shape dough into an oblong loaf about 7 x 11 inches. Pat outside of loaf generously with flour. Generously grease a baking sheet and transfer loaf to sheet. Cover with plastic wrap and let rise until doubled. Preheat oven to 350° F. and bake for 30 to 35 minutes; loaf will not brown much, but top will appear crackled. Remove from pan and cool on rack.

FARMER'S RYE BREAD

This is the bread that I grew up with on the farm in northern Minnesota. It is textured with dark rye flour. (If you cannot get it in the store, a whole wheat flour is a good substitute.)

MAKES 1 LOAF

1 package active dry yeast
¼ cup warm water,
    105° F.–115° F.

1 cup warm potato water,
    105° F.–115° F.

1 tablespoon light or dark
    brown sugar
1 tablespoon butter, lard, or
    bacon fat, melted
1½ teaspoons salt

1½ cups dark rye flour
2 to 2½ cups bread flour or
    unbleached all-purpose
    flour
Melted butter for top

In large mixing bowl dissolve yeast in warm water. Let stand 4 minutes or until yeast foams. Pour in the potato water and add the brown sugar, butter, salt, and rye flour. Beat well, then stir in bread flour until a stiff dough forms. Cover, and let rest 15 minutes. Turn out onto floured board and knead until smooth, about 10 minutes. Wash bowl and grease it; add dough to bowl, turn over to grease top, cover, and let rise in a warm place until doubled, about 1 hour, 15 minutes. Punch down; shape into a round loaf. Grease a 9-inch round cake pan. Place dough into pan and let rise again until almost doubled, 45 minutes to 1 hour. Pierce all over with a fork. Preheat oven to 375° F. Bake for 45 to 50 minutes, or until loaf sounds hollow when tapped. Remove from pan and cool on rack. Brush with butter while hot.

SWEDISH LIMPA

This is a handy overnight method for baking limpa. It accomplishes 2 things: 1. With our cooler kitchens, it is sometimes difficult to get bread to rise, and because the dough starts out with cold ingredients, the yeast grows slowly and evenly in the dough overnight without developing a yeasty taste. 2. This method is handy for busy people who do not have time to begin and finish bread-baking projects in one day. An additional feature is that the dough requires very little kneading.

MAKES 4 LOAVES

¼ cup warm water,
    105° F.–115° F.
1 package active dry yeast
1 quart cold whole milk
¼–½ teaspoon black bread
    coloring, if desired (see
    chapter introduction)
1 cup dark molasses
1 cup salad oil
1 cup dark brown sugar
1 tablespoon salt

2 teaspoons each caraway,
    fennel, and anise seeds,
    crushed
Grated rind of 1 orange
1 cup rolled oats,
    old-fashioned or
    quick-cooking
2 cups medium rye flour
11 to 12 cups bread flour or
    unbleached all-purpose
    flour

In very large mixing bowl, mix the warm water with the yeast. Let stand 5 minutes until yeast foams. Add milk, coloring if used, molasses, oil, brown sugar, salt, crushed seeds, orange rind, rolled oats, and rye flour. Stir until smooth. Add bread flour, 2 cups at a time, until 8 to 9 cups have been added and mixture is very stiff; scrape bottom and sides of bowl as you go. Cover with plastic wrap. Let stand in cool, draft-free place (such as the countertop in a cool corner of the kitchen) for 8 to 14 hours. At the end of this time, the dough will be bubbly, and look much more moist than it did in the beginning.

Sprinkle top of dough with flour, then scrape down sides of bowl using a rubber spatula. Dust work surface with more flour and turn dough out onto flour. Knead until smooth, about 5 minutes. Divide into 4 parts and shape into loaves. Grease four 9 x 5-inch bread pans and place loaves into pans. Let rise in a warm place until doubled. Preheat oven to 350° F. Bake loaves for 30 to 35 minutes, or until loaves sound hollow when tapped. Remove from pans and cool on racks.

BOHEMIAN RYE BREAD

This bread traditionally is allowed to rise in a coarsely woven basket, then inverted onto the baking sheet, the imprint of the basket remaining on the loaf. In the directions here, the dough is allowed to rise in a cloth-lined bowl because it is easier to handle and because Bohemians in this country have grown accustomed to handling the dough this way.

MAKES 1 LARGE LOAF

2 packages active dry yeast
2 cups warm water,
    105° F.–115° F.
¼ cup sugar
2 tablespoons butter, softened
4 teaspoons salt

1 teaspoon caraway seeds
3 cups light or medium rye
    flour
3-3⅓ cups bread flour
Melted butter

In a large bowl, dissolve the yeast in ¾ cup warm water and add the sugar. Let stand 10 minutes until yeast foams. Add the remaining warm water, butter, salt, caraway seeds, and rye flour. Beat well. Add bread flour, ½ cup at a time, to make a stiff dough. Turn dough out

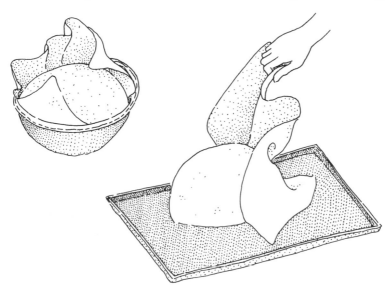

onto lightly floured surface, cover, and let rest for 15 minutes. Knead for 10 minutes or until smooth and satiny, then form into a ball. Wash the bowl, lightly grease, add the dough, and turn over once to coat it with the grease lightly. Cover and let rise in a warm place until doubled, about 1½ hours. Punch down and knead a few times on lightly floured board. Shape again into a ball. Line a 4-quart mixing bowl with a tea towel and put dough smooth side down into the bowl. Let the dough rise, covered with a tea towel, in a warm place for 1 hour or until almost doubled. Uncover the dough. Set a buttered baking sheet buttered side down over the bowl, then invert the dough onto it. Remove the towel, dampening it if necessary, and using the handle of a wooden spoon poke a hole completely through the center of the loaf. This will break up any large air holes. Bake in a preheated 450° F. oven for 10 minutes, reduce heat to 350° F., and bake 45 minutes more or until loaf sounds hollow when bottom is tapped. Transfer the loaf to a rack, brush top with melted butter, and let it cool. Cut the bread into quarters and slice each quarter.

VÖRTBRÖD—SWEDISH CHRISTMAS RYE

This is a richly flavored rye bread that in the past was made only during the holiday season because of its rather flamboyant ingredients.

MAKES 2 LOAVES

2 packages active dry yeast
1 teaspoon sugar
1 cup warm water,
    105° F.–115° F.
¼ cup butter
1½ cups (12-ounce can) dark
    beer
½ cup dark corn syrup

6 cups light or medium rye
    flour
3½ to 4½ cups bread flour or
    all-purpose flour
Grated rind of 2 oranges
2 tablespoons aniseed, crushed
2 teaspoons salt

GLAZE:

> *2 tablespoons molasses mixed*
> *with ½ cup water*

In a large mixing bowl, dissolve yeast and sugar in warm water. In saucepan, combine the butter and beer and heat until butter melts. Cool mixture to lukewarm, 105° F.–115° F. Add to yeast mixture along with the corn syrup and 3 cups of the rye flour and 1½ cups of the bread flour, the orange rind, aniseed and salt; beat until smooth. Cover and let rise in a warm place for 30 minutes or until puffy. Stir in 3 cups more rye flour and add bread flour, 1 cup at a time, until dough is stiff. Turn out onto floured surface and let rest 10 minutes. Wash bowl; grease lightly. Knead dough until smooth and satiny, about 10 minutes. Add dough to greased bowl, turn over to grease top, cover, and let rise in a warm place until doubled, about 1 hour.

Divide dough in half. Remove 1-cup piece of dough from each part and set aside. Shape remaining dough into 2 round loaves. Cover baking sheets with parchment paper or lightly grease; place loaves on prepared sheets. Cut each reserved piece of dough into 2 parts. Between hands and bread board, roll out to make strands about 10 inches long. With scissors, cut a 4-inch vertical slit in from either end of each strand (leaving a 2-inch part in the center uncut). Place cut strands in crossed fashion over the top of each loaf. Roll slit ends outward to make curliques. (See drawing). Let rise in a warm place for 1 hour or until about doubled. Bake in a preheated 375° F. oven for 15 minutes. Brush loaves with molasses and water mixture and bake for

15 to 20 minutes more, or until loaves sound hollow when tapped. Brush again with molasses mixture and cool on racks.

MINNESOTA FARMER'S BUTTERMILK RYE LOAVES

If we ever had store-bought bread when I was growing up, it was this fennel-sweetened buttermilk rye, which we bought at the local co-op. The bread was made by a baker who learned his trade in Sweden. Now when I taste this bread, I recollect those days and associate the flavor with the hot summertime, with haymaking, and with berry picking in northern Minnesota. We would make sandwiches using homemade sausage and cheese, and drink home-brewed root beer or *kalja*, a homemade Finnish malt drink, both chilled in our root cellar.

MAKES 3 LOAVES

1 cup water	½ teaspoon baking soda
¼ cup light (unsulfured) molasses	2 packages active dry yeast
¼ cup tightly packed light or dark brown sugar	¼ cup warm water, 105° F.–115° F.
2 tablespoons fennel seeds, crushed	1 teaspoon sugar
1 tablespoon butter	4 cups light or medium rye flour
1 tablespoon salt	3 to 4 cups bread flour or all-purpose flour
2 cups buttermilk	

In saucepan, combine water, molasses, brown sugar, fennel seeds, butter, and salt. Bring to a boil, then remove from heat immediately and stir until butter is melted. In large bowl, combine buttermilk and baking soda; add the molasses mixture. Stir and cool to lukewarm, 105° F.–115° F. In a small bowl, dissolve the yeast in warm water; add the sugar. Let stand 5 minutes until yeast foams. Add yeast mixture to buttermilk mixture and stir in the rye flour. Beat until smooth. Add bread flour, 1 cup at a time, until stiff dough forms. Cover and let stand 10 minutes. Turn dough out onto lightly floured board. Wash bowl; grease it. Knead dough 10 minutes or until smooth and springy.

Put dough into bowl, turn over to grease top, cover, and let rise until doubled, 1 to 1½ hours. Punch down. Divide dough into 3 parts. Cover 3 baking sheets with parchment paper or lightly grease them. Shape dough into round balls and place on the centers of prepared baking sheets. Press with palms of hands to flatten slightly. Let rise in a warm place until doubled, about 45 minutes to 1 hour. Poke the handle of a wooden spoon through the center of each loaf to make an indentation, and also to release any large air bubbles. Remove spoon. Preheat oven to 375° F. and bake loaves 35 to 40 minutes or until they sound hollow when bottoms are tapped. Transfer to racks and cool.

RYE BATONS

Thicker than breadsticks, these grainy, crusty slim breads are perfect with a hearty simmered soup or stew. Stand them in a crock for a buffet presentation.

MAKES 16

2 tablespoons active active dry yeast	¼ cup gluten flour
¾ cup warm water, 105° F.–115° F.	1 to 1½ cups bread flour or unbleached all-purpose flour
1 tablespoon sugar	¼ to ½ cup oil
2 teaspoons salt	1 egg white, beaten
1 cup dark rye flour	About ⅓ cup wheat germ

In large mixing bowl, dissolve yeast in warm water; add sugar, and let stand 5 minutes until yeast foams. Add salt and rye and gluten flours; beat well. Add bread flour until mixture is stiff. Let stand 15 minutes. Turn out onto lightly floured board and knead until dough is smooth, about 8 to 10 minutes. Cover and let rest 30 minutes. Pour oil into shallow pan with sides, such as a jellyroll pan. Cover baking sheets with parchment paper or lightly grease them. Divide dough into quarters; divide each quarter into quarters making 16 pieces. Roll out each piece between hands and work surface to about a 12-inch rope. Dip in oil, coating on all sides, and place on prepared baking sheet. Brush with egg white and sprinkle with wheat germ. Let rise 30 minutes. Preheat oven to 325° F. Bake for 30 minutes or until crusty.

SALTED RYE "STALKS": After batons are shaped and placed on baking sheets, snip about ⅓ of the way down each stalk on each side of the stick to resemble the grain on a stalk of rice. Brush with egg white and sprinkle with coarse salt.

RUSTIC SABINA RYE BREAD

This simple bread emphasizes the wonderful, clean flavor of rye. A popular rye bread in Finland, the name Sabina actually comes from an ancient tribe of people captured by the Romans in 290 B.C. It defies its namesake in ingredients, but is shaped like Italian bread.

MAKES 2 LOAVES

2 packages active dry yeast
2 cups warm water,
    105° F.–115° F.

2 tablespoons dark corn
    syrup
½ teaspoon salt

2 to 2½ cups bread flour or   *2 cups dark rye flour*
   unbleached all-purpose
   flour

In large mixing bowl dissolve the yeast in warm water and add the corn syrup; mix and let stand 5 minutes until yeast foams. Add salt and rye flour; beat well. Add the bread flour, 1 cup at a time, mixing well until stiff dough forms. Let rest 15 minutes. Turn out onto floured board and knead 8 to 10 minutes until dough is smooth. Wash bowl, grease it, and add dough to bowl; turn over to grease top of dough. Cover and let rise until doubled, about 1 hour. Punch dough down. Divide in half. On oiled surface, shape into a slender loaf about 12 inches long. Cover baking sheets with parchment paper and place loaves on sheets; let rise until about doubled. Slash lengthwise with sharp knife or razor blade. Brush with water. Preheat oven to 375° F. and bake loaves 30 to 35 minutes, or until loaves are crusty and sound hollow when tapped.

FINNISH STOUT BREAD

This makes 1 big loaf of bread fragrant with anise, fennel, and orange peel. The bread is firm and close-textured, excellent sliced thin and served with cheese.

MAKES 1 LARGE LOAF

1½ cups (12-ounce can) dark beer
½ cup milk
2½ cups dark rye flour
1 cup cracked wheat
2 teaspoons salt
1 teaspoon crushed aniseed
2 teaspoons crushed fennel seed

1 tablespoon grated orange peel
2 packages active dry yeast
¼ cup warm water, 105° F.–115° F.
1 tablespoon dark corn syrup
2 to 2½ cups bread flour or all-purpose flour

In saucepan, bring beer and milk to a boil (milk will curdle). Measure rye flour and cracked wheat into large bowl and add boiling mixture. Stir in salt, aniseed, fennel seed, and orange peel; let cool to 105° F.–115° F. In small bowl, dissolve yeast in warm water and add the corn syrup; let stand until foamy, about 5 minutes; stir into cooled mixture. Add bread flour gradually to make a stiff dough. Let stand 15 minutes. Turn out onto lightly floured board and knead for 10 minutes until dough is smooth and springy. Wash bowl, grease it, and put dough into bowl; turn over to grease top, cover, and let rise until doubled, about 1½ to 2 hours. Punch down. Turn out onto lightly oiled surface and shape into a smooth, round loaf. Cover baking sheet with

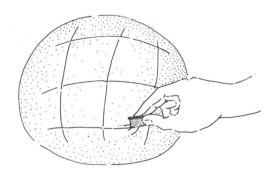

parchment paper or lightly grease it. Place loaf on prepared baking pan with smooth side up. Let rise until almost doubled, about 45 minutes to 1 hour. Slash with sharp knife or razor blade in 3 parallel cuts going each way on the loaf, making 1-inch squares. Preheat oven to 375° F. Bake for 40 to 45 minutes, or until loaf sounds hollow when tapped. Remove from pan and cool on wire rack.

RÅGBRÖD

This Scandinavian rye bread is flavored with the texture of sprouted whole rye grains. The orange rind, caraway seeds, and fennel seed combine to make the classic "Scandinavian" taste. Buttermilk adds a tartness. The addition of sprouted whole rye grains is my idea. Plan to start 2 to 3 days ahead to sprout the rye grain. If the grain has sprouted and you are not ready to bake, simply wash it in cold water, drain well, and refrigerate in a plastic bag until you are ready to use them, within 3 to 4 days.

MAKES 3 LOAVES

½ cup whole rye grain
1 cup water
½ cup light (unsulfured)
    molasses
Grated rind of 2 oranges
2 tablespoons each fennel and
    caraway seed, crushed
1 tablespoon butter
2 teaspoons salt
2 cups buttermilk

½ teaspoon baking soda
2 packages active dry yeast
¼ cup warm water,
    105° F.–115° F.
1 teaspoon sugar
4 cups light or medium rye
    flour
3 to 4 cups bread flour or
    all-purpose flour

GLAZE:

1 tablespoon molasses mixed
    with 1 tablespoon water

Two to 3 days before baking, wash the whole rye grain, and cover with lukewarm water. Let stand at room temperature 8 hours, wash again in warm water, and drain well. Put into a 1-quart jar and cover loosely. Let stand at room temperature until grain has sprouted; this may take as little as 24 hours or as long as 48 hours. Wash in lukewarm water and drain well before adding to bread dough.

In saucepan combine the water, molasses, orange rind, fennel and caraway seeds, butter, and salt. Bring to a boil, stirring, until butter is melted. In large bowl, combine the buttermilk and baking soda. Stir in the hot molasses mixture and cool to lukewarm, 105° F.–115° F. Add the sprouted rye. In a small bowl, dissolve the yeast in warm water and add the sugar. Let stand 5 minutes until foamy. Stir the yeast into the cooled molasses mixture and beat in the rye flour slowly, ½ cup at a time, until smooth. Slowly add the bread flour, stirring to make a stiff dough. Turn dough out onto lightly floured board. Let dough rest, covered, for 15 minutes. Knead for 10 minutes or until smooth and satiny, then form into a ball. Wash bowl, lightly butter it, and add dough ball to the bowl; turn over to butter top and cover. Let rise in a warm place for 1½ hours or until doubled. Punch down and knead 3 to 4 times on lightly floured surface to remove air bubbles. Divide into thirds and shape each into a round loaf. With a razor blade, cut a large X about ⅓ inch deep on each loaf, and let loaves rise, covered with towels, in a warm place until they are about doubled in bulk and crosses have opened up. Bake in a preheated 375° F. oven for 35 to 40 minutes, or until loaves sound hollow when tapped. Brush hot loaves with the molasses-water mixture. Return to oven for 5 minutes or until glaze has dried. Remove from pans and cool on wire racks.

HEIDELBERG RYE BREAD

Professional bakers will add black bread coloring (caramel color) to their doughs to add darkness to what otherwise would be a pale bread. In the introduction to this chapter I describe this ingredient, as it is most commonly used with rye breads. If you are not able to purchase the coloring, you may substitute instant coffee powder, or simply omit that ingredient and expect a lighter-colored bread. Heidelberg rye is excellent with soups, ham, cheese, or with a hearty peasant stew.

MAKES 1 LARGE LOAF OR 2 SMALLER LOAVES

3 cups bread flour or
    unbleached all-purpose
    flour
2 packages active dry yeast
2 cups water
½ teaspoon caramel coloring,
    or 2 tablespoons instant
    coffee powder

1 tablespoon caraway seeds
⅓ cup light or dark molasses
2 tablespoons butter
1 teaspoon sugar
1 teaspoon salt
3 to 3½ cups dark rye flour

In large mixer bowl, combine the bread flour and yeast. In a saucepan heat water, coloring or coffee powder, caraway seeds, molasses, butter, sugar, and salt to 120° F.–130° F. Add liquids to dry ingredients, beating at low speed for ½ minute and scraping sides of bowl constantly. Beat 3 minutes at high speed. Remove mixers and stir in enough rye flour to make a stiff dough. Turn out onto floured surface and knead about 5 minutes until smooth. Cover (you can do this right on the bread board; simply invert bowl over dough) and let rest 20 minutes. Punch dough down and either divide in half or make 1 large round loaf. Cover baking sheets with parchment paper or grease lightly. Place loaf or loaves on prepared pan and let rise in a warm place until doubled, about 1 hour. Brush with water and slash top about ¼ inch deep using a sharp knife or razor blade. Preheat oven to 400° F. Bake for 25 to 30 minutes, or until loaf sounds hollow when tapped. Remove from pan and cool on wire rack.

CARAMEL BREAD COLORING: Pour ½ cup sugar into a heavy 10-inch frying pan. Place over medium-high heat until sugar is melted; stir constantly with a fork. Continue to cook until sugar smokes and is very dark in color. When all the sugar is black, very slowly add ¾ cup boiling water and continue to cook, stirring constantly until all the sugar is dissolved and liquid is reduced to ¼ cup. Remove from heat and let cool. Store cooled syrup in a jar.

DELI ONION-RYE LOAF

Great for sandwiches of ham or cold cuts, this round braided loaf looks pretty, too!

MAKES 1 LOAF

1 package active dry yeast
½ cup warm water,
    105° F.–115° F.
1 cup milk, scalded and cooled
    to 105° F.–115° F.
2 tablespoons sugar
2 teaspoons salt
3 tablespoons minced dried
    onion

2 tablespoons butter, softened
1 cup light or medium rye
    flour
2 to 2½ cups bread flour or
    unbleached all-purpose
    flour
2 tablespoons butter, melted

In large mixing bowl, dissolve yeast in warm water; add milk and sugar; let stand until yeast foams, about 5 minutes. Add salt, onion, and softened butter. Add rye flour and gradually beat in the bread flour until dough is stiff. On floured surface, knead dough until smooth and elastic, 6 to 8 minutes, adding flour as needed. Wash bowl, grease it; add dough to bowl, turn over to grease top of loaf, cover, and let rise in a warm place until doubled, about 1 hour. Punch dough down. On oiled surface, divide into 3 parts. Shape each part into a strand about 16 inches long. Braid. Turn braid into a round loaf, sealing the ends together. Place into a greased 9-inch round cake pan in a tight spiral (start spiral in center of the pan). Brush loaf with 1 tablespoon of the melted butter. Let rise in warm place until doubled, 45 to 60 minutes. Bake in a preheated 350° F. oven for 35 to 45 minutes, or until loaf sounds hollow when lightly tapped. Remove from pan and brush with the remaining melted butter. Cool on wire rack.

PUMPERNICKEL BUFFET LOAF

If you can roll bread dough into balls, you can shape this impressive, pull-apart buffet bread.

MAKES 1 LARGE BREAD, 24 SERVINGS

2 packages active dry yeast
½ cup warm water,
    105° F.–115° F.
1 cup milk, scalded and cooled
    to 105° F.–115° F.
½ teaspoon black bread
    coloring (optional, see
    chapter introduction)
¼ cup dark molasses

1 tablespoon caraway seeds
1 teaspoon salt
½ cup butter, melted
2 eggs
2 cups dark rye flour
4 to 5 cups bread flour or
    unbleached all-purpose
    flour

GLAZE:

2 tablespoons molasses

1 tablespoon melted butter

In large mixing bowl, dissolve yeast in warm water; add milk, black
bread coloring if used, and molasses; let stand 5 minutes until yeast
foams. Stir in caraway seeds, salt, melted butter, and eggs. Add rye
flour and beat well. Gradually add the bread flour, beating after each
addition, until dough is stiff. Let rest 15 minutes. Turn out onto
floured board and knead until smooth, about 10 minutes. Cover with
inverted bowl and let rest 15 minutes. Meanwhile, grease a large
cookie sheet or pizza pan, and also grease the outside of an empty 16-
ounce can. Place can in the center of the pan. Divide dough into 4
parts. Roll each part into a 15-inch rope and cut rope into 15 equal
pieces. Shape into balls. Place dough balls to form a ring around the
can using 10 balls. Form a ring of dough balls around the first ring
using 16 balls. Form a ring around second ring using 21 balls. Last,
form a ring of 13 balls on top of the first and second rings. At this
point dough may be covered and refrigerated for up to 24 hours.
When ready to bake, let rise until doubled, about 1 hour. Preheat
oven to 350° F. Bake for 45 to 50 minutes or until golden. Mix molasses with melted butter and brush loaf with the glaze. Return to oven
for 5 minutes until glaze is set. Serve bread hot with a small bowl of
your favorite spread nestled in a custard cup in the center of the loaf.

MILWAUKEE RYE BREAD

Flavored with caraway seed and colored dark with caramel, this is an excellent loaf for sandwiches.

MAKES 2 ROUND LOAVES

1 package active dry yeast
2 cups warm water,
    105° F.–115° F.
2 tablespoons caraway seeds
1 tablespoon light or dark
    brown sugar
2 teaspoons salt
½ teaspoon black bread
    coloring (optional)
2 tablespoons shortening or
    butter, softened

2 cups dark rye flour
2½ to 3 cups bread flour or
    unbleached all-purpose
    flour
Cornmeal for dusting baking
    pans
Milk to brush top of loaves
Caraway seeds for top of
    loaves

In large mixing bowl, dissolve yeast in warm water; add the caraway seeds and brown sugar, and let stand 5 minutes until yeast foams. Stir in salt, coloring if used, and shortening. Add rye flour; beat well. Slowly beat in the bread flour to make a stiff dough. Let rest 15 minutes. Turn dough out onto floured board and knead 10 minutes or until light and springy. Wash bowl, grease it, put dough into bowl, turn over to grease top, and cover. Let rise until doubled, about 1 hour. Divide dough in half. Shape each into a round loaf. Grease 2 baking sheets and sprinkle with cornmeal. Place loaves on prepared baking sheets and let rise until doubled, about 45 minutes to 1 hour. Brush with milk and sprinkle with caraway seeds. Preheat oven to 357° F. Bake for 35 to 40 minutes, or until loaves sound hollow when tapped. Cool on rack.

WHOLE GRAIN RYE BREAD

Whole grain rye must be soaked until tender. Added to a bread dough it gives a chewy texture and a distinctive grainy flavor.

MAKES 2 ROUND LOAVES

⅓ cup whole grain rye
1 package active dry yeast
2 cups warm water,
    105° F.–115° F.
¼ cup light (unsulphured)
    molasses
2 tablespoons butter, softened

2 teaspoons salt
2 cups dark rye flour
3½ to 4 cups bread flour or
    unbleached all-purpose
    flour
Melted butter for brushing
    loaves

The night before, put washed whole grain rye into a small bowl and cover with water water; let stand overnight. Drain. In large bowl, stir yeast into warm water; add molasses, butter, salt, drained rye grain, and rye flour. Let stand 15 minutes or until yeast foams. Slowly stir in bread flour until stiff dough forms.

Cover and let stand again for 30 minutes. Turn out onto floured board and knead until smooth, about 10 minutes. Meanwhile, wash bowl and lightly oil it. Shape dough into a ball and place into bowl; turn over to grease top. Cover and let rise in a warm place until doubled, about 1 to 1½ hours. Punch dough down. Divide in half and shape each into a round ball. Place on parchment-covered baking sheet or lightly greased sheet. Let rise about 1 hour or until loaves have about doubled. Heat oven to 375° F. Brush loaves with melted butter and slash a deep X (about ½ inch deep) using a razor blade or sharp knife. Bake 30 to 40 minutes or until loaves sound hollow when

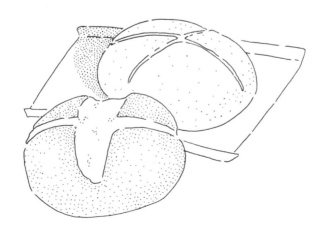

tapped. Remove from baking sheet and cool on rack. Brush again with butter.

PEPPERED RYE BERRY LOAF

Wonderfully chewy with a bite of coarsely ground pepper, this is a great party loaf. Allow 1 to 2 days for the whole grain rye to soak up liquid and become soft and chewy.

MAKES 1 LARGE LOAF

½ cup whole grain rye berries
2 packages active dry yeast
1¼ cups warm water,
*   105° F.–115° F.*
¼ cup tightly packed light or
*   dark brown sugar*
2 tablespoons vegetable oil
2 teaspoons salt
1 tablespoon coarsely ground
*   black pepper*

½ cup dark rye flour
5 to 5½ cups bread flour or
*   unbleached all-purpose*
*   flour*
Beaten egg white for top of
*   loaf*
Coarse salt, poppy seeds, or
*   caraway seeds*

Wash the whole rye grains and place in bowl, cover with lukewarm water, and let stand one to two days or until rye has become soft and chewy. The whole rye grains will measure about 2 cups after soaking. When you are ready to bake, dissolve the yeast in warm water in large mixing bowl; add brown sugar and let stand 5 minutes until yeast foams. Stir in the oil, salt, pepper, rye berries, and rye flour and beat well. Gradually beat in enough bread flour to make a stiff dough. Let dough rest for 15 minutes. Turn out onto floured board and knead 10 minutes or until dough is very smooth, elastic, and springy. Wash bowl, grease it; add dough to bowl, turn over to grease top, and cover. Let rise until doubled in a warm place, about 1 to 1½ hours. Punch dough down. Shape into an oval loaf about 10 inches long and 6 inches wide. Cover baking sheet with parchment paper or lightly grease it. Place dough on prepared sheet. Let rise until doubled. Slash across top of loaf (see diagram). Brush with beaten egg white and

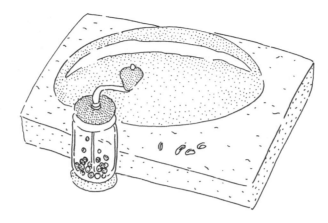

sprinkle with salt or seeds or both. Preheat oven to 375° F. Bake for 40 to 45 minutes, or until loaf sounds hollow when tapped. Cool on rack.

MY GRAND CHAMPIONSHIP FINNISH RYE BREAD

When I was a teenager and in the 4-H Club, I won a National Grand Championship for demonstrating how to prepare this bread. My hometown newspaper, the *Floodwood Forum*, printed 1,000 cards of this recipe so that I could give away copies of it!

MAKES 1 LOAF

1 package active dry yeast
¼ cup lukewarm water,
   105° F.–115° F.
1 cup warm potato water,
   105° F.–115° F. *
1 tablespoon dark or light
   brown sugar

1½ cups dark rye flour
1 tablespoon butter, melted
1½ teaspoons salt
1½ to 2 cups bread flour or
   all-purpose flour
Butter to brush loaf

* Potato water: This is the water in which pared potatoes were cooked. Instead of draining the water into the sink, I save it for use in bread like this one. Potato water should be refrigerated.

Dissolve yeast in warm water; let stand 5 minutes until yeast foams. In mixing bowl, combine potato water, brown sugar, and 1 cup of the rye flour. Add yeast mixture; beat well. Add butter, salt, and bread flour. Stir until dough forms. Turn out onto bread board; let rest 15 minutes. Knead, using the remaining rye flour to ease stickiness; the dough may not "take" the entire amount of flour. Let rise until doubled in bulk, 45 minutes to 1 hour. Punch down. Shape into a round loaf. Place onto greased baking sheet and let rise until doubled. Pierce all over with a fork. Preheat oven to 375° F. Bake for 35 to 40 minutes. Brush hot loaf with butter.

PUMPERNICKEL BAGUETTES

These long slender loaves, shaped the way French loaves are usually shaped in this country, are flavored with caraway. Serve with ham and robust cheeses.

2 LOAVES

2 packages active dry yeast
1 cup warm water,
    105° F.–115° F.
1 tablespoon sugar
1 teaspoon black bread
    coloring (optional, see
    chapter introduction)
2 teaspoons caraway seeds

1 teaspoon salt
1 cup dark rye flour
2 to 2½ cups bread flour or
    unbleached all-purpose
    flour
Cornmeal for dusting baking
    sheets

In large mixing bowl, dissolve yeast in warm water; add sugar and let stand 5 minutes until yeast foams. Add coloring, caraway seeds, salt, and rye flour and beat well. Add bread flour until mixture is stiff. Let stand 15 minutes. Turn out onto lightly floured board and knead until dough is smooth, about 8 to 10 minutes. Cover and let rest 30 minutes. Grease 2 baking sheets and coat lightly with cornmeal. Divide dough in half and shape each into a long, slender loaf. Place diagonally on prepared baking sheets to get loaves as long as possible. Let rise until doubled, about 45 minutes to 1 hour. Slash crosswise with sharp knife and brush with water. Preheat oven to 400° F. Bake until crusty and browned. Cool on rack.

RAISIN PUMPERNICKEL

Studded with raisins, this compact rye and wheat bread is exellent thinly sliced and topped with a thin slice of cheese, corned beef, or ham. It slices best the day after baking.

MAKES 1 LARGE LOAF

2 cups hot water
2 cups nonfat dry milk
4 cups dark seedless raisins
2 packages active dry yeast
½ cup warm water,
    105° F.–115° F.
2 tablespoons honey
2 tablespoons butter, melted,
    or vegetable oil
2 teaspoons salt

1½ tablespoons caraway seeds
1 cup unprocessed bran
2 cups medium rye flour or
    dark rye flour
3 cups whole wheat flour
1 to 1½ cups bread flour or
    all-purpose flour
1 cup bread flour or all
    purpose flour

GLAZE:

1 egg white beaten with
    2 tablespoons water

Coarse salt

In large mixing bowl, combine the hot water, dry milk, and raisins. In small bowl, dissolve yeast in warm water; add honey and set aside until yeast foams, about 5 minutes. Add butter, salt, caraway seeds, and bran to raisin mixture. Add rye flour, yeast mixture, and 1 cup of the whole wheat flour. Beat until smooth. Slowly add remaining whole wheat flour. Add enough bread flour to make a stiff dough. Cover and let rest 15 minutes. Turn out onto lightly floured board and knead, adding more flour as necessary to keep dough from sticking. Knead until smooth, about 10 minutes;* dough may be slightly sticky. Wash bowl, grease lightly, and add dough to bowl. Turn over to grease top, cover, and let rise 1 hour until doubled. Punch down and divide dough into 3 parts. Shape each into a strand about 20 inches long. Braid strands. Cover baking sheet with parchment or grease it lightly. Place braid in a tight spiral on prepared sheet. Cover and let rise until about doubled, about 45 minutes. Brush with egg white glaze and sprinkle with coarse salt. Preheat oven to 350° F. Bake 55 to 60 minutes, or until skewer inserted in the center comes out clean. Cool on rack.

SERBIAN PUMPERNICKEL

This is a dark, crackly-topped pumpernickel, soured by the addition of vinegar. It slices best the day after it is baked, and is delicious as a base for cold cuts and cheese.

MAKES 2 LOAVES

2 cups boiling water
1 square (1 ounce)
    unsweetened chocolate
½ cup cider vinegar
½ cup dark molasses
2 tablespoons caraway seeds
2 teaspoons instant coffee
    powder
2 packages active dry yeast
¼ cup warm water,
    105° F.–115° F.

1 tablespoon sugar
1 tablespoon salt
4 cups dark rye flour
1 cup unprocessed bran
3 to 3½ cups bread flour or
    all-purpose flour
1 egg white, slightly beaten
2 teaspoons coarse salt

Combine boiling water, chocolate, vinegar, molasses, caraway seeds, and coffee in bowl. Let stand until chocolate melts; cool to 105° F.–115° F., stirring until blended. In large mixing bowl, dissolve

* Kneading by hand in this recipe can be broken by "resting" periods as I described in the introduction to make the job easier.

yeast in warm water and let stand until foamy, about 10 minutes. Stir in chocolate mixture, sugar, and salt. Mix in rye flour and bran; add 2 cups bread flour. Turn dough out onto lightly floured board; knead, adding flour as necessary, until dough is smooth and elastic, about 10 minutes. Wash bowl, grease, add dough to bowl, turn over to grease top. Cover and let rise in a warm place until doubled, about 1½ hours. Cover 2 baking sheets with parchment paper. Turn dough out onto lightly oiled surface. Divide in half; shape into 2 round loaves. Place on baking sheet and let rise until doubled, about 1½ hours. Preheat oven to 350° F. and bake for 25 minutes. Brush top with egg white and sprinkle with salt. Continue baking another 20 minutes, until loaves sound hollow when tapped. Cool on racks.

RUSSIAN PEPPERED PUMPERNICKEL

The dark breads of Russia are fascinating. We purchased a loaf of heavy, rather coarse pumpernickel which, surprisingly, was heavily seasoned with coarsely ground black pepper. The texture of the bread becomes more solid the day after it is baked. Fresh out of the oven there is a crusty crust and a softer interior. On the second day, it is more authentic. Slice the bread about ¼ inch thick and serve it with cold cuts or cheese, or simply spread with cream cheese. Refrigerated, the bread keeps well.

MAKES 1 LARGE LOAF

2 packages active dry yeast
2 cups warm water,
    105° F.–115° F
¼ cup instant coffee powder
1 tablespoon sugar
¼ cup cider vinegar
2 teaspoons salt

2 tablespoons coarsely crushed
    black pepper
2 cups dark rye flour
2 to 2½ cups bread flour or
    all-purpose flour
Oil for coating bread
Additional coarsely crushed
    black pepper

In large mixing bowl, combine yeast, water and the coffee powder; add sugar, stir, and let stand 5 minutes until yeast foams. Stir in vinegar, salt, pepper, and rye flour, beating well. Slowly add enough bread flour to make a stiff dough. Let stand 15 minutes. Turn out onto lightly floured board and knead until smooth (dough may be sticky, but do not add a lot more flour). Wash bowl, grease, add dough to bowl, turn over to coat top, and let stand in a warm place until doubled, 2 to 2½ hours. Turn dough out onto lightly oiled board and shape into an oblong loaf about 12 inches long. Roll in additional oil and coarsely crushed black pepper. Cover baking sheet with parchment paper and place dough, smooth side up, onto it. Let rise 1 to 1½ hours longer, or until almost doubled. Preheat oven to 375° F. Bake 35 to 40 minutes, or until loaf sounds hollow when tapped. Cool on rack.

GERMAN PUMPERNICKEL

This is best served in thin slices, and it slices best on the second day when the texture has developed an even moistness throughout. This is a bread that keeps well.

MAKES 2 LOAVES

1 cup mashed potatoes	2 cups boiling water
½ cup rolled oats	½ teaspoon black bread
1 cup dark rye flour	coloring (optional)
½ cup stone-ground cornmeal	2 packages active dry yeast
⅓ cup wheat germ	¼ cup warm water,
½ cup dark molasses	105° F.–115° F.
¼ cup shortening	4 to 5 cups whole wheat flour
2 teaspoons salt	

In a large mixing bowl, combine potatoes, oats, rye flour, cornmeal, wheat germ, molasses, shortening, salt, boiling water, and coloring if used. Stir and cool to 105° F.–115° F. In small bowl, dissolve the yeast in warm water. When first mixture has cooled, add the yeast mixture to it, stirring well. Gradually stir in the whole wheat flour to make a very stiff dough. Let stand 10 minutes. Knead on floured surface until smooth, about 10 minutes; dough will not be as springy as a white-flour-based dough, but should feel well mixed. It may also be slightly sticky, but resist the temptation to add too much flour. Wash bowl, grease it, and add dough to bowl; turn dough over to grease top. Cover and let rise in a warm place until doubled, about 1½ to 2 hours. Divide in half and shape into balls. Cover; let rest 15 minutes. Shape into oblong loaves about 12 inches long. Place on lightly greased baking sheets, cover, and let rise 45 to 60 minutes; dough will not double but will appear puffy. Preheat oven to 375 ° F. and bake for 30 to 40 minutes, or until deep golden brown. Cool on rack.

CARAWAY PUMPERNICKEL RYE

Firm textured, excellent thinly sliced, this bread is dramatic when baked in a large loaf. You may wish to cut it into quarters, and wrap and freeze portions for using later.

MAKES 1 LARGE LOAF

1 package active dry yeast
½ cup water, 105° F.–115° F.
1 tablespoon sugar
⅔ cup (5½-ounce can)
    evaporated milk
1 tablespoon butter, softened
1 teaspoon salt

1 tablespoon caraway seeds
1 cup dark rye flour
1 cup whole wheat flour
1 to 1½ cups bread flour or
    unbleached all-purpose
    flour

In large mixing bowl, dissolve the yeast in warm water; add sugar and let stand 5 minutes or until yeast foams. Add the evaporated milk, butter, salt, caraway seeds, and rye flour; beat well. Add the whole wheat flour; beat well. Stir in bread flour until dough is stiff. Sprinkle remaining flour on bread board and turn dough out onto board. Let rest 15 minutes. Wash bowl, grease it, and reserve. Knead dough 10 minutes until dough is smooth. Add dough to bowl, turn over to grease top, cover, and let rise until doubled, about 1 to 1½ hours. Cover baking sheet with parchment paper or lightly grease it. Punch dough down, shape into a ball, and place dough, smooth side up, onto prepared baking sheet. With hands, flatten dough to about 2-inch thickness. Let rise until doubled in warm place, about 1 hour. Preheat oven to to 350° F. and bake for 40 to 45 minutes, or until loaf sounds hollow when tapped. Cool on wire rack.

CHRISTMAS PUMPERNICKEL

To make this dark, caraway-orange–flavored rye bread special for Christmas, the loaf is topped with a gingerbread cookie cut in the shape of a star or Christmas tree, which is baked into the top of the loaf. The easy refrigerator method of preparing this dough makes kneading simple, divides the work into 2 stages, and eliminates one rising.

MAKES 2 LOAVES

2 packages active dry yeast
¼ cup warm water,
    105° F.–115° F.
½ cup dark molasses
1 tablespoon grated orange
    peel
1 teaspoon salt
1 teaspoon caraway seeds,
    crushed

1 teaspoon fennel seed, crushed
2 cups buttermilk
2 cups light or medium rye
    flour
3 to 3½ cups bread flour or
    all-purpose flour

GLAZE:

1 tablespoon light or dark
    molasses

2 tablespoons hot water

TOPPING:

2 large cookie cut-outs (recipe
    follows)

In large mixing bowl, dissolve the yeast in warm water. Add molasses and let stand 5 minutes until yeast foams. Stir in orange peel, salt, caraway and fennel seeds, buttermilk, and rye flour; beat until smooth. Slowly stir in 3 cups of the bread flour until dough is stiff. Cover with plastic wrap and refrigerate 2 to 24 hours.

Sprinkle dough with some of the remaining flour and scrape edges down sides of bowl. Turn out onto lightly floured board and knead for 5 minutes, adding flour as necessary until dough is smooth and satiny. Divide in half. Lightly grease 2 baking sheets or cover with parchment paper. Shape dough into 2 smooth, round balls and place on prepared baking sheets with smooth side up. Flatten slightly. Let rise in a warm place until doubled, about 45 minutes. Preheat oven to 375° F. and bake for 25 minutes. Remove from oven and brush with glaze. Place large cookie cut-out (see below) on top of loaf. Return to oven for 7 to 10 minutes, or until cookie has baked and is lightly browned around the edges.

COOKIE CUT-OUTS: In bowl, add ¼ cup softened butter, ¼ cup tightly packed brown sugar, 1½ teaspoons ground cinnamon, 1 teaspoon ground ginger, ¾ teaspoon *each* ground cloves and baking soda; mix until smooth. Blend in ¾ cup all-purpose flour and stir in 2½ tablespoons water until a stiff cookie dough forms. Refrigerate at least 30 minutes. Divide in half. Roll each out to make a circle 6 inches in diameter. With tip of a knife, cut out points to make a star shape, or use large cookie cutter to cut out a star or Christmas tree. Use cut-out for decorating the top of the rye bread. Re-roll scraps, cut shapes. Place on lightly greased cookie sheet and bake in preheated 375° F. oven for 8 to 10 minutes or until lightly browned. Makes 2 large cookies and about eight 2-inch ones.

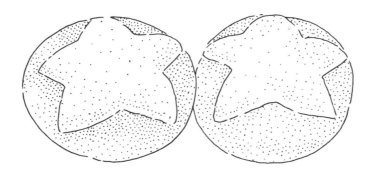

WESTPHALIAN-STYLE PUMPERNICKEL

You can buy thin slices of a heavy and moist, flavorful pumpernickel similar to this unleavened rye bread, which is much like a solid brick. A dense, compact loaf, this develops its unique texture through long, slow baking. Refrigerated, it keeps about 2 weeks, but frozen, it can be kept for months. It slices best after it has been refrigerated for a day.

MAKES 1 LARGE LOAF

¼ cup sugar
3 cups boiling water
4 cups dark rye flour
1 cup cracked wheat or
    cracked whole rye

2 teaspoons salt
2 tablespoons vegetable oil

In a heavy, preferably cast-iron, frying pan heat the sugar, stirring, until it smokes and turns black. Add the boiling water and cook, stirring, until the sugar is dissolved and a dark syrup results.* Mix the rye flour, cracked wheat, salt, and oil in large mixing bowl. Pour in the caramel and stir until well blended. Cover with plastic wrap and let stand at room temperature for 12 hours or overnight. Press the dough into a well-greased 9 x 5-inch loaf pan. Preheat oven to 200° F. Place pan in larger pan of boiling water, cover top of loaf with foil, and bake for 4 hours. Increase oven temperature to 300° F. and bake for 1½ hours longer, until loaf feels firm. Cool in pan 5 minutes; turn out to cool completely. Wrap in plastic; refrigerate several hours or until chilled. Cut into thin slices to serve.

PINWHEEL WHEAT/HERBED RYE LOAVES

After an initial mixing, divide the dough and add herbs and rye flour to one part, molasses and whole wheat flour to the other. To shape the

---

* In this case the coloring is an integral part of the mixing of the dough because the cracked wheat needs to be soaked in the hot liquid—a difference between this and other breads with caramel coloring.

bread, roll the 2 doughs together; it makes a pretty 2-tone swirled slice!

MAKES 3 LOAVES

2 packages active dry yeast
1 cup warm water,
    105° F.–115° F.
½ cup sugar
½ cup shortening
1 tablespoon salt
2 cups buttermilk, scalded and
    cooled
1 cup cold water
8 to 9 cups bread flour or
    unbleached all-purpose
    flour

1 teaspoon each dried sage,
    marjoram, and thyme
1 cup light or medium rye
    flour
¼ cup dark molasses
2½ cups whole wheat flour
1 teaspoon aniseed

In small bowl, soften yeast in warm water. In large mixer bowl, combine sugar, shortening, salt, and buttermilk; add cold water and check temperature (it should be no hotter than 115° F.), then add the yeast. With electric mixer, beat in 4 cups of the bread flour until smooth. Cover and let rise in a warm place until doubled, about 1 hour. Divide dough in half. To one part, add the herbs, rye flour, and enough bread flour to make a stiff dough. Turn out onto floured board and knead until smooth and satiny, about 10 minutes. Place into greased bowl, cover, and let rise until doubled, 1 to 1½ hours. To the second part, add the molasses, whole wheat flour, and aniseed. Beat well, and add enough of the remaining bread flour to make a stiff dough. Turn out onto floured board and knead until smooth and satiny, about 10 minutes. Place dough into greased bowl, cover, and let rise until doubled, 1 to 1½ hours. Divide both batches of dough into 3 parts. Roll out or flatten 1 section of light dough and 1 section of dark dough to make a 8 x 12-inch rectangle; place one on top of the other. Roll up tightly, being sure to pinch doughs together to avoid air pockets and starting at the 8-inch edges. Repeat for remaining dough to make 3 loaves. Place into well-greased 9 x 5-inch pans. Let rise in a warm place until doubled, about 1 hour. Preheat oven to 375° F. Bake for 45 to 50 minutes, or until loaves sound hollow when tapped. Remove from pans and cool on wire racks.

OAT BREADS

"So you and I nor no one knows how oats, peas, beans, and barley grow." I remember this folk song from quite a while back. My first-grade teacher had us all in a circle singing, clapping our hands, and stamping our feet. Even though I was the child of a farmer, I never questioned the words. Yet my father planted these grains on our farm in northern Minnesota, and I knew from his talk that oats and barley were hardy grains that grow in soil that isn't rich.

Oats were first found growing in western Europe among the barley. These were wild oats, and may have been used in the first breads along with barley because of the difficulty in separating the grains.

Oats have a wonderfully mild, nutty flavor that adds a special richness to breads and scones. Rolled oats (uncooked) as well as pre-soaked steel-cut oats (Scotch oatmeal) add an interesting grainy texture to both yeast and baking powder breads. Adding cooked oats (oatmeal) to breads will, on the other hand, give a delightfully smooth texture. If you've given up oats and oatmeal because you remember them as something your mother forced you to eat on cold winter mornings when you were a kid, you are in for a delightful surprise when you taste these delectable oat breads. What's more, oats are high in nutritional value. They are rich in protein, and are a good source for vitamins B and E.

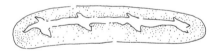

OATS FOR BREAD BAKING

OAT FLOUR

This can be bought in natural foods stores or prepared by blending rolled oats in a blender. But since oats contain no gluten, the flour must be combined with wheat flour to make yeast breads. Oat flour has the advantage of being a natural preservative, in that it has an element which is a natural anti-oxidant. An anti-oxidant prevents oils from becoming stale and rancid. Oat flour can be used in cakes and pastries successfully, and makes a very delicate dough. A Finnish flatbread called *rieska* (page 291) is often made with oat flour and has a very fine texture.

ROLLED OATS

Both the old-fashioned and the quick-cooking varieties are readily available in supermarkets, and these are the forms in which oats are most often used in breads. Rolled oats are produced by steaming and rolling the oat grains to make them quicker to cook. To toast rolled oats spread them on a baking sheet and bake for 10 to 15 minutes in a 300° F. oven to gain a more intense oat flavor. They can be added to bread dough without initial cooking, or you may cook them first and then blend them in, depending on the result you want. I often use up leftover oatmeal, a favorite cereal with my family, by adding it to bread dough (see recipe on page 124).

STEEL-CUT OATS

These are sometimes available in fancy grocery stores and natural foods stores under the name of Scotch or Irish Oatmeal. They are produced by slicing the oat kernels into thin pieces with a sharp blade, then processing them with a small amount of heat. These require a longer cooking time than rolled oats, and have a rich grainy flavor. They are delicious cooked as porridge, added to griddle cakes, or made into Scotch oatcakes and scones.

OAT GROATS

These are untreated, natural hulled oats. Just the exterior bran or "chaff" is removed. Oats in this form are the counterpart to whole wheat berries. They take a long time to cool. Groats may be soaked or cooked to soften them, then pulverized in a food processor or blender and added to bread dough. The advantage of using the whole oat grain is that the least amount of nutritional value has been destroyed through processing, and the whole grain adds an interesting crunch and chewiness to breads.

BAKING BREAD WITH OATS

Oats have a mild, slightly nutty flavor with an exceptionally smooth texture. The flavor of oats combines naturally with many favorite spices such as cinnamon, nutmeg, allspice, and cloves. Nuts such as walnuts and pecans have a natural affinity for oats. Oats blend well also with other grains, adding a mild, sweet flavor to the mixture.

OLD-FASHIONED OATMEAL BREAD

Oats give this loaf a nutty flavor. Try it toasted for breakfast with cheese and homemade jam.

MAKES 2 MEDIUM LOAVES

⅔ cup old-fashioned rolled
   oats
2 cups boiling water
½ cup nonfat dry milk
½ cup tightly packed light
   brown sugar
¼ cup butter or vegetable oil

1 teaspoon salt
1 package active dry yeast
¼ cup warm water,
   105° F.–115° F.
1 teaspoon sugar
5 to 5½ cups unbleached
   all-purpose flour

In large mixing bowl, mix oats and boiling water; stir and let stand 30 minutes. Add dry milk, brown sugar, butter, and salt. In custard cup, dissolve yeast in warm water; add sugar and let stand 5 minutes until yeast foams. When oat mixture has cooled to 105° F.–115° F., add yeast. Stir in all-purpose flour slowly to make a stiff dough. Let rest 15 minutes. Turn out onto lightly floured surface and knead for 10 minutes until dough is smooth and satiny. Wash bowl, grease it, and add dough to bowl. Turn to grease top of dough. Cover and let rise for 1 hour or until doubled. Punch down, divide in half. Shape into loaves. Grease two 8½ x 4½-inch loaf pans. Place shaped dough into pans. Cover and let rise until almost doubled, about 45 minutes. Heat oven to 375° F. Bake until loaves are golden and sound hollow when tapped, 25 to 30 minutes. Remove immediately from pans and let cool on rack.

HONEY OAT BREAD

Steel-cut oats give this bread a wonderful texture and flavor. Honey adds just a touch of sweetness. The gluten flour, available in many supermarkets as well as in natural foods stores, assures that the dough will make loaves with fine volume and texture.

MAKES 3 LOAVES

3 cups boiling water
2 cups steel-cut oats
6 tablespoons honey
2 packages active dry yeast
½ cup warm water,
    105° F.–115° F.
3 cups unbleached all-purpose
    flour

½ cup butter, melted
2 teaspoons salt
1 cup gluten flour
3 to 3½ cups whole wheat
    flour
Melted butter

In large bowl, pour boiling water over the oats; add 4 tablespoons of honey, and set aside until cooled to lukewarm. Meanwhile, dissolve yeast in warm water; add remaining honey and set aside for 5 minutes until yeast foams. When oats have cooled, stir in the yeast mixture and 2 cups of the all-purpose flour; beat well. Add butter, salt, and gluten flour and beat until smooth. Stir in whole wheat flour to make a stiff dough. Sprinkle board with some of the remaining all-purpose flour. Turn dough out onto floured surface, cover, and let rest for 15 minutes. Meanwhile, wash bowl and lightly grease it. Knead dough until elastic and springy, about 10 minutes. Return to bowl, turn over to grease top, cover, and let rise in a warm place until doubled. Punch dough down, turn out onto lightly floured board, and cut into 3 pieces. Shape into 3 round loaves. Butter three 8- or 9-inch round cake pans and place loaves smooth side up into pans; press down lightly to flatten. Let rise until doubled. Preheat oven to 350° F. and bake for 45 to 55 minutes. After loaves are golden, brush with melted butter. Turn out onto racks to cool.

MONASTERY OATMEAL LOAF

The pure flavors of whole wheat and rolled oats come out in this crusty loaf. The bread almost looks like a monastery, as the loaves during baking rise up to make little "steeples" on the top because of the way they are slashed.

MAKES 2 LARGE LOAVES

1 package active dry yeast
2 tablespoons sugar
½ cup warm water,
    105° F.–115° F.
3 cups milk, scalded
    and cooled to
    105° F.–115° F.
3 cups bread flour or
    all-purpose flour

3 to 3½ cups whole wheat
    flour
1 teaspoon salt
6 tablespoons butter or
    margarine, melted
4 cups rolled oats, quick or
    old-fashioned
Additional rolled oats for tops
    of loaves

In large mixing bowl, dissolve yeast and sugar in warm water. Let stand 5 minutes until yeast foams. Add milk, bread flour, and 3 cups of the whole wheat flour. Mix until dough is smooth, then cover and let rise 1 hour or until doubled. Sprinkle salt over. Mix melted butter and oats and stir into the dough. Sprinkle remaining whole wheat flour onto board and turn dough out onto it. Let stand 10 minutes. Meanwhile, wash bowl and lightly grease it. Knead dough 10 minutes or until springy. Put ball of dough into bowl, turn over to grease top, cover, and let rise until doubled, about 1½ hours. Grease two 9 x 5-inch loaf pans. Divide dough in half. Shape into loaves. Brush with water and roll in extra oats to coat loaf. Place in prepared pans. With a sharp knife, slash the loaves once lengthwise, then 5 times diagonally on each side of the long slash from the slash toward the edge of the pan. Let rise until doubled. Preheat oven to 375° F. Bake 35 to 40 minutes, until loaf sounds hollow when tapped. Remove from pans and cool on racks.

COUNTRY OAT LOAF

Shaped in rounds, the top textured with rolled oats and slashed before baking, this bread is pretty to serve whole on a buffet. Provide a serrated knife and have your guests slice their own. Along with a hearty vegetable soup, this is a perfect party menu. How about apple pie and cinnamon ice cream for dessert?

MAKES 2 LOAVES

2 packages active dry yeast
1¾ cups warm water,
     105° F.–115° F.
½ cup dark corn syrup
½ cup butter or margarine,
     melted
2 teaspoons salt
2 eggs, 1 separated

3 cups rolled oats, quick or
     old-fashioned
4 to 4½ cups bread flour or
     unbleached all-purpose
     flour
1 tablespoon water
¼ cup additional rolled oats

In large mixing bowl, dissolve yeast in warm water; add corn syrup and set aside 5 minutes until yeast foams. Add butter, salt, 1 egg and 1 yolk, and rolled oats. Beat well. Add flour, 1 cup at a time, beating well after each addition until dough is stiff. Cover and let rest 15 minutes. Turn out onto lightly floured board and knead until smooth and

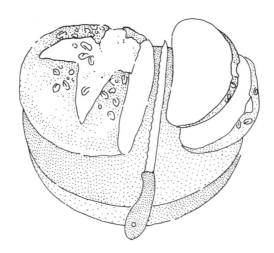

springy, about 10 minutes. Wash bowl, lightly oil it, and add dough to bowl; turn ball of dough over to oil top. Cover and let rise in warm place until doubled, about 1 hour. Punch dough down. Divide into 2 parts; shape into 2 round loaves. Lightly grease 2 baking sheets; place one loaf on each. Cover and let rise until doubled, about 1 hour. Combine reserved egg white and 1 tablespoon water; brush over loaves. Sprinkle with the additional rolled oats. With razor blade or sharp knife, slash an X across the top of each loaf, making the slashes about ½ inch deep. Heat oven to 375° F. Bake 30 to 40 minutes, or until loaves sound hollow when lightly tapped. Remove from pans and cool on racks.

WINTER MORNING OATMEAL BREAD

Steamy oatmeal porridge is one of my family's favorite breakfasts throughout the chilly season. I like to cook an oversupply and use what is left to make yeast bread. This bread is great for toasting, for sandwiches, and for quick meals during the school year. You can use any amount of leftover cooked cereal, from 1 to 3 cupfuls, in this recipe. It is simple to calculate the amount of additional liquid you need in the recipe. If you remember that when you cook oatmeal for breakfast, the formula is 1 part rolled oats to 2 parts water, you know, then, that ⅔ of each cup of leftover cereal can be counted as liquid in the recipe.

MAKES 2 LOAVES

2 packages active dry yeast
½ cup warm water,
    105° F.–115° F.
¼ cup dark or light brown
    sugar
2 tablespoons butter or
    shortening, melted, or oil
1 teaspoon salt
1 to 3 cups cooked oatmeal,
    cooled to
    105° F.–115° F.

Warm water,
    105° F.–115° F. (1⅓
    cups if you use 1 cup
    oatmeal, ⅔ cup water if
    you use 2 cups oatmeal,
    no additional water if
    you use 3 cups oatmeal)
½ cup additional rolled oats
4 to 5 cups bread flour or
    unbleached all-purpose
    flour

Honey to brush on tops of
loaves

Rolled oats to sprinkle on top
of loaves

In large mixing bowl, dissolve yeast in warm water; add the brown sugar and let stand 5 minutes until yeast foams. Stir in the butter, salt, oatmeal, and warm water. Whisk until blended. Add the rolled oats and bread flour, 1 cup at a time, beating well to keep mixture smooth, until a stiff dough forms. Let rest 15 minutes. Turn out onto lightly floured board and knead until smooth and elastic, about 10 minutes. Wash bowl, grease it, and add dough to the bowl; turn over to grease top lightly, and cover. Let rise in a warm place until doubled. Punch dough down, divide in half, and shape into 2 loaves. Place into 2 greased 8½ x 4½-inch loaf pans and let rise until doubled. Preheat oven to 375° F. Bake for 30 to 35 minutes, or until loaves sound hollow when tapped. Brush hot loaves with honey and sprinkle with rolled oats. Return to oven for 5 minutes, or until tops are dry and oats are lightly toasted. Cool on rack.

OATMEAL AND WHOLE WHEAT HEARTH BREAD

Grainy and delicious, this bread is a combination of rolled oats and stone-ground whole wheat flour, baked free-form on a sheet.

MAKES 2 LOAVES

2 cups boiling water
2 cups rolled oats, quick or
old-fashioned
2 tablespoons butter or
margarine
1½ teaspoons salt
2 packages active dry yeast

1½ cups warm water,
105° F.–115° F.
¼ cup sugar
5 to 5½ cups whole wheat
flour
Softened butter to brush on top
of loaves

In large bowl, pour boiling water over rolled oats; add butter and salt. Stir well, then set aside until mixture has cooled to 105° F.–115° F. In a small bowl, dissolve the yeast in warm water; add the sugar and let stand 5 minutes or until yeast is foamy. Add yeast mixture to the cooled oat mixture; beat well. Slowly add the whole wheat flour, beating to keep mixture smooth until a stiff dough forms. Let rest 15 minutes. Turn out onto lightly floured board and knead until dough is smooth and springy, about 10 minutes. If dough is sticky during kneading, knead 5 minutes, let rest another 10 minutes, then knead another 5 minutes; this allows the flours and oats to absorb the liquid, making it less tempting to add too much flour to the dough. Dough may still be slightly "tacky" to the touch, and should feel soft. Wash bowl, lightly grease it, and add dough to bowl; turn over to grease top. Cover and let rise 1 hour or until doubled. Punch down, and divide in half. Lightly grease 2 baking sheets or cover with parchment paper. Shape dough into balls and place smooth side up on prepared baking sheets. Flatten balls to 1 inch and let rise until puffy, about 45 minutes. Preheat oven to 375° F. Pierce all over with a fork and bake for 35 to 40 minutes, until loaves sound hollow when tapped. Brush with softened butter if desired while loaves are hot. Remove from pans and cool on racks.

GOLDEN RAISIN-OAT WHEAT BREAD

This fruit-studded hearty loaf is so good toasted that you may overlook its outstanding sandwich-making ability. Try a mild cheese, ham, or chicken filling on it for a tasty treat. Or serve it with butter and honey at teatime.

MAKES 2 LOAVES

2 packages active dry yeast
3 cups warm water,
    105° F.–115° F.
1 cup golden raisins
⅓ cup dark or light molasses
¼ cup vegetable oil
2 teaspoons salt

1 cup rolled oats, quick or
    old-fashioned
3 cups whole wheat flour
3½ to 4 cups bread flour or
    unbleached all-purpose
    flour

In large bowl sprinkle yeast over the warm water. Stir. Set aside for 5 minutes until yeast foams up. Stir in the raisins, molasses, oil, salt, rolled oats, and 2 cups of the whole wheat flour. Beat until smooth and gradually stir in the remaining wheat flour and enough bread flour to make a sitff dough. Let stand 15 minutes. Turn dough out onto a lightly floured board and knead until smooth and elastic, about 10 minutes. Wash bowl, grease it, and add dough to the bowl. Turn over to grease the top. Cover and let rise in a warm place for 1 hour or until doubled. Punch dough down, turn onto floured board, and knead to expel all the air bubbles. Divide in half. Shape into 2 loaves and place into 2 greased 9 x 5-inch loaf pans. Let rise in a warm place for 1 hour or until doubled. Preheat oven to 350° F. Bake 45 to 50 minutes, or until loaves are golden and sound hollow when tapped. Cool on wire racks.

SESAME-OAT CINNAMON SWIRL LOAF

These spicy loaves, rich with cinnamon and sesame seeds, are ideal for a Sunday brunch or afternoon tea. Try this treat toasted on a gray winter morning and see if it doesn't lift your spirits.

MAKES 2 MEDIUM LOAVES

1½ cups boiling water
1 cup rolled oats, quick or
   old-fashioned
½ cup sesame seeds
1 package active dry yeast
½ cup warm water,
   105° F.–115° F.
½ cup tightly packed dark
   brown sugar

¼ cup butter or margarine,
   melted
2 teaspoons salt
½ cup whole wheat flour
4 to 4½ cups unbleached
   all-purpose flour
1 tablespoon ground cinnamon

In large mixing bowl combine boiling water and rolled oats. Place sesame seeds in small fry pan. Toast over medium heat, stirring frequently, until seeds are golden, 3 to 5 minutes. Stir seeds into oat mixture. In mixing bowl, dissolve yeast in warm water; add brown sugar, and let stand 5 minutes until yeast bubbles. Stir in the butter, salt, and cooled oat mixture. Add whole wheat flour and beat in the all-purpose flour until mixture makes a stiff dough. Let rest 15 minutes. Turn out onto lightly floured board and knead for 10 minutes, until smooth and satiny. Wash bowl, grease it, and add dough to bowl; turn over to grease top. Cover and let rise until doubled, about 1 hour. Punch dough down and divide in half. Roll each out to make a rectangle 8 x 12 inches; sprinkle each half with half the cinnamon. Roll up tightly. Seal seams and ends. Grease two 8½ x 4½-inch loaf pans. Place loaves into pans. Let rise until doubled, about 45 minutes to 1 hour. Heat oven to 375° F. Bake until loaves are golden and sound hollow when tapped, 30 to 35 minutes. Remove immediately from pans. Cool on wire racks.

COUNTRY RAISIN-MOLASSES OAT LOAF

For the busy baker, this refrigerator method is the handiest! This crusty, moist, round loaf rises in the refrigerator—and you shape it into a loaf just after you have mixed the dough.

MAKES 1 LOAF

1 package active dry yeast	½ cup dark raisins
1 cup warm water, 105° F.–115° F.	¾ cup rolled oats, quick or old-fashioned
2 tablespoons light (unsulphured) molasses	½ cup whole wheat flour
1 egg, slightly beaten	2 to 2½ cups unbleached all-purpose flour
1 tablespoon butter or margarine, melted	1 egg white
1 teaspoon salt	Rolled oats for the top

In large mixing bowl, dissolve the yeast in warm water; let stand 5 minutes until yeast bubbles. Add molasses, egg, butter, salt, raisins, and rolled oats. Stir in the whole wheat flour. Slowly add the all-purpose flour to make a stiff dough. When dough is stiff, let rest 15 minutes. Turn out onto lightly floured board and knead until smooth and elastic, 5 to 8 minutes. Cover baking sheet with parchment paper or grease it lightly. Shape dough into a circle about 8 inches in diameter. Cover tightly with plastic wrap and let stand at room temperature about 20 minutes. Refrigerate for 8 to 24 hours. Uncover dough and let stand at room temperature 30 minutes. Heat oven to 375° F. Beat egg white with fork until foamy. Spread beaten white over bread and sprinkle with oats. Bake until evenly browned, 30 to 35 minutes. Remove from baking sheet and cool on wire rack.

HONEY-NUT OATMEAL BREAD

Before this bread goes into the oven it is spread with honey and chopped nuts.

MAKES 2 LOAVES

2 cups boiling milk
1 cup rolled oats, quick or
    old-fashioned
1 tablespoon lard or
    shortening
⅓ cup dark molasses
1 teaspoon salt
1 package active dry yeast

¼ cup warm water,
    105° F.–115° F.
4½ to 5 cups bread flour or
    unbleached all-purpose
    flour
⅓ cup honey
½ cup chopped walnuts or
    pecans

In large mixing bowl, pour milk over rolled oats; add lard, molasses, and salt. Set aside to cool to lukewarm. In small bowl, dissolve yeast in warm water; let stand until yeast foams, about 5 minutes. Add yeast to cooled oat mixture. Stir in flour gradually, beating to keep dough smooth, and adding flour until a soft, smooth dough forms. Turn out onto lightly floured board and knead until smooth and satiny, about 10 minutes. Wash bowl, grease it; turn dough over in bowl to grease top. Cover and let rise until doubled, about 1 to 1½ hours. Cover 2 baking sheets with parchment paper or grease them lightly. Divide dough in half, shape into a ball, place ball smooth side up on prepared baking sheet, and press down until dough is about 1 inch thick. Let rise until puffy again, about 45 minutes. Pierce all over with a fork.

Spread each loaf with half the honey and half the chopped nuts. Preheat oven to 350° F. Bake 30 to 35 minutes, or until golden. Cool on rack.

OATMEAL SPOON BREAD

Spoon bread is so named because it is served out of the baking dish with a spoon. This delicious variety is excellent served with melted butter and cinnamon sugar. Try it for a light supper along with a fruit salad!

MAKES 6 SERVINGS

3 cups milk	1 tablespoon sugar
1 cup rolled oats, quick or	2 tablespoons salad oil
old-fashioned	3 eggs, separated
¾ teaspoon salt	Melted butter
1 teaspoon baking powder	

Heat 2 cups of the milk in a saucepan. When milk comes to a boil, add the oats and simmer, stirring, until thickened. Remove from heat and add salt, baking powder, sugar, oil, and remaining milk. Beat egg yolks into the mixture. Whip egg whites until stiff but not dry and fold into the oat mixture. Turn into a buttered 1-quart soufflé dish and bake in a preheated 350° F. oven for 30 to 35 minutes, or until puffed and brown on top. Serve by the spoonful and top with melted butter.

CINNAMON SUGAR: In a bowl, blend ½ cup sugar with 2 teaspoons ground cinnamon.

OATMEAL WALNUT BUTTERMILK BRAID

This makes a beautiful braid for holiday entertaining. Serve it with a mushroom- or herb- or fruit-flavored cream cheese as a spread.

MAKES 1 LARGE BRAID OR WREATH

2 packages active dry yeast
¼ cup warm water,
    105° F.–115° F.
¼ cup honey
1 teaspoon salt
1 cup buttermilk, warmed to
    105° F.–115° F.

½ cup butter, melted
1½ cups rolled oats, quick or
    old-fashioned
2½ to 3 cups bread flour or
    unbleached all-purpose
    flour
½ cup chopped walnuts

GLAZE:

1 egg mixed with
    2 tablespoons milk

Rolled oats for top of loaf

In large mixing bowl, dissolve yeast in warm water; add honey; stir and let stand 5 minutes until yeast foams. Stir in salt, buttermilk, butter, rolled oats, and 2 cups of the bread flour; beat well. Slowly add enough flour to make a stiff dough, beating after each addition. When dough is stiff, let stand 15 minutes. Turn out onto lightly floured

board and knead for 10 minutes until dough is satiny and smooth. Knead in the walnuts. Wash bowl, grease it, add dough to bowl; turn over to grease top and cover. Let rise until doubled, about 1 to 1½ hours. Punch dough down and divide into 3 parts. Roll each part out between palms of hands and board to make a strand about 24 inches long. Braid. Cover baking sheet with parchment paper or lightly grease it. Place braid on baking sheet in the shape of a wreath. Trim ends and fit cut edges together. Roll trimmings out to make a thin strand of dough and shape into a bow. Place bow over the seam on the wreath. Let rise until about doubled, 45 minutes to 1 hour. Brush with the egg glaze and sprinkle with rolled oats. Preheat oven to 375° F. Bake 30 to 35 minutes or until golden. Cool on rack.

OATMEAL PITA BREADS

These flavorful pita breads are great for lunches and picnics, stuffed with a sprout and vegetable filling.

MAKES 12 PITA BREADS

1 package active dry yeast	1 cup rolled oats, quick or
1⅓ cups warm water,	old-fashioned
105° F.–115° F.	¼ cup vegetable oil
2 to 2½ cups unbleached	1 teaspoon salt
all-purpose flour	

In large bowl, dissolve yeast in warm water. Let stand 5 minutes until yeast foams. Stir in 1 cup flour, oats, oil, and salt; mix well. Add enough remaining flour to make a moderately soft dough. Knead on lightly floured surface for 8 to 10 minutes or until smooth and elastic.

Cover; let rest in warm place 20 minutes. Divide dough into 12 equal portions; shape each into a ball. Cover with plastic wrap; let rest in warm place 20 minutes. Heat oven to 450° F. On generously floured surface, roll out 2 balls, 1 at a time, to make two 7-inch circles. Place side by side on ungreased cookie sheet. Bake on lowest oven rack 5 to

6 minutes or until puffed. Or place a ceramic baking tile in oven while preheating. Transfer rolled out dough to hot tile. Bake 5 to 6 minutes. Repeat for rolling and baking remaining dough. Cool; store tightly covered at room temperature. To serve, cut pita breads in half crosswise and spoon filling into pocket of each half.

BARLEY BREADS

Most of us are familiar with the mild, nutty flavor of barley in soup, but few of us have probably eaten a barley bread. Yet this grain once was one of the most widely used in breads. In Deuteronomy the Lord promised the Israelites a land "of wheat and barley." And it was five barley loaves that Jesus divided to feed the five thousand in the story of the loaves and the fishes. Until about two centuries ago, barley was probably the chief bread grain of continental Europe and was carried to the New World by the early settlers. Today the most nutritious barley in the world is grown in the Red River Valley of Minnesota and North Dakota. This variety contains the highest amounts of protein and other nutrients.

Many of the traditional breads that use barley flour come from northern countries—northern Europe and Scandinavia—because it is one of the fastest-growing grains and will mature in the short growing season that characterizes northern countries. A classic Finnish unleavened bread, *ohrarieska*, could be included either among the flatbreads or the barley breads, but I am including it here because barley is 100 percent of the grain.

Because it has such a low gluten content, barley flour must be mixed with wheat flour to make a well-risen yeast loaf. The flavor of barley is mild, and the color is a pale gray. When it is combined with bread flour or all-purpose flour, the loaf looks almost white, but has a faint, nutty barley flavor.

Barley is available pearled—that is, the hull has been removed, then the barley has been steamed and polished. Pearled barley is sold in small packages in supermarkets. It is often used as an ingredient in soups, both to thicken and to add flavor. Unhulled barley is very difficult to cook because the hull is so tough.

Barley flour is made by grinding the barley into a meal. Because barley flour is very perishable, it is usually not available in supermarkets. However, you can often buy it in natural foods stores or by mail order. Also, if you have a grain grinder (mill), you can grind whole pearled barley yourself. The flour should always be refrigerated to keep it fresh.

BARLEY MALT EXTRACT IN BREADS

Many classic Finnish whole grain breads include malt as an ingredient. Farmers who grew their own barley made barley malt by soaking the whole grain until it sprouted, drying it in a slow oven, and pulverizing it into a coarse meal. During the drying, the malt sugar in the grain caramelizes, bringing out a malt flavor. Dried malt is available in stores that handle beer-making supplies, and can be used in breads by simply soaking in water.

Malt extract, a heavy, molasseslike syrup, is used in beer making as well as bread making. It adds a tantalizing, bitter-sweet flavor. In nonsweet breads, the result is rich and grainy—the flavor of the whole grain is emphasized by the heft of the malt. In breads that contain seeds, such as caraway, anise, or fennel, the combination is deliciously aromatic with the overtone of the flavor of hops. (Manufacturers of malt extract also use hop extract to flavor the syrup.) Malt blends pleasingly with sweet rye breads, such as the Finnish Hop-Flavored Easter Bread, blending with cardamom, egg, and butter to make a new taste sensation. In this chapter, I have included recipes that use the heavy malt syrup available wherever beer-making supplies are sold. Blue Ribbon, Premium, and the Canadian-made Sloane's are the brands I have located in Duluth. These all are barley malt extracts with a light hop flavoring.

TROLLEVIK BARLEY BREAD

This bread comes from the Finnish-Norwegian border. These are round, free-form loaves about 1½ inches thick, with a sandy-colored crumb. Barley flour produces a loaf with mild, grainy flavor and a soft, almost cakelike crumb.

MAKES 2 LOAVES

2 packages active dry yeast
2 cups warm water,
    105° F.–115° F.
1 cup nonfat dry milk
2 tablespoons sugar
2 teaspoons salt
¼ cup vegetable oil

2 cups barley flour
3 to 4 cups bread flour or
    all-purpose flour
Butter to brush tops of loaves
Additional barley flour for
    tops of loaves

In large mixing bowl, dissolve yeast in warm water; add milk and sugar; let stand 5 minutes until yeast foams. Add salt, oil, and barley flour; beat well. Gradually add the bread flour, beating well to keep mixture smooth. When mixture is stiff, let rest 15 minutes. Sprinkle board with remaining flour, turn dough out onto board, and knead until smooth and elastic, about 10 minutes. Wash bowl, grease it, add dough to bowl, and turn over. Cover and let rise until doubled, about 1 to 1½ hours. Punch down. On lightly oiled surface, divide dough in half. Cover baking sheets with parchment paper. Shape each half of dough into a ball and place on prepared baking sheet with smooth side up. Flatten with palms of hands until loaves are about ½ inch thick. Let rise until doubled (about 45 minutes to 1 hour). Preheat oven to 375° F. and bake for 30 to 35 minutes, until loaves are lightly browned and sound hollow when tapped. Brush tops of loaves with butter while hot and dust lightly with additional barley flour. Cool on rack.

FIVE BARLEY LOAVES

This is my idea of what the 5 barley loaves might have looked like that went with the 2 fish which Jesus used to feed the five thousand. It's one of my favorite Bible stories. These are delicious, chewy loaves that are good served with soup. Also, these make wonderful large, individual "hoagie" sandwiches if you split them horizontally and stuff them with any favorite filling.

MAKES 5 LOAVES, ABOUT 4 x 8 INCHES EACH

2 cups water	¼ cup lard, melted
½ cup pearled barley	1½ cups barley flour
2 packages active dry yeast	2 to 3 cups bread flour or
½ cup warm water,	unbleached all-purpose
105° F.–115° F.	flour
¼ cup sugar	Water
2 teaspoons salt	Barley flour for tops of loaves

Combine water and pearled barley in saucepan, bring to a boil, lower heat, and simmer 45 minutes or until barley is tender. Cool. In large

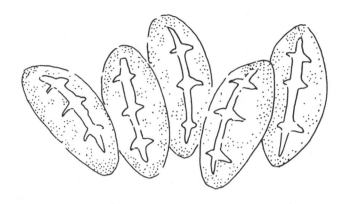

mixing bowl, dissolve yeast in warm water; add sugar, salt, lard, and cooked barley. Add barley flour; beat well. Beat in the bread flour, 1 cup at a time, until a soft dough forms. Sprinkle bread board with remaining flour and turn dough out onto board. Knead until smooth and satiny, about 10 minutes (dough should be well mixed and smooth, but will be tacky to the touch and rather soft). Wash bowl, grease it, add dough to bowl, turn over to grease top. Cover and let rise 45 minutes to 1 hour until doubled. Cover 2 baking sheets with parchment paper or grease them. Sprinkle sheets with barley flour. Punch dough down and divide into 5 parts. Shape each into an oval about 3 x 5 inches and place on baking sheets. Brush tops with water and sprinkle with barley flour. Let rise until puffy. Slash lengthwise, then across, making the cuts about ⅛ inch deep. Preheat oven to 375° F. Bake 30 to 35 minutes, or until loaves sound hollow when tapped. Cool on wire racks.

BARLEY MALT RYE BREAD

Large, round, and slightly flat, this is a coarse-textured, chewy bread. With no sweetening added, the malt extract adds a bitter tang almost like a sourdough. This bread can stand up to the flavor of the most robust of the soft cheeses. I love it with a well-aged Wisconsin brick cheese and even a Limburger!

MAKES 1 LARGE, FLAT LOAF

1 cup warm water, 105° F.–115° F.	*2 teaspoons salt*
1 package active dry yeast	*2 cups dark rye flour*
1 cup buttermilk, warmed to 105° F.–115° F.	*2½ to 3 cups bread flour or unbleached all-purpose flour*
2 tablespoons barley malt extract	

In large bowl, combine the warm water and yeast; let stand 5 minutes until yeast foams. Stir in the buttermilk, malt extract, salt, and rye flour; beat until smooth. Let stand, covered, for 15 minutes. Gradually add the bread flour, beating well after adding each cupful. When dough is stiff, sprinkle board with some of the remaining flour and turn dough out onto flour. Knead for 10 minutes or until smooth and satiny. Dough may still be slightly tacky. Wash bowl, grease it, and put dough into bowl; turn over to grease top. Cover and let rise in a warm place until doubled, about 1 to 1½ hours. Punch down. Turn out onto lightly oiled surface and shape into a smooth, rather flat loaf about 12 inches in diameter. Lightly grease baking sheet or cover with parchment paper. Place loaf on prepared sheet with smooth side up. Let rise until about doubled, about 45 minutes to 1 hour. Slash, using a serrated knife or razor blade, to make 1-inch squares all over the top of the loaf, making the cuts about ⅛ inch deep. Brush generously with water and sprinkle with about 2 teaspoons rye flour. Preheat oven to 375° F. Bake 40 to 45 minutes, or until loaf sounds hollow when tapped. Remove from pan and cool on wire rack.

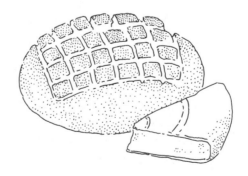

OHRARIESKA (FINNISH BARLEY FLATBREAD)

This chewy bread is wonderfully grainy and rich-tasting. It is made in different thicknesses throughout Finland. The farther north you go, the thinner the *rieska*. I like to make it rather thin, and bake it in a 12-inch pizza pan. It cooks quickly in a very hot oven. Cut it into wedges, and serve it hot from the oven, spread with butter; it is excellent with soups. Traditionally, this bread has no leavening added. However, with the addition of baking powder it takes on a biscuitlike texture. If you leave out the baking powder, the bread is soft and pliable, and to some American tastes this might seem "doughy."

MAKES ONE 12-INCH FLAT LOAF

1 cup milk
2 cups barley flour
2 tablespoons butter, melted
1 tablespoon sugar

2 teaspoons baking powder
  (optional; see above)
½ teaspoon salt
Butter for pan

Mix the milk, barley flour, butter, sugar, baking powder, and salt until smooth. Butter a 12-inch pizza pan generously; pour batter into pan. Bake in a preheated 500° F. oven for 15 minutes or until bread feels firm to the touch and is lightly browned. Cut in wedges and serve hot.

OHRARIESKA WITH BACON: Cook ¼ pound bacon until crisp; chop or crumble. Add to the batter before pouring into the pan.

MALTED CHRISTMAS BREAD

In Sweden, one fancy bread was baked early in the Advent season, and it was the table decoration throughout the Christmas season. This bread was called "sowing bread" because, on Knut's Day (January 13), it was taken from the kitchen table and buried in the grain bin. On the first day of sowing in the spring, the bread was softened in beer, cut into pieces, and distributed to every member of the household including the horse. This was a ceremony intended to give everybody the strength to do what needed to be done.

This practice is no longer in existence; however, the fancy bread is still part of the holiday season, simply called "Christmas bread."

I thought all the references to beer during the holiday celebrations would make hop-flavored barley malt a good addition to this aromatic, spicy, nonsweet bread. The malt adds a tang which almost makes this taste like sourdough!

MAKES 1 LARGE LOAF

2 cups warm potato water or
    plain water,
    105° F.–115° F.
2 tablespoons golden syrup or
    dark corn syrup
2 tablespoons barley malt
    extract
2 packages active dry yeast
2 teaspoons salt

1 teaspoon ground ginger
1 teaspoon ground cloves
Grated rind of 1 orange
¼ cup butter, melted
2 cups medium rye flour
3½ to 4 cups bread flour or
    unbleached all-purpose
    flour

In large bowl, combine the potato water, syrup, malt extract, and yeast; stir and let stand 5 minutes until yeast foams. Stir in the salt, ginger, cloves, orange, butter, and rye flour; beat until mixture is very satiny and smooth. Beat in the bread flour, 1 cup at a time, until dough is stiff. Scrape down sides of bowl frequently. Cover and let rest 15 minutes. Sprinkle board with some of the remaining flour and turn dough out onto the board. Knead for 10 minutes or until very smooth and satiny. Dough may be tacky to the touch and you should be careful not to knead in excess flour. If dough seems difficult to work with, let it rest a few minutes before continuing to knead. (One kneading technique that is helpful with sticky doughs is to pick up the ball of dough and drop it on the work surface several times.) Wash bowl, grease it lightly, and add dough to bowl. Cover and let rise in a warm place until doubled, about 1 to 1½ hours.

Turn out onto lightly floured surface and cut off about ⅙ of the dough; set aside. Shape remainder of the dough into a large, smooth ball about 10 inches in diameter and about 2 inches thick. Cover baking sheet with parchment paper or lightly grease it. Place dough ball on prepared sheet with smooth side up; smooth and even out the dough to make a perfect loaf. Brush with water. Divide the reserved

dough into 3 parts. Roll one of the parts out to make a strand of dough about 20 inches long. Cut into 3 parts and place on loaf, curling the ends and crossing the strands at the center of the loaf. Roll out the second part as flat as possible (it springs back a lot, but if you work at it you can succeed at getting it to about a 6-inch square). With knife or cookie cutters, cut out to make stars, half-moons, flowers, leaves, or any other fanciful shapes. Place onto loaf. Shape remaining part of dough into little balls and fasten to the loaf to complete the decoration. Brush all over with water. Let rise until about doubled, 45 minutes to 1 hour. Preheat oven to 375° F. Bake for 40 to 45 minutes, or until nicely browned and loaf tests done in the center.

Note: To fasten decorations on the loaf, it may be necessary to skewer them with toothpicks.

FINNISH HOP-FLAVORED EASTER BREAD

Finnish Easter bread traditionally is baked in a milk pail, resulting in a bread with a huge, mushroomlike shape. In this cardamom-perfumed sweet bread, hop-flavored barley malt adds both authenticity and a wonderful, satisfying quality. You have a choice of baking this bread in a 4-quart pail (a pail from camping set is perfect), in a round braided wreath, or in 3 standard loaf pans. This bread is delicious toasted and served with a spreading of cream cheese.

MAKES 1 LARGE LOAF OR THREE 9 x 5-INCH LOAVES

1 package active dry yeast
⅓ cup warm water,
*   105° F.–115° F.*
2 tablespoons barley malt
*   extract*
2 teaspoons freshly ground
*   cardamon seeds*
4 eggs
1 can (13 ounces) evaporated
*   milk*

⅔ cup light or dark
*   well-packed brown sugar*
2 teaspoons salt
2 cups medium rye flour
½ cup butter, melted
5 to 5½ cups bread flour or
*   unbleached all-purpose*
*   flour*

GLAZE:

1 egg mixed with
*   2 tablespoons milk*

DECORATION:

Chopped blanched almonds

In large mixing bowl, dissolve yeast in warm water; let stand 5 minutes until yeast foams. Add the malt extract, cardamom, eggs, evaporated milk, and brown sugar. Add the rye flour and beat until satiny and smooth. Stir in the butter. Add bread flour gradually, keeping mixture smooth. After 4 cups flour are added, let rest 15 to 30 minutes, covered. Sprinkle some of the remaining flour on board, turn dough out onto board, and sprinkle with more flour. Knead dough until flour is worked into the dough and dough is smooth and satiny, but not too stiff; it should feel tacky to the touch.* For final kneading, pick up the dough and drop it on the counter 25 times to further develop the gluten. Wash bowl, grease it, and add dough to bowl. Cover, and let rise until doubled, 1½ to 2 hours.

Punch down. For a large loaf, shape dough into a ball and fit into a 4-quart, well-greased, straight-sided metal pail such as one that fits a camping set.

Or divide dough into quarters. Between palms of hands and

---

* A dough that is well kneaded will have a satiny appearance and be rather smooth but should be a little tacky (like masking tape).

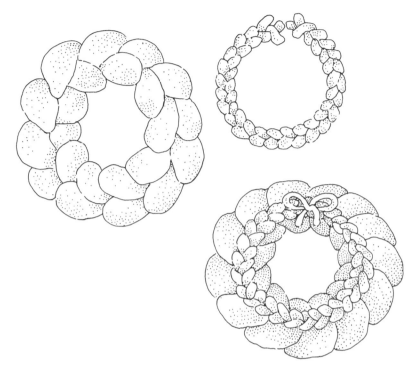

board, roll out 3 pieces to make strands about 36 inches long. Braid the 3 strands and place on a greased baking sheet in a large wreath about 12 inches in diameter. Cut ends of braid to even out, and reserve trimmings. Fuse the cut ends to close the bread wreath. Divide last quarter of dough into 3 parts and roll out each to make a long strand, about 36 inches long. Braid these 3 strands, making a long, skinny braid. Trim ends and reserve scraps. Place small wreath on top of the large wreath. Press it down firmly to fuse. Roll out dough scraps to make a 16-inch-long strand and shape into a bow. Place bow over seam on wreath.

Or divide dough into 3 parts and shape each into a loaf; fit into 3 well-greased 9 x 5-inch loaf pans. Cover and let rise until doubled. (Or, if desired, you may shape each of the 3 parts into braids and fit them into the 9 x 5-inch pans.) Let rise until doubled, 45 minutes to 1 hour. Brush with egg glaze and sprinkle with chopped almonds. Preheat oven to 350° F. Bake 45 to 50 minutes for large loaf in a pail, or until a wooden skewer inserted in the center comes out clean. Bake wreath and individual loaves for 30 to 35 minutes, or until they test done. Remove from pans and cool on racks.

CORNBREADS

Corn is one of the first foods that the American Indians introduced to the English settlers in America. And very soon after, colonial women were using ground corn to make all sorts of breads. Recent interest in regional cooking and in interesting breads has restored cornbreads to a place of honor on American tables. Once again advocates of Southern cornbread vie with Yankee diehards to lay claim to the best cornbread recipes. To those of us outside the fray, both Northern and Southern versions seem delicious and we like to alternate. But there are also some excellent yeast breads that have cornmeal combined with wheat flour. Because cornmeal adds a slightly crunchy texture and a touch of sweetness to breads, many of these recipes are especially popular for breakfasts and brunches. But they are also wonderful at baked bean suppers, summer barbecues, and soup-and-dessert suppers.

CORN IN WHOLE GRAIN BREAD

The use of cornmeal in bread differs the farther south you go in the United States. Northerners use a smaller percentage of cornmeal in cornbread; Southerners might go 100 percent cornmeal. Though it is not often used in a yeast-risen bread in the South, cornmeal may be cooked into a mush and then mixed into a bread dough.

I've included nonyeast-risen breads in this chapter because they are so classic to the topic of cornbreads. Because the tortilla of Mexico is a classic cornbread I have that included in this chapter, too.

FORMS OF CORN

WHITE CORNMEAL

This is coarsely ground whole white corn. It is not refined from yellow meal, but is ground from a variety of corn kernel that is white. It has a milder flavor than yellow cornmeal and is traditional in southern spoon bread and johnnycakes. It is sweeter and lighter than yellow cornmeal, but contains less vitamin A. White cornmeal is available in most well-stocked supermarkets and may be found in the cereal or baking products section of the store, as well as in natural and whole foods stores. The quality of the cornmeal may vary from one market to another, which affects the flavor of bread made with the meal.

YELLOW CORNMEAL

This meal is ground from whole yellow corn. It is important for cornbread, cornsticks, pancakes, waffles, and hoecakes. Yellow cornmeal is higher in protein than white cornmeal, but it is not the protein necessary for good gluten development in bread. For this reason, cornmeals—both yellow and white—must be mixed with wheat flour when making yeast breads. Yellow cornmeal is available in most well-stocked supermarkets as well as natural and whole foods stores. It may be found in the cereal or baking products sections of some stores. The quality of the cornmeal may vary from one brand to another, which affects the flavor of the finished product. The very best cornmeal I have used is that which is labeled "stone-ground," which contains the flavorful germ and feels moist. The lowest quality cornmeal I have used comes in a cardboard box, is "degermed," and is a dry granular meal.

MASA HARINA

The flavor of Mexican masa harina is richer than that of most cornmeals available in the United States. This is because the meal is made from hominy (hulled corn) instead of the whole kernel. The corn kernel (white) is first soaked in lime to remove the hulls, then ground finely in a stone mill or mortar. Masa harina is used to make tortillas, tamales, and many other Mexican specialties. Masa harina is available in 5- and 10-pound bags in supermarkets and specialty food stores in the South and Southwest, as well as in well-stocked markets in the North.

YEAST-RAISED HONEY CORNBREAD

Yeast, honey, and whole wheat give this pan of cornbread a character different from the traditional. Serve it with bowls of hearty vegetable soup for supper, and try softened cream cheese and butter on top!

MAKES ONE 9-INCH SQUARE

1 package active dry yeast
1 cup warm water,
    105° F.–115° F.
⅔ cup nonfat dry milk
2 eggs, lightly beaten
1 tablespoon vegetable or salad
    oil

2 tablespoons honey
1 cup yellow cornmeal
1 cup whole wheat flour
1 teaspoon salt
¼ cup butter, melted (optional)

In large mixing bowl, dissolve the yeast in warm water; add the milk, eggs, oil, honey, cornmeal, whole wheat flour, and salt. Beat until very well blended. Turn into well-buttered 9-inch square pan. Cover and let rise in a warm place until doubled, about 30 minutes. Preheat oven to 350° F. Bake 30 minutes or until bread tests done. Drizzle top with melted butter, if desired. Serve warm, cut into squares.

PIONEER BREAD

Cornmeal was a staple food of the pioneers who settled the American frontier. And pioneer women used the meal to make both yeast-raised and quick breads. Serve these delightful, round yeast breads with a tureen of steaming vegetable chowder, a New England fish chowder, or an old-fashioned split-pea soup.

MAKES 2 ROUND LOAVES

1 package active dry yeast
⅓ cup sugar
1 cup warm water,
    105° F.–115° F.
2 eggs, beaten
1 teaspoon salt
⅓ cup butter or margarine,
    melted

⅔ cup yellow cornmeal
3½ to 4 cups bread flour or
    unbleached all-purpose
    flour
Butter for brushing tops of
    loaves

In large mixing bowl, dissolve yeast and sugar in warm water; let stand 5 minutes until yeast foams. Add eggs, salt, butter, and cornmeal. Slowly add the bread flour until dough is stiff and smooth. Let rest 15 minutes. Turn out onto lightly floured board and knead for 10 minutes, until smooth and satiny. Wash bowl, grease it, and put dough into bowl. Turn over to grease top. Cover and let rise in a warm place until doubled, about 1 hour. Punch dough down, divide in half, and shape into 2 round loaves. Grease two 9-inch round cake pans and place loaves smooth side up into pans. Let rise until doubled, about 45 minutes to 1 hour. Preheat oven to 375° F. Bake loaves 25 to 30 minutes, or until they sound hollow when tapped. Remove from pans and cool on wire racks. Brush with butter while hot.

ANADAMA BREAD

According to legend, a 19th-century fisherman was enraged that his wife, Anna, who always served him cornmeal mush for dinner, refused to change the menu. The fisherman took the mush, threw in flour and yeast, then baked the bread and sat down to eat mumbling, "Anna, damn her!" Hence the name Anadama Bread.

MAKES 1 LOAF

¼ cup yellow cornmeal
½ cup boiling water
1 package active dry yeast
½ cup warm water,
    105° F.–115° F.
¼ cup dark molasses
2 tablespoons butter or
    margarine, softened

1 teaspoon salt
2½ to 3 cups bread flour or
    unbleached all-purpose
    flour
Butter or margarine to brush
    top of loaf

In small bowl, mix cornmeal and boiling water; stir and let stand until cool. In large mixing bowl, dissolve yeast in warm water; let stand 5 minutes until yeast foams. Add molasses, butter, salt, and the cornmeal mixture. Stir in bread flour, slowly keeping batter smooth, until stiff dough forms. Let rest 15 minutes. Turn out onto lightly floured board and knead for 5 to 8 minutes or until dough is smooth and elastic. Wash bowl, grease it, and add dough to bowl; turn over to grease top. Cover and let rise until doubled, about 1 hour. Punch dough down and shape dough into a ball. Generously grease a 9-inch pie pan. Place dough smooth side up into greased pan. Let rise until doubled, about 1 hour. Preheat oven to 375° F. Bake until loaf is golden and sounds hollow when tapped, 30 to 35 minutes. Remove from pan immediately, brush with butter, and cool on rack.

COUNTRY CORN LOAVES

Crisp bits of bacon, stone-ground yellow cornmeal, and wheat germ combine to give this rustic bread a rich, country flavor.

MAKES TWO 9-INCH ROUND LOAVES

½ pound bacon, cut into
    ½-inch pieces
1½ cups yellow cornmeal,
    preferably stone-ground
2 packages active dry yeast
2½ cups warm water,
    105° F.–115° F.
1 cup wheat germ

4 to 4½ cups bread flour
1½ teaspoons salt
½ teaspoon freshly ground
    black pepper
1 egg white
Additional cornmeal for tops
    of loaves

Separate bacon pieces and place into heavy skillet over medium heat; cook, stirring occasionally until golden and crisp, about 4 minutes. Drain off fat; reserve. Drain bacon bits on paper towels. Spread cornmeal over a cookie sheet and bake at 350° F. for 20 minutes. Cool. In large bowl, dissolve yeast in warm water; add roasted cornmeal, wheat germ, and 1 cup of bread flour. Beat well, cover, and let rise for 1 hour or until bubbly. Stir in salt, pepper, 2 tablespoons of the reserved bacon fat, and enough of the remaining flour to make a stiff dough. Knead on lightly floured board until smooth and elastic, about 10 minutes. Shape into a ball. Wash bowl, grease lightly, and add dough to bowl; turn over to grease top. Cover and let rise in a warm place until doubled, about 1½ hours. Punch dough down. Knead in the bacon. Let rest, covered, for 10 minutes. Divide dough in half. Shape each into a smooth, round ball. Grease two 9-inch round cake pans and place dough, smooth side up, into pans. Press down slightly to make even loaves. Let rise at room temperature until doubled, about 1 hour. Preheat oven to 400° F. Brush loaves with egg white; sprinkle with cornmeal. Slash tops of loaves with razor blade, making deep crosswise cuts. Bake for 35 minutes or until loaves sound hollow when tapped. Remove from pans and cool on racks.

SOUTHERN WHITE CORNMEAL BREAD

Real southern cornbread has no wheat flour and no sweetening; there is question whether the cornmeal is to be white or yellow. Fresh stone-ground cornmeal is the best, as the flavor and texture do not compare with the cornmeal available in average grocery stores, which is more dry and coarse. This batter can be baked in a cast-iron cornstick pan or in one of those pretty old-fashioned cast-iron muffin pans with a variety of shapes.

MAKES 6 SERVINGS

1 egg
1 cup buttermilk
2 teaspoons baking powder
1 teaspoon baking soda
½ teaspoon salt

1 cup white cornmeal,
* preferably fresh*
* stone-ground*
4 tablespoons bacon fat or
* butter*

In small mixer bowl, beat egg until light; add buttermilk, baking powder, soda, and salt. Add cornmeal and stir until smooth. Put bacon fat into heavy cast-iron skillet, about 8 inches in diameter. Heat until a drop of water sizzles furiously. Tilt pan so that all sides are coated, then pour batter into pan and let cook on medium-high heat for 3 to 5 minutes, until bottom is crisp and brown. Preheat oven to 375° F. Place in the oven and bake 20 minutes, until top is browned and cornbread is cooked through. Serve hot cut in wedges.

TO BAKE CORNBREAD IN A CORNSTICK PAN OR CAST-IRON FANCY MUFFIN PAN: Grease indentations with the bacon fat. Place into oven until bacon fat sizzles. Brush to coat all sides of cups or molds and add

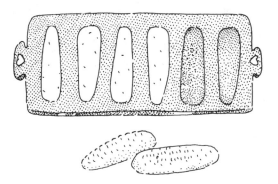

cornmeal batter to each cup or mold. Return to oven and bake for 10 to 15 minutes, or until browned and cooked through.

YANKEE CORNBREAD

Northern-style cornbread has a smaller proportion of cornmeal and a lighter texture. The beauty of any cornbread is how quickly it can be ready to serve. In muffin pans, it bakes in less than 20 minutes. In many gift stores you can find prettily shaped muffin pans—stars, hearts, diamonds—which you might like to use for baking this bread. The addition of nuts or fruits to the batter is strictly optional, but an interesting addition. I like to blend fruit right into the batter, but sprinkle the nuts over the top before baking.

MAKES 12 MUFFINS OR ONE 9-INCH SQUARE

1½ cups unbleached
    all-purpose flour
½ cup yellow cornmeal
¼ cup sugar
2 teaspoons baking powder
1 teaspoon salt
2 eggs

1 cup milk
¼ cup butter or bacon
    drippings, melted
1 cup chopped walnuts or
    chopped dates, raisins, or
    fresh blueberries
    (optional)

In large mixing bowl combine flour, cornmeal, sugar, baking powder, and salt. In another bowl, beat eggs; add milk and melted butter or bacon drippings. Pour liquid mixture over dry ingredients and stir just until moistened; batter may still be lumpy. Add fruits if desired. Pour into a well-buttered 9-inch square pan; sprinkle with nuts if desired. (Or portion into a well-buttered cornstick pan, or into 12 large well-buttered muffin cups. Sprinkle muffins with nuts if desired.) Preheat oven to 425° F. Bake for 15 to 20 minutes, or until golden around the edges and center springs back when touched. Remove from pans and cool on racks.

OLD-FASHIONED CORNBREAD

Quick-to-mix cornbread is a staple menu item in most parts of the South. I like to serve it hot from the oven for breakfast with jam and scrambled eggs, at lunch with a fruit salad, or for supper with fried chicken. Once cooled and a day old, the cornbread will be dry; it is best, then, to crumble it into a cornbread stuffing.

MAKES ONE 9-INCH SQUARE

¾ cup yellow cornmeal
1 cup unbleached all-purpose
  flour
⅓ cup sugar
3 teaspoons baking powder

¾ teaspoon salt
1 cup milk
1 egg, beaten
2 tablespoons butter, melted

In large mixing bowl, blend the cornmeal, flour, sugar, baking powder, and salt. In another smaller bowl, mix the milk, egg, and butter. Stir liquid mixture into dry ingredients just until blended. Pour into a well-buttered 9-inch square pan. Preheat oven to 425° F. Bake 20 minutes, or until center springs back when touched. Serve hot with butter.

FEATHER-LIGHT SPOON BREAD

Spoon bread, of course, gets its name because you serve it with a spoon. I love it with plenty of melted butter. This bread is delicate, soufflélike, and, although it will sink somewhat shortly after you remove it from the oven, as you spoon it onto each plate the bread will be light in texture.

MAKES 4 SERVINGS

2 cups milk
2 tablespoons butter
½ teaspoon salt

¾ cup yellow cornmeal
5 eggs, separated

In a large saucepan, combine milk, butter, and salt; bring to a boil. Add cornmeal gradually, stirring with a whisk to keep mixture smooth; cook 5 minutes until thick. Remove from heat. Beat egg yolks in bowl. Add 1 cup of the hot mixture to eggs, then stir egg mixture into hot mixture. Whip egg whites until stiff and fold into batter. Turn into a well-buttered 1-quart casserole or soufflé dish. Preheat oven to 375° F. Bake 30 to 35 minutes, or until a wooden skewer inserted in the middle comes out clean. Serve from baking dish at once.

OZARK HOECAKE

For those who live outside the Ozarks, trying to establish the difference among "hoecakes," "ash cakes," and "corn pone" is the source of some confusion. The truth is that to define any of these is to start an argument, which to me indicates authentic regional foods. When I lived in Missouri, I gathered an armload of colorful Ozark cookbooks and cooking pamphlets. Some books say that the reason these pancakes are called "hoecakes" is that they were originally baked right on a hoe over an open fire. These are made with 100 percent cornmeal, and may have a crumbly texture if the cornmeal is dry or coarse. The best cornmeal to use for this is a fresh, stone-ground cornmeal, which has the germ ground in and is moister than degermed cornmeal.

MAKES **12** CAKES

1 pound bacon, sliced	1 tablespoon bacon drippings
1 cup yellow cornmeal	or other melted fat
½ teaspoon salt	½ to ¾ cup water, enough to
½ teaspoon baking powder	make a soft dough

Fry bacon in skillet or on griddle until crisp. Drain and reserve fat. Combine the cornmeal, salt, and baking powder. Add fat and stir in enough water to make a soft dough. Make into small cakes about ¼ inch thick and 3 inches in diameter. Cook on a hot greased griddle until browned on one side; turn over and brown on other side. Serve hot with honey and butter, along with the bacon.

CRANBERRY CORNBREAD MINILOAVES

These delicious, small, quick bread loaves combine 2 foods that the Indians introduced to the first American settlers. They are quick to make, unusually nutritious, and wonderfully rich tasting. These seem especially suited to brunches and parties at Thanksgiving time, but don't keep them just for that time of year.

MAKES **4** MINILOAVES

1 cup unbleached all-purpose flour	½ cup chopped walnuts
½ cup whole wheat flour	2 cups buttermilk
½ cup sugar	¾ cup salad oil or butter, melted
1½ teaspoons salt	2 eggs, lightly beaten
1¼ teaspoons baking soda	1 cup coarsely chopped fresh or frozen cranberries
2 cups yellow cornmeal	
1 cup wheat germ	

In large bowl, stir together flours, sugar, salt, and soda until thoroughly blended. Mix in cornmeal, wheat germ, and nuts. In a separate bowl, mix buttermilk, oil or butter, and eggs. Stir liquid mixture into dry ingredients just until blended. Fold in the cranberries. Pour into 4 greased 5½ x 3-inch loaf pans. Preheat oven to 375° F. Bake for 30 to 35 minutes or until a wooden skewer inserted in the center comes out clean. Cool in pans for 5 minutes, then remove and cool completely on a wire rack.

CORN TORTILLAS

There are only 2 necessary ingredients for making tortillas: one of them is water, the other is a very finely ground cornmeal called masa harina. Don't try to substitute regular cornmeal. However, many supermarkets today carry masa harina in 5-pound bags. Once you've tasted homemade tortillas, the store-bought variety seem tasteless. In specialty cookware stores, you can purchase a tortilla press, which is handy for flattening out the tortilla dough. But tortillas are not difficult to make without the press, and they make heavenly enchiladas and tacos. Or simply top them with green chilies and melted Monterey Jack cheese for a great snack.

MAKES 12

2 cups masa harina
1¼ cups water

Dash salt (optional)

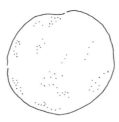

In mixing bowl, mix masa harina, water and salt together with a fork, then with your hands to make a stiff dough. If you have a food processor, put everything into it using the steel blade. Process until dough is very smooth. Divide into 12 equal balls. Roll each ball on an unfloured surface, or between sheets of waxed paper, to ⅛ inch thick, 6 inches across. Trim edges with a knife. Heat an ungreased griddle to 450° F. Cook tortillas one at a time for 2 to 3 minutes on each side. Stack as they are finished and then wrap in plastic or store in a plastic bag. Prepare and serve as you would for any dish that calls for tortillas.

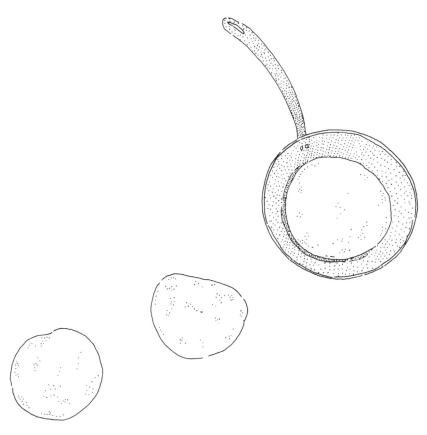

MULTIPLE GRAIN
BREADS

Many a newcomer to the art of bread baking gets tempted by the thought of combining grains to produce the best-tasting *and* most nutritious loaf of all time. But it is easy to go too far and end up with bread that has lost the rich, nutty flavor and firm, chewy texture of the well-balanced loaf and which acquires a disappointingly gritty texture and lackluster flavor. There is an art to mixing grains!

One is always safe combining wheat, triticale,* rye, and oats. The textures of these balance each other when cooked. The flavors blend well, too. Wheat is nutty and rather sweet; rye has a grainy flavor; triticale, being a cross between the two grains, also has a flavor with the sweetness of wheat and graininess of rye; oats are bland, but add smoothness to the texture.

Ground millet and cornmeal look alike and behave in similar ways in a bread mixture—they can make it dry, a bit crumbly. A little of either, however, adds an interesting crunch to the crumb.

I have enjoyed wonderful 3-grain breads as well as breads that have a flavor which cannot be created except by combining the grains. Not just any grains, however. A good way to start is to explore a natural foods store and purchase a multiple-grain cereal to make a bread. The grains in those cereals are usually some combination of wheat, oats, triticale, millet, soy, corn, rye, barley, buckwheat, and rice. It will not necessarily include all of these grains, but several in a balance that has already been deemed good-tasting. These pre-mixed grains are sold as breakfast cereals and so a good way to check the flavor is to cook a little of the cereal and taste it.

In this book there are chapters which cover the qualities and available forms of wheat, oats, triticale, corn, buckwheat, rye, and barley. Millet, soy, and rice are not usually used in large quantities in breads, but they have special qualities which add flavor, texture, and nutrition to whole grain breads.

BREAD GRAINS

MILLET

Millet is a very tiny, round grain that looks a lot like a mustard seed. It is the seed of a grass which was first cultivated in Asia or Africa. Millet, when cooked, has a mild flavor and chewy texture that

* Triticale is a hybrid grain produced by combining wheat and rye. See page 188.

resembles barley or brown rice. Added whole to bread, it gives a nutty flavor, seedy quality, and intriguing texture. When ground, millet resembles cornmeal, and can be used also in bread. Too much millet added to a whole grain bread can make the bread crumbly. It is best used for texture and flavor. The nutritional value of millet is similar to wheat, except that it does not have sufficient gluten to produce a dough that will rise well.

SOY

Soy has received a lot of attention in recent years because of its high protein content. The soybean contains a valuable mix of amino acids which makes it easier to get complete protein from grain sources. For bread making, even though soy flour is high in protein, it does not contain sufficient gluten to make good bread by itself. For bread baking the flour must be mixed with wheat flour to make a loaf that will rise successfully. Soy flour adds a beanlike flavor to mixtures, and therefore must be used in careful balance with other ingredients to get a good-flavored yeast bread.

RICE

White and brown rice are available in most well-stocked supermarkets. Brown rice has undergone a minimum of processing as only the hull and a small portion of the bran have been removed. White rice has had the hull and bran removed and has also been polished. Although you can interchange brown and white rice in recipes calling for rice, brown rice usually requires a longer cooking time.

Both brown and white rice flour is available in whole foods and nutrition stores; these are flours that can be used in a bread dough to replace whole wheat flour and give extra softness to the crumb. White rice flour has less flavor and nutritional value than brown rice flour. Both can be used in combination with soy, rye, buckwheat, or oat flour for wheat-free recipes. Rice flour does not have sufficient gluten to produce a successful yeast dough, but it can be used alone in non-yeasted nut breads (see recipe page 310) and unleavened flat breads.

WILD RICE

Despite its name, wild rice is not a true rice, as it is only distantly related to commercial white rice. The grain is dark, long, and slender. Because of its relatively high protein content (compared with wheat, which has 11.1 percent protein, wild rice has 14.6 percent), it has been the staple food of American Indians. Wild rice is an aquatic plant and grows in marshy regions along the Great Lakes from Manitoba to the Atlantic coast, south along the coast to the Gulf of Mexico, and west to Texas. The most significant production is in northern Minnesota. Some wild rice has been successfully cultivated in California, but the best production is still in its natural, wild stands.

Wild rice must be cooked before being added to breads. It adds a rich grainy taste, crunchy texture, and dark flecks of color. Because it is expensive, and also because wild rice has a good strong flavor, it can be used in small amounts just as you would add nuts to bread for flavor and texture.

Wild rice flour has at times been available from wild rice producers, but is not in large enough supply to rely on for recipe development. If you happen to get some, use it in breads, muffins, and pancakes in place of a small amount of another flour to add a rich, grainy taste.

SEVEN-GRAIN BREAD

Seven-grain cereals are available in health and natural foods stores, and although different brands may have different proportions, all work equally well in this recipe. The usual combination consists of some blending of wheat, oats, triticale, millet, soybeans, buckwheat, and yellow corn.

MAKES 1 LOAF

½ cup boiling water
⅓ cup seven-grain cereal
2 tablespoons salad oil
2 tablespoons honey
¾ teaspoon salt
¼ cup warm water,
    105° F.–115° F.

1 package active dry yeast
1 egg
2 to 2½ cups whole wheat
    flour

In large mixing bowl, mix the boiling water and cereal; let stand until cooled. Add the oil, honey, and salt to cereal. In small bowl or cup, mix the warm water into the yeast. Let stand 5 minutes or until yeast is foamy. When cereal mixture has cooled to 105° F.–115° F., add yeast and egg. Stir in enough whole wheat flour to make a stiff dough; let stand 15 minutes. Turn out onto lightly floured board and knead until smooth, about 5 minutes. Wash bowl, lightly grease it, add dough to bowl, turn over to grease top, and let rise in a warm place until doubled, about 1 to 2 hours.

Punch dough down and shape into an oblong loaf. Lightly grease an 8½ x 4½-inch loaf pan. Place dough into pan. Let rise in warm place until doubled, about 1 hour. Preheat oven to 375° F. Bake 30 to 35 minutes, or until loaf is browned and sounds hollow when tapped. Remove from pan and cool on rack.

PILGRIM'S HEARTH BREAD

A rustic loaf that combines cornmeal with whole wheat and rye flour and is ideal to serve with a harvest vegetable soup.

MAKES 1 LARGE FREE-FORM LOAF OR 2 PAN LOAVES

½ cup yellow cornmeal
½ cup well-packed brown
    sugar
2 teaspoons salt
2 cups boiling water
¼ cup vegetable oil
2 packages active dry yeast
½ cup warm water,
    105° F.–115° F.

1 cup whole wheat flour,
    preferably stone-ground
½ cup rye flour, preferably
    stone-ground
4 to 4½ cups bread flour or
    unbleached all-purpose
    flour

GLAZE:

1 egg white beaten with
    2 tablespoons water

2 tablespoons yellow cornmeal
    for tops of loaves

In a medium mixing bowl, mix the cornmeal, brown sugar, salt, boiling water, and oil. Let stand until cooled to lukewarm, 105° F.–115° F., and liquid is absorbed. In large mixing bowl, dissolve yeast in warm water; let stand 5 minutes until yeast foams. Add cooled cornmeal mixture, whole wheat flour, and rye flour; beat until smooth. Gradually add the bread flour to make a stiff dough. Turn out onto lightly floured surface. Let rest 15 minutes. Knead until smooth and elastic, about 10 minutes. Wash bowl, grease lightly, add dough to bowl, and turn over. Cover and let rise in a warm place until doubled (about 1 hour). Punch down. Shape into one large round loaf or divide in half and shape into loaves to fit two 9 x 5-inch breadpans. Place round loaf on baking sheet covered with parchment paper or in lightly greased bread pans. Let rise until doubled. Brush with egg white glaze and sprinkle with the cornmeal. With sharp knife or razor blade, slash large loaf to make a criss-cross pattern on top; slash pan loaves once along the length of the loaf. Preheat oven to 375° F. Bake 40 to 45 minutes or until loaves sound hollow when tapped. Remove from pans or sheet and cool on wire rack.

WILD RICE THREE-GRAIN BREAD

Wild rice gives this bread a texture and flavor that is unique. Shaped into a braid and curled into a wreath, it makes a pretty presentation for a holiday table.

MAKES 1 LARGE WREATH

1 package active dry yeast
½ cup warm water,
    105° F.–115° F.
2 cups milk, scalded
    and cooled to
    105° F.–115° F.
2 tablespoons butter or lard,
    melted and cooled
1 tablespoon salt
½ cup honey
1 cup rolled oats

1 cup dark rye flour
1 cup whole wheat flour
4 to 4½ cups bread flour or
    unbleached all-purpose
    flour
2 cups cooked wild rice
1 egg beaten with 1 tablespoon
    water
½ cup hulled sunflower seeds,
    plain or salted

In large bowl, dissolve yeast in warm water; let stand 5 minutes until yeast foams. Add milk, butter, salt, and honey. Stir in oats, rye flour, whole wheat flour, and 2 cups of the bread flour or enough to make a soft dough. Add wild rice. Cover dough; let rest for 15 minutes. Stir in enough bread flour to make a stiff dough. Turn out onto a board and knead 10 minutes. Add flour as necessary to keep dough from sticking.

Wash bowl, grease it, place dough into bowl, turn dough over, cover, and let rise until doubled, about 2 hours. Punch down and knead briefly on lightly oiled board. To shape, divide dough into 3 parts and shape into strands like a rope by rolling between hands and oiled surface. Braid, and place on baking sheet to make a wreath. Let rise until doubled, about 45 minutes. Brush top of wreath with egg mixed with water, then sprinkle with sunflower seeds. Bake in a preheated 375° F. oven for 40 to 45 minutes or until loaves sound hollow when tapped. Cool on rack.

FOUR-SEED HEALTH BREAD

The crunchy texture in this healthy bread comes from millet, sunflower, sesame, and poppy seeds. Excellent for breakfast!

MAKES 1 LOAF

2 packages active dry yeast
½ cup light or dark molasses
2 cups warm water,
    105° F.–115° F.
¼ cup butter, melted, or
    vegetable oil
1 teaspoon salt
½ cup sunflower seeds

½ cup millet
¼ cup sesame seeds
2 tablespoons poppy seeds
½ cup gluten flour
½ cup unprocessed bran
1 cup light or dark rye flour
3 to 3½ cups whole wheat
    flour

In large bowl, combine yeast, molasses, and warm water. Let stand 5 minutes until yeast foams. Stir in butter, salt, seeds, millet, and gluten flour; beat until smooth. Add the bran and rye flour. Slowly stir in the whole wheat flour until a stiff dough forms. Let rest 15 minutes. Turn out onto lightly floured board and knead until dough is smooth and springy, about 10 minutes.

Grease a 9 x 5-inch loaf pan. Shape dough into loaf and place into pan. Cover with plastic wrap. Let rise in a warm place until dough is doubled, about 1 to 1½ hours. Preheat oven to 350° F. and bake until loaf sounds hollow when tapped, about 40 to 45 minutes. Turn out of pan. Cool on rack.

TRIPLE PARTY LOAF

This is for a big party! It's a show-off bread that is basically 3 kinds of bread—white, rye, and wheat—all braided together to make a large loaf. The easiest way to mix the bread is in 3 separate bowls all at one time. Otherwise, you can use 1 bowl and start with the white bread, continue with the rye, and follow with the whole wheat.

MAKES ABOUT 24 SERVINGS

3 packages active dry yeast	2 teaspoons fennel seeds
3 teaspoons sugar	2 teaspoons caraway seeds
3 cups warm water,	5 to 5½ cups bread flour or
105° F.–115° F.	unbleached all-purpose
3 eggs	flour
6 teaspoons salt	1 cup light or dark rye flour
6 tablespoons butter or	3 cups whole wheat flour
margarine, melted	1 cup chopped walnuts

GLAZE:

1 egg beaten with
    2 tablespoons milk

Line up 3 mixing bowls. Put 1 package of yeast into each, add 1 teaspoon sugar to each, and add 1 cup warm water to each. Stir all 3 and let stand 5 minutes until yeast foams. Add 1 egg to each bowl, 2 teaspoons salt, and 2 tablespoons melted butter to each; mix well. To the

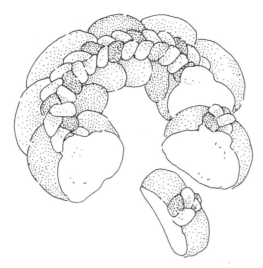

first bowl, add the fennel seeds; to the second add the caraway seeds. Stir 3 cups of the bread flour slowly into the bowl with the fennel seeds until dough is stiff. Set aside for a few minutes. Add 1 cup rye flour and 2 cups of bread flour to the bowl with the caraway seeds; stir until dough is stiff. Add the whole wheat flour to the third bowl and stir until dough is stiff. Beginning with the white dough, knead 5 minutes on lightly floured board or until dough is satiny and smooth. Return to bowl, cover, and let rise until doubled, about 45 minutes. Turn out rye dough and knead 5 minutes or until dough is satiny and smooth. Return to bowl, cover, and let rise until doubled, about 45 minutes. Turn out whole wheat dough and knead for 5 minutes or until dough is satiny and smooth. Return to bowl. Let rise 45 minutes or until about doubled. Line a baking sheet with parchment paper or sprinkle with cornmeal. When doughs have risen, add chopped walnuts to the whole wheat dough; knead in until blended. Cut off ¼ of the dough and reserve. Roll out to make a strand about 36 inches long. Cut off and reserve ¼ of the dough from both white and rye breads. Roll remaining portions out to make strands 36 inches long. You should have 3 strands. Braid the 3 strands together. Place in a wreath shape on cookie sheet covered with parchment paper. Pinch ends to seal together. Roll out reserved dough to make 3 strands. Braid the 3 strands together to make a thin braid. Brush top of first braid with egg-milk glaze. Place smaller braid on top and pinch ends to seal. Brush all over with glaze. Let rise until doubled in a warm place, about

45 minutes to 1 hour. Preheat oven to 375° F. Bake for 30 to 35 minutes or until loaf is lightly browned. Cool on a rack.

MENNONITE COMMUNITY THREE-FLOUR BREAD

The Mennonites are dedicated to feeding the world's hungry. But to do so, all people must learn to consume less of the world's limited resources. Breads and whole grains are part of the plan. This bread, besides being deliciously grainy in flavor, is simple to make.

MAKES 3 LOAVES

2 packages active dry yeast
4 cups warm water,
    105° F.–115° F.
2 teaspoons salt
¼ cup vegetable oil
¼ cup honey or molasses
1 cup nonfat dry milk

1 cup rye flour
¼ cup soy flour
¼ cup wheat germ
4 cups whole wheat flour
5 to 5½ cups bread flour or
    unbleached all-purpose
    flour

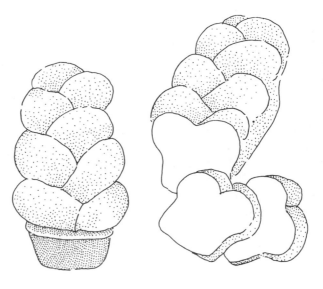

In large mixing bowl, dissolve the yeast in 1 cup of the warm water. Let stand 5 minutes until yeast foams. Stir in the salt, oil, honey or molasses, remaining water, and dry milk. Mix in the rye flour, soy flour, wheat germ, and whole wheat flour; beat well. Add bread flour, 1 cup at a time, beating well until stiff dough forms. Turn dough out onto lightly floured board and knead until smooth and elastic, about 10 minutes. Wash bowl, grease it, and add dough to bowl. Turn over to grease top of dough. Cover and let rise in a warm place until doubled, about 1½ to 2 hours. Grease three 9 x 5-inch loaf pans. Punch dough down. Divide into 3 parts. Shape each into a loaf and place into greased pans. Or divide each of the 3 parts into 3 more parts and shape each into a rope about 15 inches long by rolling between hands and oiled surface. Braid each set of 3 strands together, then ease each braid into the loaf pan. Let rise until about doubled. Preheat over to 375° F. Bake for 25 to 30 minutes or until loaves sound hollow when tapped. Remove from pans and cool on rack.

THREE-GRAIN HONEY CROWN

A fancy loaf with a clever shaping technique, this bread is pretty on a buffet table.

MAKES 1 LOAF

2 packages active dry yeast
1 cup warm water,
      105° F.–115° F.
¼ cup honey
¼ cup vegetable oil
1½ teaspoons salt
½ cup rolled oats

½ cup dark rye flour
1 cup whole wheat flour
½ cup bread flour or
      unbleached all-purpose
      flour
Vegetable oil to brush top of
      loaf

GLAZE:

1 egg beaten with
      1 tablespoon water

Wheat germ to sprinkle over
      top

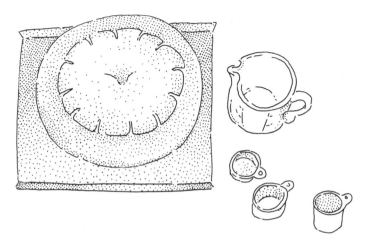

In large bowl, dissolve yeast in warm water; add honey and stir; let stand 5 minutes until yeast foams. Add oil, salt, oats, rye flour, and whole wheat flour until dough is stiff. Let stand 15 minutes. Sprinkle board with bread flour; turn dough out onto board and knead about 10 minutes until dough is smooth and elastic. Wash bowl, grease it, add dough to bowl, and turn to coat all sides. Cover and let rise until doubled, 1½ to 2 hours. Punch down. Divide into 2 parts, one slightly larger than the other. Shape large piece into a ball and flatten to make a 6-inch round. Place on greased baking sheet. Shape other piece of dough into a ball and flatten to make a 5-inch round. Place on top of the first round; press together firmly. Press finger through both rounds to make a deep indentation right through the center of the loaf; as you press you should touch the baking pan. Let rise 45 minutes or until doubled. Brush dough with beaten egg, then slash surface of top layer using a sharp knife, razor, or steel blade of a food processor to make 12 cuts ½ inch deep. Sprinkle with wheat germ. Bake in a 375° F. oven for 35 to 40 minutes, until loaf sounds hollow when tapped. Remove from sheet and cool on wire rack.

HOLIDAY BREAD WREATH

This is a delicious bread with whole grain texture and chewiness, but with an interesting combination of seed flavors. Anise blended with oat dough and caraway with rye results in a contrasting combination of flavors unlike that which results when they are all blended together. This bread is pretty enough to feature on a holiday appetizer buffet.

MAKES 1 LARGE WREATH

2 cups warm water,
105° F.–115° F.
1½ tablespoons sugar
2 packages active dry yeast
2 teaspoons salt
2 tablespoons butter, melted
4 to 4½ cups bread flour or
unbleached all-purpose
flour

1 teaspoon caramel coloring
(see page 84), or 2
tablespoons instant coffee
dissolved in 1 tablespoon
water (optional)
1 cup light or dark rye flour
1 tablespoon caraway seeds
1 teaspoon aniseeds
1 cup rolled oats, quick or
old-fashioned

GLAZE:
1 egg beaten with
2 tablespoons milk

In large bowl, combine warm water, sugar, and yeast. Let stand 5 minutes until yeast foams. Add salt, butter, and 3 cups of the bread flour. Beat until smooth and elastic. Pour half the mixture into another bowl. Add caramel coloring, if desired, rye flour, and caraway seeds to one bowl. Beat well. Add more all-purpose flour to make a stiff dough. Cover and let rest 15 minutes. Add aniseeds and oats to second bowl. Beat well. Add enough all-purpose flour to make a stiff dough. Cover and let rest 15 minutes. On a floured board, turn out one of the doughs at a time and knead each for 10 minutes or until smooth and satiny. Wash mixing bowls, grease them, and return dough to bowls; cover and let rise until doubled, about 1 hour.

Turn doughs out onto lightly oiled board. Divide each in half and shape each half into a strand about 30 inches long. Making a 4-stranded braid, weave the strands together. Trim ends to make even and place dough onto a parchment-covered or lightly greased cookie sheet, fusing the cut ends together to shape a wreath. With palm of hands, flatten out the dough trimmings (it will be marbleized with

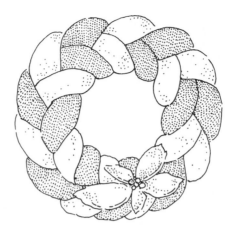

both dark and light dough). With pastry cutter or knife, cut out long, slender "leaves." Place the leaves over the seam on the wreath to fashion a poinsettia. Roll extra dough trimmings into little balls and place them in the center of the poinsettia. Touch the edges of the poinsettia with glaze. Very lightly brush the entire wreath to highlight its contours with the glaze. Let rise until doubled, about 45 minutes. Preheat oven to 375° F. Bake 25 to 30 minutes or until golden and light.

NO-KNEAD QUICK-MIX THREE-GRAIN BREAD

This should appeal to the timid, or to the cook without much time, or to anyone who loves the flavor of a multiple grain bread. The loaf has a higher percentage of liquid to flour, so it is more tender, needs no kneading—just a good beating—and rises quickly.

MAKES 2 LOAVES

½ cup whole wheat flour
½ cup light or dark rye flour
½ cup quick or old-fashioned
 rolled oats
¼ cup sugar
2 packages active dry yeast

2 cups milk
¼ cup vegetable oil
1 egg
2½ to 3 cups bread flour or
 unbleached all-purpose
 flour

In large mixer bowl, combine the whole wheat flour, rye flour, rolled oats, sugar, and yeast. In saucepan, heat the milk to between 120° F. and 130° F. Add hot liquid, oil, and egg to dry ingredients and mix at low speed until moistened. Beat 3 minutes at medium speed, then stir in by hand enough bread flour to make a very stiff batter. Cover and let rise until doubled. Meanwhile, grease two 8½ x 4½-inch loaf pans. Spoon batter into the pans. Let rise until doubled, 30 to 35 minutes. Preheat oven to 375° F. Bake 35 to 40 minutes or until loaves sound hollow when tapped. Remove loaves from pan and cool on rack.

BUCKWHEAT BREADS

Golden brown pancakes with maple syrup are what most people think of when they hear the word *buckwheat*. Or they conjure up buckwheat blini, those Russian yeast-raised pancakes served with dollops of sour cream and caviar. In Finland, buckwheat blinis with their traditional trimmings are a classic Shrove Tuesday meal. And they have become so popular that they are often served as a first course other times of the year as well, especially when served with fresh whitefish caviar.

But buckwheat flour has been used in many different countries to make a variety of breads. It has been used, for example, in the sourdoughs of Germany, Eastern Europe, and Finland. In the chapter on Sourdough Breads, there are a number of these old favorites.

In the United States, buckwheat grows from Pennsylvania north into Canada. It is a hardy plant which develops such a strong root system that it is often used for planting along roadsides to choke out weeds. Planted along the turnpikes of the United States, buckwheat is seldom allowed to develop to the point at which the grain will form. However, it is often allowed to flower, making it an important crop for the production of honey. Buckwheat honey is delicious and has a flowery taste. It is a naturally compatible topping for bread along with butter. Because of the importance of these flowers, most buckwheat is not sprayed with pesticides since they would kill the bees.

Buckwheat flour is fine, dark in color, and—when used without diluting with another flour—has a rather strong flavor. When it is added to bread dough, buckwheat flour adds a distinctive tart taste. The classic Shrove Tuesday buckwheat blini are yeast-risen; however, the dough is allowed to "sour" overnight to develop the flavor even further.

Because it is low in protein, especially gluten, buckwheat flour must be mixed with a high gluten flour to produce a light and well-risen yeast bread. Buckwheat is high in the B vitamins.

Buckwheat groats (the whole grain) can be purchased in health food, whole food, and nutrition shops. They can be cooked as would be any other cereal or soaked and used in pilaf, as a stuffing, in meat loaves, and in casseroles. Cooked or soaked buckwheat groats are excellent in bread. They impart a distinctive flavor and texture to yeast breads. *Kasha* is another name for buckwheat groats and can sometimes be purchased in supermarkets as well as specialty food stores.

BUCKWHEAT RAISIN BREAD

In this bread, the groats are first soaked, then combined with the bread dough along with finely ground buckwheat flour. The sweetness of the raisins balances the tartness of the buckwheat flavor.

MAKES 2 LARGE LOAVES

½ cup buckwheat groats
1 cup boiling water
2 packages active dry yeast
1½ cups warm water,
    105° F.–115° F.
½ cup dark molasses
3 tablespoons butter, softened
    or melted
2 tablespoons caraway seeds

1 teaspoon salt
1 cup dark raisins
½ cup buckwheat flour
5 to 5½ cups bread flour or
    unbleached all-purpose
    flour
Butter to brush on tops of
    loaves

In large mixing bowl, combine buckwheat groats and boiling water. Set aside for 30 minutes until buckwheat has softened. In small bowl, combine yeast and warm water; add molasses and stir; let stand 5 to 10 minutes or until mixture begins to foam. Stir yeast mixture into cooled buckwheat mixture; add butter, caraway seeds, salt, raisins, and buckwheat flour; beat well. Slowly add the bread flour, beating to keep smooth, until a slightly stiff dough forms. Cover and let stand 15 minutes. Turn out onto lightly floured board and knead 10 minutes or until dough is springy and smooth; it may be slightly tacky, but should have an even texture. Wash bowl, grease it, add dough to bowl, turn over to grease top. Cover and let rise until doubled, about 1 to 1½ hours. Grease two 9-inch round cake pans or 2 loaf pans 9 x 5 inches. Punch dough down. Divide in half and shape into loaves to fit pans. Let rise until doubled, about 45 minutes to 1 hour. Preheat oven to 375° F. Bake 35 to 40 minutes. Brush tops of hot loaves with butter. Remove from pans and cool on wire racks.

BUCKWHEAT MOLASSES BREAD

The slightly pungent flavor of buckwheat, blended with molasses and anise, makes this bread wonderful for sandwiches filled with either corned beef and Swiss cheese or an all vegetable filling such as shredded, crunchy vegetables (carrots, sprouts, lettuce, and avocado).

MAKES 2 LOAVES

2 packages active dry yeast
2 cups warm water,
    105° F.–115° F.
1 cup nonfat dry milk
½ cup blackstrap molasses
¼ cup lard, oil, or butter,
    melted
1 tablespoon anisseed
2 teaspoons salt
2 cups buckwheat flour

4 to 5 cups bread flour or
    unbleached all-purpose
    flour
About ⅓ cup wheat germ
    (optional)
About ⅓ cup dark raisins
    (optional)
Butter to brush tops of loaves
    (optional)

In large mixing bowl, dissolve yeast in warm water; add the dry milk and molasses. Let stand 5 minutes until yeast foams. Add lard, aniseed, salt, buckwheat flour, and 2 cups of the bread flour; beat until smooth. Gradually add more flour, stirring to make a stiff dough. Let stand 15 minutes. Turn dough out onto board sprinkled with some of the remaining flour. Knead 10 minutes or until dough is smooth and springy. Wash bowl, grease it, and add dough to bowl. Turn over to grease top. Let rise in warm place until doubled, about 1 to 1½ hours. Punch dough down, divide in half, and, on an oiled surface, roll out to make a rectangle 8 by 12 inches. Sprinkle loaves with either wheat germ or raisins, using ⅓ cup of either for each loaf. Roll up tightly, sealing well, starting with an 8-inch side. Seal ends. Place into greased 8½ x 4½-inch baking pans. Let rise until doubled, 45 minutes to 1 hour. Preheat oven to 375° F. Bake 35 to 40 minutes, or until loaves are well browned and sound hollow when tapped. Remove from pans, cool on rack, and brush loaves while still hot with butter if desired.

BUCKWHEAT SUNBURST BREAD

Buckwheat and whole wheat flour give this bread a grainy flavor and texture. Shaped into a braid that is spiraled into a round cake pan and crusted with sunflower seeds, this loaf is a showpiece as well.

MAKES 2 LOAVES

1 package active dry yeast
2 cups warm water,
   105° F.–115° F.
¼ cup honey
2 teaspoons salt
2 tablespoons vegetable oil

¼ cup nonfat dry milk
1½ cups buckwheat flour
2 cups whole wheat flour
1 to 1½ cups bread flour or
   unbleached all-purpose
   flour

GLAZE:

1 egg mixed with
   2 tablespoons water

½ cup shelled sunflower seeds

In large mixing bowl, dissolve yeast in warm water; add 1 tablespoon of the honey; set aside for 5 minutes until yeast foams. Add remaining honey, salt, oil, dry milk, and buckwheat flour; beat well. Beat in the whole wheat flour until mixture is smooth. Cover and let stand 30 minutes. Stir in the bread flour until a stiff dough forms. Turn out

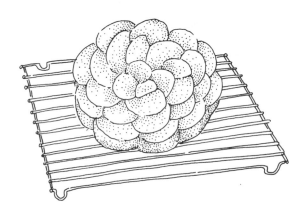

onto lightly floured board and knead 8 to 10 minutes or until dough is smooth and springy; it may still be slightly tacky, but resist the temptation to add more flour. Wash bowl, grease it, and add dough to bowl; turn over to grease top. Cover and let rise in a warm place until dough has doubled, 1 to 1½ hours. Divide in half. Divide each half into 3 parts. Roll each out into a strand about 20 inches long. Braid the strands. Grease two 9-inch round cake pans. Place the braids in spirals into the cake pans, making the spirals very tight in the center (top of braid remains on the top of the loaf). Pinch ends to seal together, and with hands shape loaf into a perfect round. Let rise until doubled, about 45 minutes. Brush with glaze and sprinkle with sunflower seeds. Preheat oven to 375° F. Bake 30 minutes or until golden. Remove from pans and cool on wire racks.

BUCKWHEAT BLINI

In Finland, these little pancakes are always served on the Tuesday evening before Lent begins. They are enjoyed with a topping of sour cream and fresh caviar. Served this way, they make a spectacular first course, especially if you add chopped green onion and a pinch of ground allspice to each serving. There's no reason why you can't serve these as ordinary pancakes, too, with melted butter and syrup. To achieve the proper flavor and texture, the dough should be made the night before, or at least 8 hours in advance. The cakes should be cooked just before serving, though they may be served after they have cooled to room temperature if you are using them as a first course with caviar.

MAKES 16 PANCAKES

½ package active dry yeast
¼ cup warm water,
    105° F.–115° F.
2 teaspoons sugar

1 cup milk, scalded and cooled
    to 105° F.–115° F.
1 egg, slightly beaten
1 cup buckwheat flour

The night before, or 8 hours in advance, dissolve yeast in warm water in large mixing bowl; add sugar, milk, egg, and flour. Beat until a soft, smooth batter forms. Cover and let stand overnight or for at least 8 hours. Before serving, heat griddle and use 2 to 3 tablespoons of the batter for each cake. Cakes should be no more than 4 inches in diameter.

BUCKWHEAT BUTTERMILK YEAST BISCUITS

Tangy with the flavor of buckwheat, lightly soured with buttermilk, and topped with walnuts, these yeast-risen biscuits are a perfect accompaniment to a hearty potato chowder.

MAKES 16 TO 18 BISCUITS

1 package active dry yeast
¼ cup warm water,
    105° F.–115° F.
2 tablespoons dark molasses
2 tablespoons sugar
2 cups buttermilk, warmed to
    105° F.–115° F.

¾ cup butter, melted
1½ cups buckwheat flour
3½ to 4 cups unbleached
    all-purpose flour
1½ teaspoons salt
2 egg whites, lightly beaten
½ cup chopped walnuts

In large mixing bowl, dissolve the yeast in warm water. Add the molasses and let stand 5 minutes until mixture foams. Stir in the sugar, buttermilk, ¼ cup of the butter, and 1 cup of the buckwheat flour. Beat well, cover, and let stand in warm place for 30 minutes. Mix in the remaining buckwheat flour, 1 cup of the all-purpose flour, and salt. Beat well. Stir in enough additional flour to make a stiff dough. Turn out onto floured surface, cover, and let stand 15 minutes. Knead 5 minutes or until smooth and velvety. Wash bowl, grease it, and put dough into the bowl. Turn over to grease top. Cover with plastic wrap and let rise until doubled in bulk, about 1 hour. Punch down and let rise again until doubled, about ½ hour. Punch down and roll out to make a flat of dough about 1 inch thick. With biscuit cutter, cut out rounds of dough. Dip in remaining melted butter and place on ungreased baking sheet. Let rise for 30 minutes or until about doubled. Preheat oven to 400° F. Bake 15 minutes. Remove from oven and brush tops with egg white; sprinkle with chopped nuts; return to oven just until nuts are browned, another 5 to 10 minutes. Serve hot. Or, you may split and toast cooled biscuits.

SUNFLOWER SEED–CRUSTED BUCKWHEAT FLATBREAD

The textured crust of sunflower seeds gives crunch and contrast to the smooth inside of this rather unusual flatbread. The basic recipe comes from Ulla Kakonen, a native Karelian who wrote a book called *Natural Cooking the Finnish Way*. In her book, she states that this bread was baked for special occasions by baker-caterers hired by the host of the party. I bake it in a jellyroll pan, and spread the dough about ½ inch thick. The batter is soured overnight, and the flavor develops from a blend of the potato starter with the bitter tartness of the buckwheat flour. It is best served hot from the oven. After baking and while it is still hot, cut squares of the bread to make it easy for stuffing with sandwich fillings.

MAKES 16 SERVINGS, ABOUT 4 INCHES SQUARE

½ pound (2 large) potatoes, scrubbed	⅓ cup warm water, 105° F.–115° F.
3 cups water	2 cups buckwheat flour
1½ teaspoons salt	½ cup buttermilk
1 package active dry yeast	1 cup gluten flour

GLAZE:

1 egg, beaten	¼ cup butter, melted
½ cup shelled sunflower seeds, plain or salted	(optional)

The day before you plan to bake this bread, put the potatoes in water with ½ teaspoon salt. Cook until potatoes are soft, about 20 to 25 minutes. Reserve the cooking liquid. Peel the potatoes and mash while still warm. Add 2 cups of the cooking liquid, mixing well.

Press potato mixture through a sieve into a bowl. Cool to lukewarm. Mix the yeast with the warm water. Add the potato purée. Add 1 cup of the buckwheat flour. Let stand in a warm place 8 hours or overnight. The dough should ferment and develop a sweet-sour odor. Add buttermilk, remaining buckwheat flour, gluten flour, and salt. Stir until smooth. Dough will be the consistency of a thick porridge.

Generously butter a 10 x 15-inch jellyroll pan. Spread dough evenly in pan. Brush top of dough with beaten egg and sprinkle with the sunflower seeds. Preheat oven to 450° F. Bake 20 minutes or until seeds are toasted and bread is done. Brush with melted butter if desired. Cut into squares and serve while warm.

TRITICALE BREADS

Triticale is a rather new variety of grain that is a hybrid—a cross of rye, durum wheat, and red winter wheat. It is high in protein, containing a complex of amino acids that combines with other grains to increase the utilization of protein in the diet. You can purchase triticale as a whole grain, in flakes, or ground into flour. All are available from natural foods stores.

Cooked whole triticale is delicious as a hot breakfast cereal. Flaked triticale has been rolled to produce a texture similar to rolled oats; it too can be cooked and added to bread or eaten as a cereal. Ground triticale flour is ready to use in yeast breads, pancakes, quick breads, or waffles, and you can use it as you would use another whole flour to give a nutty–grainy flavor to favorite recipes.

The flour made from triticale has a natural sweet taste and, when combined with white flour, also imparts a creamy color. Triticale has a flavor that combines well with other whole grains. My favorite is to combine it with either whole wheat or rye flour.

Even though triticale flour is high in protein, it does not in itself have enough gluten to make a good yeast bread. Therefore, at least half of the flour in the dough mixture should be a high-gluten bread flour or an all-purpose flour. A delicious and chewy bread results when triticale is mixed half and half with whole wheat flour, but the resulting loaf will have a dense, heavy texture.

We have 2 basic recipes for triticale breads—one that uses the flour, the other that is for the cooked whole grain.

TRITICALE HONEY LOAF

This is a pale, slightly nutty-flavored bread that is excellent for toast, sandwiches, or as a meal accompaniment. If I were serving it for a holiday or guest meal, I would shape it into a pretty braid.

MAKES 2 LOAVES

1 package active dry yeast	¼ cup vegetable oil
2 cups warm water,	2 teaspoons salt
105° F.–115° F.	1 cup nonfat dry milk
¼ cup honey	2½ cups triticale flour

2½ to 3 cups bread flour or *Butter to brush tops of loaves*
unbleached all-purpose
flour

In large mixing bowl, dissolve yeast in warm water; add the honey, stir, and let stand 5 minutes until yeast foams. Add the oil, salt, milk, and triticale flour; beat with spoon until smooth and satiny. Add the bread flour, 1 cup at a time, beating well after each addition. When dough is stiff, cover and let stand 15 to 20 minutes. Sprinkle board with remaining flour and turn dough out onto it. Knead 5 to 10 minutes until dough is smooth and satiny. Wash bowl, grease it, and add dough to bowl. Cover and let rise in a warm place until doubled, about 1 hour. Divide in half. Shape into 2 loaves. Place into 2 greased 8½ x 4½-inch loaf pans. Let rise until doubled again, about 45 minutes to 1 hour. Preheat oven to 350° F. Bake 45 to 50 minutes. Brush hot loaves with butter. Remove from pans and cool on wire racks.

CRUSTY TRITICALE BRAIDED BREAD

Prepare dough as directed above. Instead of shaping into 2 loaves, divide entire batch into 3 parts. Shape each part into a strand about 30 inches long. Shape into a braid and shape into a wreath. Pinch ends together to seal. Cover baking sheet with parchment paper or lightly grease it. Place loaf on baking sheet. Let rise until doubled. Before baking, brush with water. Preheat oven to 350° F. Bake 45 to 50 minutes, brushing once with water during baking. Remove from pan and cool on rack.

WHOLE GRAIN TRITICALE BREAD

Whole triticale grains can be cooked until tender, then added to a bread dough to give a crunchy texture and a distinctive, slightly sweet and nutty taste.

MAKES 2 ROUND LOAVES

⅓ cup whole triticale	*¼ cup wheat germ*
1 package active dry yeast	*5 cups whole wheat flour*
2½ cups warm water,	*½ to 1 cup bread flour or*
105° F.–115° F.	*unbleached all purpose*
¼ cup honey	*flour*
2 tablespoons butter, softened	*Melted butter for brushing*
2 teaspoons salt	*loaves*

The night before, put whole triticale into a small bowl and cover with warm water; let stand overnight. Drain. In large bowl, stir yeast into warm water; add honey, butter, salt, wheat germ, and 2 cups of the whole wheat flour. Let stand 15 minutes or until yeast foams. Add drained triticale. Slowly stir in remaining whole wheat flour until stiff dough forms. Cover and let stand again for 30 minutes. Stir in enough bread flour to make dough no longer sticky. Turn out onto floured board and knead until smooth, about 10 minutes. Meanwhile, wash bowl and lightly oil it. Shape dough into a ball and place into bowl; turn over to grease top. Cover and let rise in a warm place until doubled, about 1 to 1½ hours. Punch dough down. Divide in half and shape each into a round ball. Place on parchment-covered or lightly greased baking sheet. Let rise about 1 hour or until loaves have about doubled. Heat oven to 375° F. Brush loaves with melted butter and slash a deep X (about ½ inch) using a razor blade or a sharp knife. Bake 30 to 40 minutes, or until loaves sound hollow when tapped. Remove from baking sheet and cool on rack. Brush with butter.

SOURDOUGH BREADS

SOURDOUGH—THE LEGEND, THE STARTER, THE BREAD

As the gold miners in the 1840s rushed to California, many carried with them, in a pouch strapped to their bodies, a sourdough starter. In the evening, flour and water were added to the contents of the pouch and it expanded to more than twice its volume. In the morning, a portion was saved and the remainder made into pancake batter.

Today we tend to think of sourdough breads as being made with white flour, but in the days of the early prospectors and settlers, when they "ground their own," the flour was whole wheat, not white, and certainly not bleached.

It was because of gristmills and saw mills that gold was discovered in the California streams. As workers were building these water-powered mills, they noticed flecks of gold in the rocks along the riverbanks. Colonel Sutter, owner of vast areas in the West, asked that the workers please keep this a secret until the mills were completed. Secrets such as these are never kept, and the rush began.

Sourdough, however, had its beginnings in many countries of the world, and dates back to days before the discovery of yeast, when a portion of the active dough was held over from each day's baking to leaven that of the next batch. Sourdough is exactly what it says it is— "sour dough." Fermented dough, made active by the yeast which is available all around us in nature. Some "wild" yeasts are more active than others, and only a microbiologist would be able to separate them in a laboratory. But the active variety is more abundant than not, and it is possible to "catch" the wild yeast and start your own sourdough starter (just as the early pioneers must have when theirs was lost or ruined).

When we spent a year in Finland, I was sold on Finnish sourdough rye bread. The early Finns depended on sourdough to get their bread to rise. They did, however, have 2 different methods, depending on which part of Finland they were from; the customs were different. In eastern Finland—Karelia, the province closest to the Russian border—it was the custom to bake fat rye loaves every day. Karelian sourdough rye bread was "started" with a rye flour starter which was continually active. A portion of the dough was saved for the next day's baking, and the starter was always wet. In western Finland—the provinces closest to the Swedish border—it was the custom to bake bread twice a year, and then in vast quantities. These were the flattish loaves that have a hole in the center. The holes had a purpose. The loaves were strung on poles and hung in the *aitta,* or grainery, to dry. Hundreds of loaves that were made in the fall lasted through the winter, and those baked in the spring were enough to sustain the Finnish farmers through the summer. The starter for this bread was made by mixing the unbaked "crust," that which formed in the unwashed wooden bread-mixing bowl, with rye flour and water. The mixture was then allowed to ferment until it was very active, and then the dough was mixed. If, however, there was no crust from an unwashed bowl, some Finnish bakers used actual crusts from the previously baked loaves to flavor the dough, and they made the active starter by simply fermenting the mixture of rye flour and water.

Even though sourdough starter and sourdough bread are made using similar methods, the ingredients affect the flavors a lot. The flour makes a big difference. Soured rye bread has a tanginess entirely separate from unsoured rye bread. Rye flour carries the sour flavor very well, and is one of the most commonly "soured" breads in Europe. Whole wheat flour in a sourdough bread is a sweeter flavor, though tangy. White sourdough is the mildest of all, even though it is the variety most of us know best.

The older and more developed the sourdough starter, the tangier the bread will be, regardless of the flour used. White sourdough bread, for instance, may be so mildly flavored you can hardly detect it. The tanginess develops as you save the starter for next time. This is one reason I recommend maintaining the "starter pot" rather than saving a bit of the dough from each baking. You can develop a tangy starter more quickly using the pot method, because the starter is less diluted with flour and liquid each time you bake. To use the starter pot, remove part of the starter and add it to the beginning of the bread dough before souring overnight. At the same time, add flour and milk or water to the starter pot, let it bubble up overnight, and return it to the refrigerator.

Whether or not you regularly bake bread using the starter, it is smart to take the starter out of the refrigerator every now and then and add fresh flour and liquid to it. Let it bubble up overnight, and again refrigerate it. Even though my starter has sometimes gone as long as 6 months without attention, it has remained active. Sometimes I have frozen it when we have been gone for extended periods of time. It's best, though, to refresh the starter every couple of weeks or so.

You can use these sourdough starters interchangeably in recipes that call for sourdough starter. The only exception is the potato starter, which is very liquid; if you use this starter, use ½ cup of the starter plus ½ cup flour to equal the 1 cup of sourdough starter which most recipes call for.

I have found no problem using whole wheat flour as a starter in rye bread and vice versa. In fact, if you wish to make the starters using all-purpose flour, that works fine, too, except that the sour flavor will not be as pronounced.

Tangy sourdough pancakes are a good first experience for the beginning sourdough cook. From there, graduate into crispy, light Sourdough Waffles, Old-Fashioned Sourdough Wheat Biscuits, and then sourdough bread.

STARTING THE STARTER

Sourdough starter is not difficult to "start." There are several popular methods and each one is successful, and though each produces a slightly different-flavored starter, each does accomplish, in time, the task of sharpening the sour flavor of bread.

ORIGINAL MILK-BASED STARTER

With this method, you set out to "catch" wild yeasts in a bowl of milk before adding flour. If you use whole milk, the flavor is less tart than if you use skim milk. The flavor and aroma should be rather sweet-sour in the successful starter; if not, discard and start again.

MAKES ABOUT 2 CUPS

> *1 cup milk, whole homogenized*   *1 cup whole wheat flour*
> *or skim*

Pour milk into a nonmetal bowl or crock and cover with cheesecloth or with a piece of waxed paper placed loosely over the top. Let stand 24 hours in an airy, cool, but not cold place. (I do it on the windowsill above the sink). Stir in the flour and cover loosely again; let stand 3 to 5 days, stirring every day once or twice until mixture is bubbly and has a sweet-sour aroma. At this point the starter is ready to use or should be covered and refrigerated. Each time you use some of the starter in the following recipes, replenish the starter with equal parts of flour and milk. Let stand overnight at room temperature until the starter bubbles, cover loosely, and refrigerate. (A cover on the starter pot should be loose so that gases can escape.)

RYE FLOUR STARTER

Prepare starter as directed in previous recipe, using rye flour (any grind) in place of the whole wheat flour.

YOGURT-BASED STARTER

This popular sourdough starter uses cultured yogurt to "help" the fermentation and achieve a tart flavor.

MAKES 1½ CUPS

1 cup plain natural yogurt   *1 cup whole wheat flour*

Turn yogurt into bowl and place over another bowl filled with hot tap water. Stir until yogurt is no longer "chilly," but is about body temperature. Add the flour, stir, and let stand until it is bubbly and has a pleasantly sour smell, 2 to 3 days. It is now ready to use, or cover and refrigerate until ready to use. To replenish after using, add an equal amount of skim milk and flour, cover, and let stand in a warm place until it has bubbles, then refrigerate again. Starter should be used every couple of weeks. If you choose to use the entire amount in a batch of bread dough, be sure to remove 1½ cups for next time.

RYE YOGURT STARTER

Prepare Yogurt-based Starter as directed in previous recipe, using rye flour (any grind), in place of the whole wheat flour.

POTATO STARTER

This old-fashioned starter develops a good, sour flavor in 3 to 5 days depending on the temperature of the room. In the early days neighbors often shared the contents of their jar of this starter to use it regularly and keep it active. It is renewed each time you remove some of the starter, and does contain added yeast. Unlike the other starters, this is a liquid mixture, and can be used in place of yeast when baking bread. About ½ cup of this starter replaces 1 package of active dry yeast and ½ cup liquid in the bread mixture.

MAKES ABOUT 4 CUPS

4 medium potatoes, pared
4 cups water
2 teaspoons salt
3 tablespoons sugar

1 package active dry yeast
¼ cup warm water,
    105° F.–115° F.

Dice the potatoes and place in saucepan; add water and cook until tender, about 20 minutes. Remove potatoes and mash until smooth. Add the salt and sugar and potato cooking water; cool to lukewarm. Meanwhile, dissolve the yeast in warm water; add to potato mixture after it has cooled. Turn into a 2-quart nonmetal container (a jar or crock is fine) and cover loosely. Let stand at room temperature for 3 to 5 days, stirring occasionally until mixture has a sweet-sour aroma and has stopped rising furiously. Refrigerate. Before using, stir starter thoroughly in the jar. Replenish when mixture is down to last ½ cup by adding 2 teaspoons active dry yeast dissolved in ½ cup water. Let stand again until mixture bubbles up, then refrigerate, covered.

WHOLE WHEAT BANANA STARTER

Use a banana that has blackened and is so ripe that the flesh is soft and mushy. After souring there will be just a hint of banana aroma. You can use this starter in any recipe that calls for sourdough starter.

MAKES ABOUT 1½ CUPS

1 very ripe banana	*½ cup nonfat dry milk*
1 cup warm water	*1 cup whole wheat flour*

In a nonmetal bowl or crock, blend the banana with the warm water and dry milk until banana is puréed. Cover lightly and let stand at room temperature 24 hours. Stir in the whole wheat flour and let stand for 3 to 5 days, stirring each day, until mixture is fermented and bubbly. Stir down and refrigerate or use in recipes that call for sourdough starter. To replenish, add equal parts of skim milk (or dry skim milk and water) and flour to the starter; stir and let stand again until bubbly, about 24 hours.

BAKING SOURDOUGH WHOLE GRAIN BREADS

The sourdough enthusiast will be delighted with the flavor whole grains achieve. Whole grains (whole wheat and rye) will produce a tangy, rich, sour flavor more quickly than white flour.

Try first the pancakes, waffles, and biscuits. Then try the Gold Prospector's Whole Wheat Sourdough loaves. Hot from the oven, all the flavors are intense; later, slice and toast the bread for breakfast or snacks!

I have provided several sourdough starter recipes, but as I have indicated in the recipes, most of them can be used interchangeably. They all give excellent results, but the ingredients and methods of one may appeal to you more than another. Or try them all! After my testing I simply combined all of the starters, and now my abundant sourdough pot is ready for any "rush hour" of baking!

MIXING SOURDOUGH BREADS

When you mix the dough for sourdough breads (after the souring step), the dough may tend to "loosen" as you add flour. This is because of the intense souring action which is converting starch in the flour to carbon dioxide and a simple sugar. The gas escapes and sugar thins out the bread dough. Sourdough breads require a lot of kneading and "working in" of more flour. That is why the recipes seem to call for more flour in relation to liquid than other recipes in this book.

TO USE YOUR FOOD PROCESSOR FOR KNEADING

If all that kneading is too strenuous for you, it can be done in a food processor. Even if your food processor is a small one, you can knead the dough in small amounts after mixing and combine the kneaded dough in a bowl.

Follow this procedure:

1. Prepare the bread according to the recipe, up to the kneading step.

2. Fit food processor with plastic dough mixing blade or steel blade.

3. Remove 2-cup amounts of dough from the bowl and place into food processor.

4. Turn processor on; if dough is sticky and clings to edges of bowl and blade, scrape sides down with spatula and sprinkle with 1 to 2 tablespoons flour. Process again. Repeat until dough forms a rather firm ball that cleans the sides of the bowl and spins around the bowl. Process until dough spins around bowl 100 times. This may seem like a lot, but the more kneading the dough gets, the better. The only problem with excessive processing is if the dough becomes so warm that it kills the yeast. Stop processing halfway through and feel the dough. If it seems very warm to the touch, stop; let it cool, and process again later. (To be sure, you can insert an instant-reading thermometer into the center of the dough. It should read no more than 115° F.)

5. Continue processing remaining dough in batches, then combine the kneaded dough and proceed with shaping, rising, and baking as recipe instructs.

WHAT TO DO IF YOU KILL THE YEAST (too high a dough temperature)

1. Dissolve 1 package active dry yeast in ¼ cup warm water (no cooler than 105° F. and no warmer than 115° F.). Let stand a few minutes until yeast foams.

2. Work yeast mixture into dough by cutting and kneading it in, either by hand or in the food processor or in the bowl of a heavy-duty mixer with a dough hook.

SOURDOUGH WHOLE WHEAT PANCAKES

Start this pancake batter the night before. You'll be surprised how moist and light they are! Consider the waffle variations; most of these sourdough pancakes are easily converted to crisp and delicious waffles.

MAKES ABOUT 18 PANCAKES

½ cup sourdough starter (any but the potato starter)
1½ cups warm water
1 cup nonfat dry milk
1 cup whole wheat flour
¾ cup unbleached all-purpose flour

2 eggs
2 tablespoons sugar
½ teaspoon salt
1 teaspoon baking soda

The night before, combine starter, warm water, dry milk, and whole wheat and all-purpose flours in a large bowl; blend and leave at room temperature, covered. The next morning, add eggs, sugar, salt, and soda; mix well. Preheat pancake griddle to 375° F. Use ¼ cup batter to make 4 to 5 inch pancakes. Bake until golden on one side, about 1½ to 2 minutes, turn over and bake until browned on opposite side, about 1 minute. Serve hot.

BUCKWHEAT PANCAKES: Prepare sourdough pancakes as directed, but use 1 cup buckwheat flour in place of the whole wheat flour.

SOURDOUGH OAT AND WHEAT CAKES: Prepare sourdough pancakes as directed, but use 1 cup rolled oats and ½ cup whole wheat flour in place of the 1 cup of whole wheat flour.

SOURDOUGH CORNMEAL PANCAKES: Prepare sourdough pancakes as directed, but substitute cornmeal for the whole wheat flour.

SOURDOUGH WAFFLES: Prepare pancake batter and add 3 tablespoons salad oil or melted butter to the batter before baking.

CORNMEAL WAFFLES: Prepare as for regular sourdough waffles, but substitute cornmeal for the whole wheat flour.

OLD-FASHIONED SOURDOUGH WHEAT BISCUITS

Delicious hot from the oven, these biscuits become very firm when cold. Begin this dough at least 8 hours before you plan to serve the biscuits.

MAKES 9 TO 12 BISCUITS

½ cup sourdough starter (any but the potato starter)
1 cup whole milk
1 cup whole wheat flour
1½ cups unbleached all-purpose flour

½ teaspoon salt
2 teaspoons sugar
1 teaspoon baking powder
½ teaspoon baking soda
¼ cup butter, melted

In large bowl, mix the starter, milk, and whole wheat flour. Cover and let rise at room temperature for 8 or more hours (up to 16 hours). Blend ½ cup of the all-purpose flour with salt, sugar, baking powder, and soda. Stir into the dough. Sprinkle board with remaining flour and turn dough out onto it. Mix and knead until smooth. Roll out to ½-inch thickness. Cut biscuits with a 3-inch cutter and dip biscuits in warm, melted butter. Place close together in a 9-inch square pan and set in a warm place for ½ hour until biscuits look puffed but not doubled in bulk. Preheat oven to 375° F. Bake 25 to 30 minutes, until browned. Serve hot.

GOLD PROSPECTOR'S WHOLE WHEAT SOURDOUGH

The tangy flavor of this bread will please the sourdough enthusiast. Use any starter except the potato starter for this bread to develop the rich taste. This loaf has yeast added for quicker rising; however, you can eliminate the yeast and let the dough rise for 24 to 36 hours in the first step instead of just 1½ to 2 hours. Because this bread requires a lot of kneading, it is helpful to use a machine with a dough hook, or divide the batch into 3 smaller parts after mixing and process in the food processor for 100 turns for each part; recombine them in the bowl for rising.

MAKES 1 LARGE ROUND LOAF OR 2 SLENDER OVAL LOAVES

1½ cups warm water,
105° F.–115° F.
1 package active dry yeast
1 cup sourdough starter

2 teaspoons sugar
2 teaspoons salt
4 to 4½ cups whole wheat
flour

In large mixer or mixing bowl, combine the warm water, yeast, and starter; add sugar and let stand 5 minutes until yeast foams. Add salt and stir in 4 cups of the whole wheat flour, mixing to keep dough smooth. Dough should be very stiff. Let rest 15 minutes. Turn out onto board sprinkled with flour and knead for 15 to 20 minutes until very smooth and quite stiff. If mixing in electric mixer, mix for 15 minutes (or at this point you may divide dough into 3 parts and knead in food processor as described on page 198). Turn out into a large greased bowl, cover with plastic wrap or a towel, and let rise in a warm place until doubled in bulk, 1½ to 2 hours.

Shape dough into 1 large round loaf or divide in half and shape into 2 oblong loaves. Place on lightly greased or cornmeal-covered baking sheet. Cover and let rise until doubled, another 1½ to 2 hours. Slash large round loaf 5 times straight across using a razor blade, making cuts ⅛ inch deep, or slash oblong loaves lengthwise and then crosswise. Brush with warm water. Bake in a hot oven (375° F.) until loaves sound hollow when tapped, 45 to 50 minutes for large loaf or 35 to 40 minutes for oblong loaves.

For a heavier and tougher crust, 10 minutes before loaves are done, brush with a mixture of ½ cup water and 1 tablespoon salt. Return to oven and increase temperature to 425° F. to bake the remaining time.

POTATO SOUR RYE BREAD

Use the potato starter in this delicious soured rye bread.

MAKES 3 LOAVES

2 cups warm water, 105° F.–115° F.	2 tablespoons barley malt extract (explained in barley chapter)
1 cup potato starter	
½ cup dark or light molasses	1½ teaspoons salt
3 cups light or dark rye flour	4 tablespoons lard, softened
½ teaspoon ground ginger dissolved in 2 teaspoons warm water	4 cups bread flour or unbleached all-purpose flour

In large bowl, combine the warm water, starter, molasses, and rye flour. Beat well and let stand, tightly covered, in a warm place overnight or for several hours until very spongy and light. Add ginger dissolved in warm water, malt extract, salt, lard, and 3 cups of the bread flour; beat until dough is smooth and cleans the bowl. Sprinkle board with remaining flour and turn dough out onto board. Cover and let rest for 15 minutes. Knead for 10 minutes or until smooth and springy. Wash bowl, grease it, and place dough into the bowl; turn over to grease top. Cover and let rise in a warm place until doubled in bulk, about 1 hour. Punch dough down and divide into 3 parts. Shape into loaves and place in greased 8½ x 4½-inch loaf pans. Let rise until doubled. Preheat oven to 350° F. Bake 30 to 35 minutes, or until loaves sound hollow when tapped with finger.

FINNISH SOUR RYE BREAD

This sour rye bread is the loaf Finns are talking about when they say "bread." Its history is as fun to chew on as the crust. As in many cultures, before yeast was available in neat little packets, bread was leavened with a starter mixture. Salt was an expensive commodity generations ago, so Finns used a sour starter to provide the tang that salt might otherwise provide. The loaf is made big and flat with a hole in the center, so it resembles a large flat doughnut. The loaves

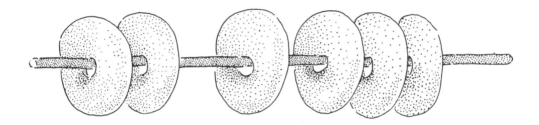

were strung on poles and kept in the *aitta,* as described earlier. Today, of course, Finns buy the bread from good local bakeries. To make this bread, read the directions first, and you will see that there are long waiting periods. In a recent trip to Finland, I discovered that many Finnish bakers use a slice of previously baked bread in place of the sour bread starter. You can use a commercially available sour Finnish crisp bread in place of a starter to give the bread its piquant flavor.

MAKES 2 LARGE ROUND LOAVES

*½ cup sour rye bread starter
   (recipe follows) or 1 slice
   sour rye bread
2 cups warm potato water or
   plain water
3½ cups dark rye flour*

*2 packages active dry yeast
¼ cup warm water,
   105° F.–115° F.
2 teaspoons salt
3 to 3½ cups bread flour or
   all-purpose flour*

Turn the sour rye bread starter into a large mixing bowl and stir in the warm potato water (saved from cooking potatoes) or plain water. If you do not use the sour rye bread starter, crumble the slice of sour rye bread and add half the yeast to the water. Blend in 1 cup of the rye flour and stir well. Cover and let stand in a warm place (85° F.), for 20 to 40 hours, depending on the degree of sourness desired.

Dissolve the yeast (remaining yeast if you are using the slice of sour rye bread) in the warm water. Let stand 5 minutes until yeast foams. Stir into the mixture in the large bowl. Add salt and very gradually beat in the remaining rye flour. Add the bread flour a little at a time, beating well after each addition. (Note: To make the really old-fashioned rye bread, use all rye flour, replacing the 3 to 3½ cups bread flour with rye flour.) When dough is stiff, let rest for 15 minutes. Turn out onto floured board and knead until smooth. Wash bowl, grease lightly, and turn dough into bowl. Turn over to grease top. Cover and let rise in a warm place until doubled, about 1 to 1½ hours. Turn dough out onto lightly floured board and divide in half. (You may reserve ½ cup of the dough and keep it refrigerated to make a sour starter for your next batch of bread.)

Grease 2 baking sheets, or cover with parchment paper. Flatten each ball of dough on a baking sheet to make a big, even round about 1 inch thick. With fingers, make a hole in the center of each loaf and stretch it to about 2 inches in diameter. Dust top of each loaf lightly with rye flour. Cover and let rise in a warm place until puffy and smooth but not doubled in bulk, 30 to 45 minutes. Pierce all over with tines of a fork. Preheat oven to 375° F. Bake for 45 minutes, until loaves are lightly browned. If desired, brush with butter while hot and cool on racks.

SOUR RYE BREAD STARTER: Two to 4 days before you plan to make sour rye bread, mix ½ cup whole milk (at room temperature) with ½ cup rye flour. Let stand, uncovered, in a warm place until the mixture begins to bubble and has a pleasantly sour odor. You may refrigerate the starter at this point or use it immediately.

GERMAN SOURED RYE AND WHEAT BREAD

To sour this bread, do not use a sourdough starter; rather, start the dough as much as 4 days in advance to "sour" the sponge.

MAKES 2 LOAVES

2 packages active dry yeast
2½ cups warm water,
    105° F.–115° F.
4 cups dark rye flour
1 tablespoon salt
1 tablespoon dark molasses
1 tablespoon lard or
    shortening, softened

1 to 2 cups bread flour,
    unbleached all-purpose
    flour, or whole wheat
    flour
Additional rye flour to coat
    loaves

At least 24 hours ahead of baking (or up to 4 days before), combine in
a large bowl 1 package yeast, 1½ cups warm water, and 2 cups of the
rye flour; beat well, cover with plastic wrap, and leave at room temperature. Stir down once each day. When ready to proceed, stir down
the soured sponge and add remaining water, the remaining yeast, and
the salt, molasses, and lard. Stir in remaining rye flour and 1½ cups of
the all-purpose or whole wheat flour. Dough will be soft and rather
sticky. Let stand for 15 minutes. Sprinkle board with remaining flour;
turn dough out onto board and knead by folding dough carefully onto
itself. (It is easy to get your hands all sticky, so keep them well
floured.) Knead until dough feels smooth and holds its shape in a ball,
about 10 minutes, but do not add so much flour to it that the texture is
hard (like play-dough). Wash bowl, grease it, add dough to bowl, turn
over to grease top, cover, and let rise until doubled, about 1 hour.
Punch down to knead 2 to 3 times. Divide in half. Shape each into a
round ball, coating the outside of the loaf with additional rye flour.
Place onto greased baking sheets. Brush with water and coat with ad-

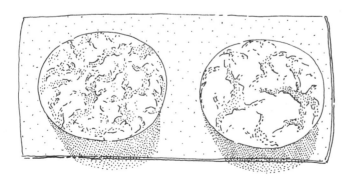

ditional rye flour. Let rise until puffy, about 1 hour. (Rye coating will have a "pulled apart" appearance.) Preheat oven to 275° F. Bake 40 to 45 minutes, until loaves are well browned and sound hollow when tapped. Remove from pans and cool on racks.

RIKE MEZKER'S SOUR ROGGENBROT

My friend Rike Mezker bakes this bread in an outdoor wood-fired brick oven once every 2 weeks or so. Each baking consists of 12 to 14 loaves. Rike is a purist. In her kitchen are sacks of whole rye and wheat grains, which she grinds herself for each baking. I have cut the recipe down to 2 round loaves that are wonderfully grainy and taste just like the original. Start making this bread the day before to develop the sour flavor.

MAKES 2 LOAVES

2 cups dark rye flour	2 tablespoons dark molasses
2 cups warm water, about 100° F.	2 teaspoons salt
	2 teaspoons ground coriander
1 cup sourdough starter	2 teaspoons caraway seeds
1 package active dry yeast	4 to 4½ cups bread flour or
¼ cup warm water, 105° F.–115° F.	unbleached all-purpose flour

In large mixing bowl, stir together rye flour, warm water, and sourdough starter. Cover and let stand in a warm place overnight or up to 24 hours. Remove 1½ cups of the mixture, place into a jar, and refrigerate for the next baking. (You may do this, as Rike does, or simply replenish the sourdough starter pot as directed in the starter recipes.) In a custard cup, dissolve yeast in warm water; add molasses and let stand 5 minutes until mixture foams. Add to the soured mixture along with the salt, coriander, and caraway seeds. Beat well. Gradually add the bread flour until a stiff dough forms. Turn out onto lightly floured board and let rest for 15 minutes. Wash bowl, grease it, and have ready. Knead dough 15 to 20 minutes or until smooth and springy. Place into bowl, cover, and let rise until doubled, about 1 hour. Punch down and divide in half. Place loaves, smooth side up, onto greased pans. Let rise again until doubled, 45 minutes to 1 hour. Preheat oven to 350° F. Bake 35 to 40 minutes, or until loaves sound hollow when tapped. Cool on wire racks.

CRISPY CRUSTED SOURDOUGH BAGUETTES

Delicious with blue cheese and butter, these long, slim loaves are irresistible hot from the oven! Baking soda adds a burst of leavening power.

MAKES 2 SLIM LOAVES

> ½ cup warm water,
>   105° F.–115° F.
> 2 teaspoons sugar
> 1 cup sourdough starter
>
> 2 to 3 cups whole wheat flour
> 1 package active dry yeast
> 1½ teaspoons salt

In large mixing bowl, combine ¼ cup of the warm water, 1 teaspoon sugar, and the sourdough starter with 1 cup of the whole wheat flour. Mixture will seem rather thick and dry; let stand in a warm place for 24 hours. During that time mixture will sour and bubble. Dissolve the yeast with remaining warm water and remaining sugar. Let stand 5 minutes until yeast foams. Stir into soured mixture along with the salt. Sprinkle board with remaining flour and turn dough out onto board; knead for 5 to 10 minutes or until smooth, adding flour as necessary. Divide in half. Shape each part into a long, narrow loaf and place on greased baking sheet. Brush tops of loaves with water. Cover and let rise until doubled, about 1 to 1½ hours. Brush again with water and slash tops of loaves with sharp knife or razor blade. Preheat oven to 400° F. Bake 25 to 30 minutes, or until crusty and golden.

SOURDOUGH OAT BREAD

Rolled oats in a sourdough bread has an appealing, tangy, yet nutty flavor. This bread is great toasted.

MAKES 4 SLIM LOAVES

1 cup sourdough starter
2½ cups warm water,
    105° F.–115° F.
2 cups nonfat dry milk
1 cup quick or old-fashioned
    rolled oats
6 to 6½ cups bread flour or
    unbleached all-purpose
    flour

1 package active dry yeast
2 tablespoons sugar
2 teaspoons salt
3 tablespoons butter, melted
Butter to brush tops of loaves
Additional rolled oats for tops
    of loaves

In large mixing bowl, combine starter, 2 cups of warm water, the dry milk, rolled oats, and 4 cups of the flour. Mix well and cover; let stand in a warm place for 24 hours or until mixture has bubbled up.

Dissolve yeast in the remaining warm water and add the sugar; let stand 5 minutes until yeast foams. Stir into soured mixture along with the salt and butter; beat well. Add remaining flour enough to make a stiff dough. Turn out onto floured board and knead for 10 minutes or until smooth, adding flour as necessary. Divide dough into 4 parts. Shape into oval loaves about 10 inches long and 4 to 5 inches wide. Place on parchment-covered or lightly greased baking sheets. Let rise in a warm place until about doubled, 1½ to 2 hours. Brush with melted butter and sprinkle with additional rolled oats. Slash tops of loaves about ¼ inch deep lengthwise. Preheat oven. Bake at 400° F. for 25 to 30 minutes or until golden. Cool loaves on wire racks.

SOURDOUGH OATMEAL BUTTERHORNS

MAKES 32 BUTTERHORNS

1 recipe Sourdough Oat Bread
Additional rolled oats
1 cup butter, melted

⅓ cup sugar (optional)
2 teaspoons ground cinnamon
    (optional)
Additional melted butter

After dividing dough into 4 parts, sprinkle work surface with rolled oats. Roll out 1 part at a time to make a circle 16 inches in diameter. Brush with melted butter. If desired, mix sugar and cinnamon and sprinkle surface with the mixture. With straight knife, cut into 8 pie-shaped wedges. Starting with the wide end of a wedge, roll up toward the tip; place each roll in a crescent shape on a prepared baking sheet, being sure to place the narrow tip of the roll on the underside. Repeat for all 4 parts. Let rise for 45 minutes to 1 hour or until puffy; brush with melted butter and bake at 400° F. for 15 to 20 minutes or until golden.

SOURDOUGH CORNBREAD

Just stir this up with sourdough starter and it's ready to bake.

MAKES ONE 10-INCH ROUND LOAF OR ONE 9-INCH SQUARE LOAF

1 cup sourdough starter
1⅔ cups yellow cornmeal
1⅔ cups (13 ounces)
  evaporated milk
2 eggs, beaten

2 tablespoons sugar
¼ cup butter, melted but still
  warm
½ teaspoon salt
1 teaspoon baking soda

In large mixing bowl, combine the starter, cornmeal, evaporated milk, eggs, and sugar in a large bowl. Stir in melted butter, salt, and soda. Pour into a greased 10-inch cast-iron skillet or a 9-inch square baking pan. Preheat oven to 400° F. Bake 25 to 30 minutes or until golden. Cut in squares or wedges. Serve hot.

WHOLE GRAIN
COFFEE BREADS AND
SWEET ROLLS

Now that we are aware of the nutritional bounty of whole grain flours, it seems only natural that home bakers should turn to creating delicious whole grain coffee breads and mouth-watering sweet rolls. Whole grain flours have an innate nuttiness and richness that seem an ideal marriage with the spices, fruits, and nuts usually found in sweet breads. Think of a cinnamon-scented apple-walnut filling for sweet whole wheat rolls or a cinnamon-pecan streusel topping for a quick, light whole wheat coffeecake. And raisins, almonds, or citrus peels also combine superbly with hearty whole grain flours.

For holiday time and other festive occasions, I've created several new variations on old favorites, including a delectable Apple-filled Brioche and a Whole Wheat Stollen that is laden with fruits and scented with brandy. But don't reserve any of these delicious breads and rolls just for holiday celebrations. They can brighten any gathering, from a family birthday to a casual Sunday supper for friends.

And all of these whole grain delights make wonderful gifts. Simply wrap a loaf in cellophane or combine a bread with other treats, perhaps some packets of spiced tea mix, or mulled wine spices, or a couple pounds of exotic coffee. Remember, too, that when you give these to friends who bake, it's a nice idea to include the recipe on a decorative recipe card.

BASIC WHOLE WHEAT REFRIGERATOR DOUGH

With this handy refrigerator dough you can make a variety of coffee breads, baking just one part of the dough—or all of it if you wish; you may keep the dough refrigerated up to 4 days.

MAKES ENOUGH FOR 2 COFFEECAKES

2 packages active dry yeast
½ cup warm water,
    105° F.–115° F.
1 cup milk, scalded and cooled
    to 105° F.–115° F.
½ cup butter, melted
½ cup well-packed light or
    dark brown sugar

3 eggs, slightly beaten
1 teaspoon salt
2 cups whole wheat flour
3 cups bread flour or
    unbleached all-purpose
    flour

In a large mixing bowl, dissolve yeast in warm water; let stand 5 minutes until yeast foams. Stir in milk, butter, brown sugar, eggs, salt, and whole wheat flour. Beat until smooth, using electric mixer or wooden spoon. Stir in bread flour to make a dough that is stiff, but too soft to knead. Cover and refrigerate at least 2 hours or up to 2 days. Use as directed in the following recipes.

MAPLE PECAN COFFEECAKE

MAKES ONE 9-INCH ROUND COFFEECAKE

¾ cup well-packed light or
   dark brown sugar
¼ cup maple syrup
⅓ cup butter, at room
   temperature

¾ cup coarsely chopped pecans
1 teaspoon vanilla extract
½ recipe Basic Whole Wheat
   Refrigerator Dough

In small bowl, cream together the brown sugar, syrup, and butter. Add pecans and vanilla extract. Spread mixture over the bottom of a

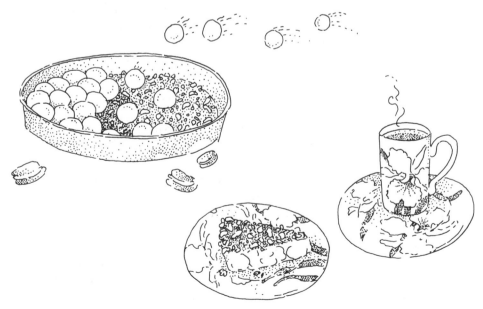

well-buttered 9-inch round cake pan. Divide dough into 32 equal pieces. (Cut into quarters; cut each quarter into quarters, then cut each piece in half to equal 32 pieces.) Shape each into a smooth ball. Set balls on the pecan mixture in 1 layer, leaving a little space around each. Cover with plastic wrap and let rise in a warm place for 1 to 1½ hours or until doubled. Preheat oven to 350° F. Bake 25 to 30 minutes. Cool in pan 5 minutes, then invert onto serving dish.

WHEAT GERM ALMOND-FILLED BRAID

Each strand in this braid is filled with toasted wheat germ and ground almonds, combined to give a wholesome whole-grain flavor.

MAKES ONE 16-INCH BRAID

½ cup toasted wheat germ (with brown sugar and honey), or whole wheat flakes
½ cup blanched almonds
¼ cup light or dark brown sugar

1 egg white
1 tablespoon butter, at room temperature
½ teaspoon almond extract
½ recipe Basic Whole Wheat Refrigerator Dough

GLAZE:

1 egg beaten with 1 tablespoon cream or milk

¼ cup sliced almonds

In food processor with metal blade in place, process the wheat germ, almonds, sugar, egg white, butter, and almond extract until a smooth paste forms. Divide dough into 3 equal parts. On lightly floured surface, roll out each portion to make an 18 x 3½-inch strip. Spoon ⅓ of the wheat germ mixture down the length of each strip. Bring edges together and pinch lightly to make a round strand. Place strips side by side, seam sides down on a greased or parchment-covered 14 x 17-inch baking sheet. Starting from the center, braid the 3 strips, taking

care not to stretch the dough. Pinch ends together and tuck under. Cover the plastic wrap and let rise in a warm place until doubled (about 1 hour). Mix egg and cream for glaze and brush over top of braid. Sprinkle with sliced almonds. Preheat oven to 350° F. Bake 35 to 40 minutes or until golden.

WHOLE WHEAT STOLLEN

This classic German Christmas bread is extra-special when made with whole wheat dough. Keep one and give one as a gift!

MAKES TWO 15-INCH STOLLEN

⅔ cup golden raisins
1 cup candied orange or lemon
    peel or combination of
    both
¼ cup plus 2 tablespoons
    cognac or brandy
Grated rind of 1 lemon
Grated rind of 1 orange
2 tablespoons unbleached
    all-purpose flour

1 recipe Basic Whole Wheat
    Refrigerator Dough
Filbert-Almond Filling (recipe
    follows)
1 egg white mixed with 1
    tablespoon water
Powdered sugar

Soak raisins and candied peel in ¼ cup cognac for 30 minutes. Combine raisin mixture with lemon and orange rinds in small bowl; sprinkle with the flour. Stir to coat all pieces with flour, then knead into the Refrigerator Dough. Divide dough in half. On lightly floured surface, roll each half out to make an oval about 15 x 9 inches. Spread each lengthwise half of dough with half the filling to about ½ inch from edge. Press uncovered half down firmly to seal and cover filling; transfer to greased or parchment-covered baking sheet. Cover and let rise until about doubled, 1 to 1½ hours. Brush top of each stollen with the egg white and water mixture. Sprinkle with sugar. Preheat oven to 375° F. Bake 20 to 25 minutes or until lightly browned. Drizzle hot stollen with remaining cognac or brandy. Cool on wire rack. Dust with powdered sugar.

FILBERT-ALMOND FILLING: In a wide frying pan over medium heat, melt 3 tablespoons butter. Add 1½ cups chopped filberts (hazelnuts), pecans, or almonds in any combination. Cook, stirring, until nuts are toasted and pale gold in the center. Add ½ cup firmly packed light or dark brown sugar and ½ teaspoon ground cinnamon. Cool.

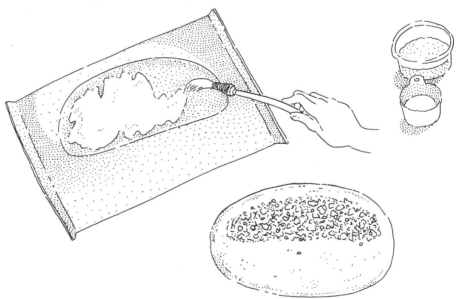

WHEAT FARMER'S CINNAMON BRAID

Each strand of this bread, before braiding, is coated with cinnamon sugar; you then fold the braid and place the fold into a loaf pan. When baked, the loaf is attractive, and each slice has an interesting pattern of cinnamon sugar swirls and raisins. Serve it toasted for breakfast with softened cream cheese.

MAKES 1 LOAF

1 package active dry yeast
1 cup warm water,
    105° F.–115° F.
¼ cup nonfat dry milk
⅓ cup instant potato flakes
¼ cup butter or margarine,
    softened
1 teaspoon salt
1 egg

1 cup whole wheat flour
1½ to 2 cups unbleached
    all-purpose flour
½ cup dark raisins
¼ cup wheat germ
¼ cup sugar blended with 1
    tablespoon ground
    cinnamon
Powdered sugar (optional)

In large mixing bowl, dissolve yeast in warm water; add the dry milk and let stand 5 minutes until yeast foams. Add potato flakes, butter, salt, and egg; beat well. Stir in whole wheat flour; beat well. Slowly add all-purpose flour until dough is stiff. Let rest 15 minutes. Sprinkle some of the remaining flour on board. Turn dough out onto board and knead until smooth and elastic, about 8 to 10 minutes. Wash bowl, grease it, and add dough to the bowl; turn over to grease top. Cover and let rise until doubled, about 1 hour in warm place. Turn out onto lightly oiled work surface. Knead in the raisins and wheat germ. Divide into 3 parts. Roll out each part to make a strand about 20 inches long. Roll each strand in sugar-cinnamon mixture. Grease a 9 x 5-inch loaf pan. Fold braid into thirds lengthwise, and place into pan with what were the edges of the braid upward. Let rise in a warm place until doubled, about 45 minutes to 1 hour. Preheat oven to 350° F. Bake 35 to 40 minutes, until loaf sounds hollow when tapped. Remove from pan and cool on wire rack. Dust with powdered sugar if desired.

CINNAMON-WHEAT KUGELHUPF

This is a cinnamon and walnut-filled yeast-risen sweet bread that is baked in a fancy "kugelhupf" mold. Kugelhupf is also called "Turk's Head," so named when the Turks ruled Hungary.

MAKES 1 LARGE RING MOLD

2 packages active dry yeast
½ cup warm water,
    105° F.–115° F.
½ cup sugar
1 cup milk, scalded and cooled
    to 105° F.–115° F.
4 egg yolks
¼ cup sour cream

½ teaspoon salt
2 cups whole wheat flour
2 to 2½ cups unbleached
    all-purpose flour
½ cup butter, melted and
    cooled
½ cup toasted wheat germ
Powdered sugar

FILLING:

2 egg whites, stiffly beaten
1 cup sugar
½ pound walnuts, pulverized

½ tablespoon ground
    cinnamon

In large mixing bowl, dissolve yeast in warm water; add sugar, and set aside for 5 minutes until yeast foams. Add milk, egg yolks, sour

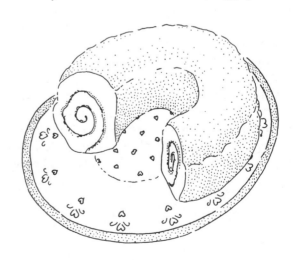

cream, salt, and whole wheat flour; beat well. Beat in all-purpose flour to make a smooth, blistery batter, gradually adding the melted butter. Cover dough and set aside in a warm place for 1 hour or until dough doubles in bulk.

Meanwhile, prepare filling. Fold egg whites into the sugar; add the walnuts and cinnamon. Set aside. Turn dough out onto lightly floured board; knead until air bubbles are removed. Roll dough out to ½ inch thickness; sprinkle with wheat germ and spread with the walnut filling. Roll up like a jellyroll. Generously butter a 12-cup fancy tube mold. Put roll into the pan; pan should be about half full. Let rise until dough fills pan, 45 minutes to 1 hour. Preheat oven to 325° F. Bake 60 minutes, until golden. Invert on rack to cool. Sprinkle with powdered sugar.

STREUSEL WHEAT COFFEECAKE

Whole grain coffeecakes take well to the the usual coffeecake embellishments: streusel toppings, spices, apples, and nuts. This is a quick batter bread.

MAKES ONE 13 x 9-INCH COFFEECAKE

COFFEECAKE:

1 package active dry yeast
¼ cup warm water,
    105° F.–115° F.
½ cup milk, scalded
    and cooled to
    105° F.–115° F.
¾ cup butter, melted

⅓ cup sugar
1 teaspoon salt
1 teaspoon ground cinnamon
3 eggs
1 cup whole wheat flour
1¼ cups unbleached
    all-purpose flour

CINNAMON STREUSEL TOPPING:

½ cup sugar
¾ cup whole wheat flour
¼ cup butter, softened

2 teaspoons ground cinnamon
¼ cup chopped pecans or
    walnuts

In large mixer bowl, dissolve yeast for coffeecake in warm water; let stand 5 minutes until yeast foams. Add the milk, butter, sugar, salt, cinnamon, and eggs; beat well. Beat in the whole wheat flour and all-purpose flour. With spoon or electric mixer beat until very smooth and elastic. Cover and let rise in warm place for 30 minutes. Beat down and spread in well-buttered 9 x 13-inch pan. Combine the ingredients for streusel topping mixture until crumbly. Sprinkle over the top. Cover; let rise until doubled, 30 to 45 minutes. Preheat oven to 350° F. Bake 25 to 30 minutes or until golden. If desired, frost while warm with a vanilla glaze.

VANILLA GLAZE: Blend 1 cup powdered sugar with 2 to 3 tablespoons hot coffee and ½ teaspoon vanilla extract to make a smooth glaze which you can drizzle over the coffeecake.

STATE FAIR SPICED RAISIN ROLLS

Just like grandma used to make and take to the fair! These raisin-studded swirls rise up so that the center pops out when you bake them close together in a pan.

MAKES 18 ROLLS

1 package active dry yeast
½ cup warm water,
        105° F.–115° F.
¼ cup light or dark brown
        sugar
½ cup milk, scalded
        and cooled to
        105° F.–115° F.

½ cup butter, softened
1 egg
1 cup whole wheat flour
1 teaspoon salt
2 to 2½ cups unbleached
        all-purpose flour

FILLING:

¼ cup butter, softened
⅓ cup sugar
⅓ cup brown sugar

½ cup dark or light raisins
2 teaspoons ground cinnamon

In large mixing bowl, dissolve yeast in warm water; add 1 tablespoon of the brown sugar; stir and let stand 5 minutes until yeast foams. Add milk, butter, egg, whole wheat flour, remainder of brown sugar, and salt; beat well. Add the all-purpose flour gradually until dough is stiff; turn out onto board sprinkled with flour and knead until smooth and satiny, about 5 minutes. Wash bowl, grease it, add dough to bowl, turn over, and cover. Let rise in a warm place until doubled, 1 to 1½ hours. Punch down and roll out to make a 12 x 18-inch rectangle. Generously butter a 9 x 13-inch baking pan. Spread dough with the softened butter for the filling. Combine sugars, raisins, and cinnamon, and sprinkle over dough. Roll up, starting with the 18-inch side. Cut into 1-inch slices. Place slices cut side down in pan. Cover and let rise about 1 hour, or until light and doubled. Preheat oven to 375° F. Bake 25 to 30 minutes. Frost if desired with your favorite confectioners' sugar icing or use the vanilla glaze of the Streusel Wheat Coffeecake on page 219.

APPLE-FILLED BRIOCHE

MAKES 10 TO 12 SERVINGS

1 recipe Whole Wheat
   Brioche (page 66)
2 lemons
¼ cup butter
3½ pounds Golden Delicious
   apples, cored, peeled, and
   thinly sliced

½ cup dark brown sugar
2 egg yolks
½ cup heavy cream
Powdered sugar
Whipped cream for serving

Prepare brioche dough and, while dough is rising, prepare filling. Grate lemon rind and squeeze juice; you should have ⅓ cup lemon juice. Melt butter in large skillet and add apples, brown sugar, lemon rind, and juice. Stir and cook, covered, for 4 to 5 minutes until apples begin to soften. Cook until moisture has evaporated. Cool to room temperature.

    Punch down risen dough. Pat out in large, lightly greased,

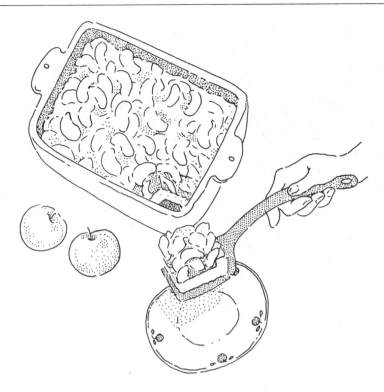

rimmed pan about 13 x 18 inches, spreading dough out to corners and forming a 1-inch rim all around. Let rise for 30 minutes. Spread apple mixture evenly over top of dough. Preheat oven to 375° F. Bake 15 minutes. Meanwhile, mix egg yolks and cream; after brioche has baked 15 minutes, remove from oven and spread the egg-cream mixture evenly over apples. Bake for 20 to 25 minutes more until edges are browned. Remove from pan and cool on rack. Sprinkle with powdered sugar. Serve with whipped cream.

WHOLE WHEAT CINNAMON REFRIGERATOR ROLLS

This is a handy refrigerator dough recipe for making rolls. You may use all of the dough at once as directed in the recipe, or just bake a portion of it. This is also good shaped into individual dinner rolls.

MAKES 4 DOZEN ROLLS

2 packages active dry yeast
½ cup warm water,
    105° F.–115° F.
1 cup milk, scalded and cooled
    to 105° F.–115° F.
½ cup butter, melted
½ cup well-packed light or
    dark brown sugar

3 eggs, lightly beaten
1 teaspoon salt
2 cups whole wheat flour
3 cups bread flour or
    unbleached all-purpose
    flour

FILLING:

½ cup butter, softened

½ cup sugar mixed with 1
    tablespoon ground
    cinnamon

GLAZE:

1 cup powdered sugar

2 to 3 tablespoons hot coffee

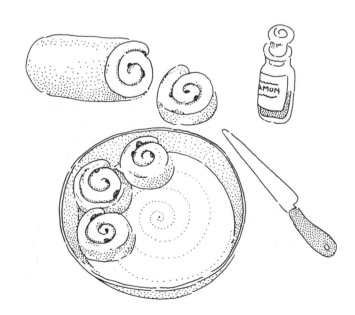

In a large mixer bowl, dissolve yeast in warm water; let stand 5 minutes until yeast foams. Stir in milk, butter, brown sugar, eggs, salt, and whole wheat flour. Beat until smooth using an electric mixer or wooden spoon. Stir in bread flour to make a dough that is stiff, but too soft to knead. Cover and refrigerate at least 2 hours or up to 2 days. Cut dough into 4 parts. Roll out, 1 part at a time, to make a 12-inch square. Spread with 2 tablespoons of the softened butter and sprinkle with 2 tablespoons of the cinnamon sugar. Roll up, jellyroll fashion. Cut into 1-inch slices. Grease an 8-inch round pan. Place cut slices, evenly spaced, in the pan. Repeat for remaining portions of the dough. Let rise until doubled, about 1 hour, 15 minutes. Preheat oven to 375° F. and bake rolls 15 to 20 minutes or until golden. While rolls bake, mix powdered sugar and coffee to make a smooth, thin glaze. Remove hot rolls from pan and cool on rack. While rolls are hot, drizzle with the glaze.

WHOLE WHEAT APPLE-MAPLE-NUT ROLLS

These whole grain rolls, stuffed with apples and nuts and drizzled with maple syrup, are great for breakfast or brunch, or make a perfect bread to go with creamy scrambled eggs or a fruit salad.

MAKES 24 ROLLS

2 packages active dry yeast
1 cup warm water,
    105° F.–115° F.
½ cup nonfat dry milk
¼ cup light or dark brown
    sugar
1 teaspoon salt
6 tablespoons butter or
    margarine, softened or
    melted

1 egg
1 to 1¼ cups whole wheat
    flour
2 cups bread flour or
    unbleached all-purpose
    flour
2 tablespoons maple syrup
Powdered sugar icing
    (optional)
Vanilla Glaze p. 220
    (optional)

FILLING:

4 raw apples, pared and
   sliced
2 tablespoons lemon juice
1 cup well-packed brown sugar

2 teaspoons ground cinnamon
½ cup butter or margarine,
   softened
½ cup chopped walnuts

In large mixing bowl, dissolve the yeast in warm water; add the dry milk and brown sugar; stir and let rest 5 minutes or until yeast foams. Add salt, butter, egg, and 1 cup of the whole wheat flour; beat well. Slowly add the bread flour, beating well. Cover and let rest 15 minutes. Turn out onto board sprinkled with remaining whole wheat flour. Wash bowl, grease it, and reserve. Knead dough until smooth and elastic, about 5 minutes, working in the whole wheat flour as needed. Put kneaded dough into bowl, turn over to grease top, cover, and let rise 1 hour or until doubled. Meanwhile, prepare filling: mix apples and lemon juice; add brown sugar and cinnamon. When dough is risen, turn out onto lightly oiled surface and roll out to make a rectangle about 20 inches square. Spread with the butter and sprinkle with nuts. Cover with the apple mixture evenly. Roll up as tightly as possible. Butter a 9 x 13-inch baking pan and drizzle with the maple syrup. Cut apple-filled roll into 24 slices and place into pan close together. Let rise until doubled. Preheat oven to 375° F. Bake 25 to 30 minutes or until golden. Drizzle with powdered sugar icing if desired. Serve hot.

YEASTED WHOLE WHEAT DOUGHNUTS

If you've never made homemade doughnuts, here's the recipe to try. It's an easy refrigerator dough which requires no kneading. If you wish, you may bake the doughnuts instead of deep-frying.

MAKES 36 DOUGHNUTS

2 packages active dry yeast	1 teaspoon salt
1 cup warm water,	1 teaspoon mace
105° F.–115° F.	1 cup unprocessed bran
½ cup nonfat dry milk	5 cups whole wheat flour
1 cup honey	Powdered sugar or cinnamon
3 eggs	sugar (optional)
½ cup butter, melted	

In large mixing bowl, dissolve yeast in warm water; add dry milk and let stand 5 minutes until yeast foams. Stir in honey, eggs, butter, salt, mace, bran, and half the flour; beat very well, with electric mixer if you wish. Slowly add the remaining whole wheat flour to make a smooth, elastic dough. Cover and refrigerate 2 to 24 hours. Turn dough out onto a lighty floured board and roll out to about ½ inch thickness, adding more flour if necessary to keep dough from sticking. Cut out doughnuts with doughnut cutter or a wide-mouthed canning jar. Place the rounds on a greased cookie sheet and let rise until puffy, about 1 hour. Heat at least 2 inches of oil to 370° F. (or preheat oven to 375° F.). Fry doughnuts in hot oil, turning when they begin to rise and are browned on one side. Turn and cook on other side; total cooking time will be about 10 minutes in the fat. If you prefer to bake the doughnuts, bake at 375° F. for 12 to 15 minutes or until golden. Dust with powdered sugar or cinnamon sugar if desired.

OAT-CINNAMON FLATS

Mix this no-knead batter bread with your electric mixer. These turn out to be thin, crisp, cinnamon-crusted rolls ideal for brunch or morning coffee.

MAKES 18 ROLLS

1 package active dry yeast	1 cup unbleached all-purpose
½ cup whole wheat flour	flour
½ cup rolled oats	2 tablespoons sugar

¼ cup butter   ¾ cup hot milk,
1 teaspoon salt   120° F.–130° F.
2 eggs

TO COAT ROLLS:

¼ cup butter, melted   2 teaspoons ground cinnamon
1 cup well-packed light or
    dark brown sugar

GLAZE:

1 cup powdered sugar   2 tablespoons hot coffee

Place ingredients into mixing bowl in this order: yeast, whole wheat
flour, rolled oats, all-purpose flour, sugar, butter, salt, eggs, and hot

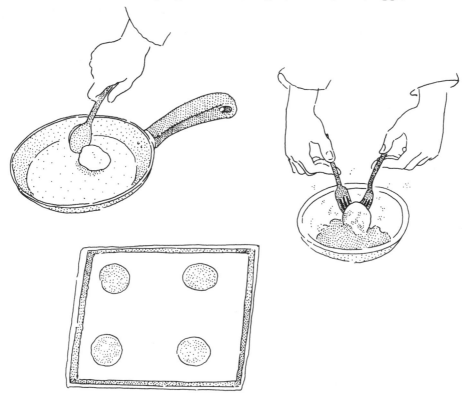

milk. Beat at medium-low speed for 3 minutes. Have melted butter in a shallow pan. Mix brown sugar and cinnamon and have ready in bowl. Drop a tablespoon of batter into butter. With 2 forks, lift to brown sugar–cinnamon mixture; turn to coat. Cover baking sheets with parchment paper or grease well. Place rolls 4 inches apart on prepared baking sheets. Flatten with fork to ¼ inch thickness. Sprinkle leftover cinnamon sugar over rolls. Cover; let rise in warm place for 30 minutes or until puffy. Bake at 400° F. for 12 to 15 minutes or until golden. Remove from sheets immediately if not using parchment paper. Drizzle glaze over rolls.

WHOLE GRAIN BREADS WITH FRUIT

Fruits combine with whole grains in breads as naturally as they do with nuts in any other kind of baking. In fact, fruits add a delicious moistness to breads that might otherwise be dry or a bit dull. One day when I was tired of making loaf after loaf of whole wheat bread, I chopped up some tart apples and kneaded them into the dough. The result was a delicious, rustic, rather peasanty loaf that we (and a few friends) devoured along with a hunk of well-aged Jarlsberg cheese.

Here is a selection of different fruits either kneaded into the breads or puréed and mixed with the liquid ingredients. In all cases, they remain identifiable with their fruity overtones while they complement the goodness of whole grains in these breads.

APPLE-HONEY WHEAT BREAD

This moist and tasty bread can be baked either in the standard loaf pans or as a big loaf ideal for a party. Put it on a rustic board next to a round of well-aged Cheddar cheese.

MAKES 2 9 X 5-INCH LOAVES, OR 1 LARGE ROUND LOAF

> 1 package active dry yeast
> 1½ cups warm water,
>   105° F.–115° F.
> 2 eggs, at room temperature
> ¼ cup honey
> 2 teaspoons salt
> ¼ cup lard, melted and cooled
> 3 cups whole wheat flour

> 1½ to 2 cups bread flour or
>   unbleached all-purpose
>   flour
> ½ to 1 cup wheat germ (with
>   honey and brown sugar)
> 3 cups chopped fresh tart green
>   apples, pared and cored

In large bowl, dissolve yeast in warm water; let stand 5 minutes until yeast begins to foam. Add eggs, honey, salt, lard, and whole wheat flour; beat until smooth. Let stand, covered, for 30 minutes or until mixture looks puffy. Beat in the bread flour, ½ cup at a time, until dough is stiff. Let stand 15 minutes. Turn out onto floured board and knead until smooth, about 10 minutes. Wash bowl, grease lightly; add dough to bowl, turn over to grease top. Cover and let rise in a warm place until doubled, about 1 hour; punch down. Sprinkle board with

wheat germ. Turn dough out onto board and knead in the chopped apple. The dough may get quite sticky and soft; however, resist the temptation to add any flour; simply coat the dough with wheat germ. Shape into 1 long loaf about 15 or 16 inches long. Place onto a baking sheet covered with parchment paper or well greased and coated with cornmeal; arrange the long piece of dough in a *U* shape, then cross the open ends. Or divide dough in half and shape into loaves, then place into two 9 x 5-inch greased loaf pans. Let rise until doubled, 45 minutes to 1 hour; bake in a preheated 375° F. oven for 30 to 35 minutes, or until loaves sound hollow when tapped. Remove from pans and cool on racks.

WALNUT-RAISIN-RUM BREAD

One day, as I was contemplating a variety of breads to serve at a casual party, I came up with the idea of soaking raisins in rum, then adding them to a whole grain bread. It turned out to be a bread with a natural affinity to cheese. We served it with Brie, Camembert, and cream cheese rolled in coarsely ground black pepper.

MAKES 2 LONG, SLENDER LOAVES

1 cup dark raisins
½ cup dark rum
1 package active dry yeast
2½ cups warm water,
    105° F.–115° F.
¼ cup well-packed light or
    dark brown sugar
2 tablespoons butter, softened
2 teaspoons salt

¼ cup wheat germ
5 cups whole wheat flour
1½ to 2 cups bread flour or
    unbleached all-purpose
    flour
2 cups coarsely chopped
    walnuts
Melted butter for brushing
    loaves

In small bowl, combine raisins and rum; let stand 30 minutes or until raisins are plumped.

In large bowl, stir yeast into warm water; add brown sugar, butter, salt, wheat germ, and rum-soaked raisins, including liquid. Add 2 cups of the whole wheat flour; let stand 15 minutes or until yeast bubbles. Slowly stir in remaining whole wheat flour until stiff dough forms. Cover and let stand again for 30 minutes. Stir in enough bread flour to make dough no longer sticky. Turn out onto floured board and knead until smooth, about 10 minutes.

Meanwhile, wash bowl and lightly oil it. Shape dough into a ball and place into bowl; turn over to grease top. Cover and let rise in a warm place until doubled, about 1 to 1½ hours. Punch dough down. Knead in the walnuts until evenly incorporated into the dough.

Divide in half. Shape each into a long, slender loaf and place on parchment-covered or greased and cornmeal-sprinkled baking sheets. Let rise until doubled, about 1 hour. Heat oven to 375° F. Brush loaves with melted butter and slash diagonally along the length of the loaves, making cuts 2 inches apart using a razor blade or a sharp knife. Bake 30 to 40 minutes or until loaves sound hollow when tapped. Remove from baking sheets and cool on rack. Brush with butter.

BLUEBERRY CORNMEAL RING

In cross section, this is pretty, with the swirls filled with blueberries. If you use frozen blueberries, it's best not to thaw them; however, frozen berries do make the dough cold and rising after shaping may take twice as long.

MAKES 1 LOAF

⅓ cup yellow cornmeal
1 cup boiling water
1 tablespoon butter, softened
⅓ cup honey
1 egg
1 package active dry yeast
¼ cup warm water,
    105° F.–115° F.

3½ to 4 cups bread flour or
    unbleached all-purpose
    flour
2 cups blueberries, fresh or
    frozen

In saucepan, stir cornmeal into the boiling water. Cook, stirring until mixture thickens. Remove from heat and stir in the butter, honey, and egg; cool to 105° F.–115° F.

In large mixing bowl, dissolve yeast in warm water; let stand 5 minutes until yeast foams. Stir in enough flour to make a stiff dough. Turn mixture out onto a floured board; let rest 15 minutes. Knead until smooth and elastic, about 10 minutes. Wash bowl, grease it, and add dough to the bowl; turn over to grease top, cover, and let rise until doubled, about 1 hour. Punch dough down and roll on a lightly floured surface into an 18-inch square. Sprinkle the blueberries over

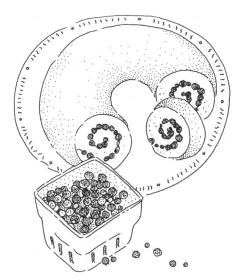

the square and press into dough gently. Roll up jellyroll fashion, tucking under the ends, and put loaf, seam side down, onto a well-greased or parchment-lined baking sheet. Shape the roll into a doughnutlike ring loaf; seal ends together. Cover and let rise until doubled, about 45 minutes (if blueberries were frozen, rising time will be longer). Preheat oven to 375° F. Bake 45 to 50 minutes or until loaf sounds hollow when tapped on the bottom. Cool on a rack.

PEAR-ANISE WHOLE WHEAT BREAD

What do you do with a boxful of slightly over-ripe pears? Cook and purée them, and make them into bread! This I did; and I packed the extra purée into plastic 2-cup freezer bags for use in making this bread the next time around. Pears contribute in a very special way to the flavor, texture, moistness, and lightness of this whole grain bread. A touch of anise gives a slightly sweet aroma and flavor to the bread; gluten flour adds both flavor and chewiness; it can be obtained in most well-stocked natural foods stores.

MAKES 2 LOAVES, 1 LARGE DOUBLE BRAID, OR 1 LARGE CIRCLE BREAD

1 package active dry yeast
¼ cup warm water,
     105° F.–115° F.
¼ cup light or dark brown
     sugar
1 tablespoon aniseed
1½ teaspoons salt
2 tablespoons butter, melted,
     or oil

2 cups puréed cooked pears
½ cup gluten flour
2 cups whole wheat flour
3 to 3½ cups bread flour or
     unbleached all-purpose
     flour

In large bowl, dissolve yeast in warm water; add brown sugar and let stand 5 minutes until yeast is foamy. Add aniseed, salt, butter, and puréed pears. Mix the gluten flour with the whole wheat flour. Add the mixed flour to the yeast mixture and beat well. Add all-purpose flour to make a stiff dough. Let rest 15 minutes. Turn out onto a floured board and knead until dough is smooth and springy, about 10 minutes. Wash bowl, grease it, place dough into bowl, turn over. Cover and let rise until doubled, about 1 to 1½ hours. Punch down and turn out onto lightly oiled surface. To make a large double braid, cut off ⅓ of the dough and reserve. Cut the larger part into 3 parts. Shape into a strand about 16 inches long by rolling between palms of hands and board. Braid into a 3-stranded braid. Cover baking sheet with parchment paper. Place braid in a wreath shape on the prepared baking sheet. Pinch ends to seal together. Cut the smaller part of dough into 3 parts and roll into long, skinny strands, making a braid just as long as the first one. Place small braid on top of the large one in the center. With finger, poke a hole in 4 equally spaced places through both the small and the large braid to the bottom. This will seal the 2 braids together. To make a big circle loaf (which looks like a big donut), roll out entire batch of dough to make a 20-inch-long single rope. Place on prepared baking sheet in the form of a circle. Pinch ends together to seal. Let rise in a warm place until about doubled. Make a ½-inch slash all around the center of the bread shaped like a donut. Preheat oven to 375° F. and bake for 35 to 40 minutes, or until loaf sounds hollow when tapped. Remove from pan and cool on rack.

If desired, you may simply divide the dough in half and shape into 2 loaves; place into 2 greased 9 x 5-inch loaf pans, let rise, and bake as for the braid.

SPICED LAUREL WREATH

This bread looks like a laurel wreath because first you shape it into a braid, then snip the bumps on the braid to resemble leaves. Although it is not a sweet bread, it is flavored with sweet spices and raisins. Serve it with any sharp cheese.

MAKES 1 LARGE WREATH

2 cups boiling water
¼ cup lard or vegetable
    shortening
2 teaspoons salt
⅓ cup dark molasses
½ cup rolled oats, quick or
    old-fashioned
½ cup unprocessed bran
½ cup wheat germ
2 packages active dry yeast
1 teaspoon sugar
½ cup warm water,
    105° F.–115° F.

1 teaspoon ground nutmeg
1 teaspoon ground cinnamon
½ teaspoon ground ginger
½ cup raisins, dark or light
½ cup gluten flour
2 cups whole wheat flour
2 to 2½ cups bread flour or
    unbleached all-purpose
    flour
Molasses to brush on top

In large bowl, combine the boiling water, lard, salt, molasses, oats, bran, and wheat germ. Stir and cool to lukewarm. In small bowl, dissolve yeast and sugar in warm water; add nutmeg, cinnamon, and ginger. Let stand 5 minutes or until yeast foams. Add yeast mixture to cooled molasses mixture along with the raisins, gluten flour, and whole wheat flour; beat well. Add bread flour, 1 cup at a time, beating after each addition to keep dough very smooth and elastic. When dough is stiff, let rest for 15 minutes. Wash bowl, grease it, and have ready.

Turn dough out onto lightly floured board and knead until

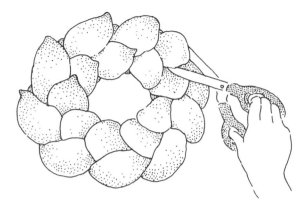

smooth and springy, about 10 minutes. Place dough into prepared bowl, turn over to grease top, cover, and let rise in a warm place until doubled, about 1 hour. Turn out onto lightly oiled work surface and divide into 3 parts. Roll each part out to make a strand 36 inches long. Lightly grease baking sheet or cover with parchment paper and place braided strand on baking sheet making a wreath; pinch ends together to seal. Let rise until doubled, about 45 minutes. With scissors, cut a 2-inch "leaf" by snipping horizontally into each section of the braid; continue to snip leaves all around the wreath; the leaves will lift themselves up as the bread bakes. Preheat oven to 375° F. Bake 35 to 40 minutes or until loaf sounds hollow when tapped. Brush hot loaf lightly with molasses, brushing just the top side of each leaf and the inside and outside of the wreath. Cool on wire rack.

BANANA WHOLE WHEAT YEAST BREAD

What do you do with black bananas? Banana breads are a popular quick bread, but I had never encountered a yeast-risen banana bread, so I tried it. It was heavenly hot from the oven, and even better toasted and spread with honey.

MAKES 1 LARGE LOAF OR TWO 9 x 5-INCH LOAVES

1 package active dry yeast

1 cup warm water,
105° F.–115° F.

¼ cup light or dark brown
sugar

1½ teaspoons salt

1 teaspoon ground nutmeg

¼ cup butter, melted

2 eggs

2 cups mashed very ripe
bananas

½ cup wheat germ

3 cups whole wheat flour

3 to 3½ cups bread flour or
unbleached all-purpose
flour

GLAZE:

1 egg, beaten with
2 tablespoons water

Wheat germ to sprinkle top

In large mixing bowl, dissolve yeast in warm water; add brown sugar
and let stand 5 minutes until yeast foams. Add salt, nutmeg, butter,
eggs, bananas, wheat germ, and whole wheat flour; beat 50 strokes
until very smooth. Add the bread flour, 1 cup at a time, keeping mixture smooth. When dough is stiff, turn out onto lightly floured board
and let stand 15 minutes. Knead 10 minutes until dough is smooth
and springy. Wash bowl, grease it, add dough to bowl, turn over to
grease top, and let rise until doubled, about 1 to 1½ hours. Turn
dough out onto lightly oiled surface and knead out the bubbles of air.
Shape into a 6-stranded braid (see page 64), or shape into 1 long sau-
sagelike log 24 inches long. Place on a baking sheet that is covered
with parchment paper or that is well greased. Shape into a circle to
form a large doughnut. Seal ends together. Brush with egg-water glaze
and sprinkle with wheat germ. With sharp knife, make slashes in the
bread every 1 inch, radiating from the "hole" of the doughnut out toward the outer edge. Make the slashes about ½ inch deep. Let rise
until about doubled, 45 minutes to 1 hour. Preheat oven to 375° F.
Bake for 40 to 45 minutes or until loaf sounds hollow when tapped.
Remove from pan and cool on rack. If desired, you may simply divide
the dough in half and shape into 2 loaves; place into 2 greased 9 x 5-
inch loaf pans, let rise, and bake as for the braid. Baking time for the
loaves may be 5 to 10 minutes less.

FRUIT-STUFFED OAT BRIOCHE

The whole grain flavor of oats pairs with the spicy, fruity filling of this loaf. Fruit and spices are rolled in an unusual way into the center of the bread. The whole thing is covered with a thin shell of the dough, and the top is decorated with scraps of dough. This is a pretty bread for holiday entertaining.

MAKES 1 LOAF

OAT BRIOCHE:

1 package active dry yeast
⅓ cup warm water,
    105° F.–115° F.
½ tablespoon sugar
1 teaspoon salt
2 eggs, at room temperature

½ cup butter, at room
    temperature
1 cup rolled oats, quick or
    old-fashioned
1¾ to 2¼ cups unbleached
    all-purpose flour

SPICED FRUIT FILLING:

¼ cup sugar
1 teaspoon each ground
    cinnamon and nutmeg
½ teaspoon ground cloves
1 cup golden raisins
1 cup mixed candied whole
    cherries and pineapple
    chunks

1 package (8 ounces) chopped,
    pitted dates
2 tablespoons dark rum
¼ cup butter, softened
Melted butter

GLAZE:

1 egg mixed with
    2 tablespoons milk

In large mixing bowl, dissolve the yeast in warm water; add sugar, stir, and let stand 5 minutes until yeast foams. Add salt and eggs; beat well. Cut butter into small pieces and, with a whisk, blend into the

mixture (it will not blend in; rather it will float in small pieces on top of the liquid). Stir in the oats and 1 cup of the flour; beat well. Add enough flour to make a firm but still soft dough. Let stand 15 minutes. Turn dough out onto lightly floured board and pick it up. Slap it down onto the board 100 times, or knead for 8 to 10 minutes until very satiny, adding just enough flour to keep dough from sticking at first. Wash bowl, grease it lightly, and add dough to bowl; cover and let rise in a warm place until doubled, 1 to 2 hours. Meanwhile, prepare filling. Mix sugar with cinnamon, nutmeg, and cloves; set aside. Mix the raisins, cherries, pineapple, and dates and sprinkle with rum. Stir until blended. Set aside. Remove ⅙ of the dough and set aside.

Roll remaining dough out to make a 12 x 18-inch rectangle; trim edges and reserve trimmings. Brush dough with softened butter. Sprinkle with half the spiced sugar. Top with the fruits, spreading fruits to within 1 inch of the edges. Sprinkle with remaining spiced sugar. Fold dough lengthwise to make 3 layers. Brush top with melted butter and curl up loosely in a spiral with the original folds at the edges. Take care not to break the dough, as it is fragile. Place roll on end in a buttered 9-inch pie pan or cake pan. Roll reserved dough and trimmings to make a thin circle 12 inches in diameter. Cover spiral of dough with the dough circle, tucking down edges so it is completely covered. Brush with more melted butter. Roll out scraps to make petals, leaves, and a stem for a flower decoration on top. "Glue" down with egg glaze. Brush entire loaf with egg glaze. Let rise 30 minutes. Preheat oven to 350° F. Bake 45 minutes or until golden. Cool before cutting; serve slightly warm.

WHOLE GRAIN BREADS
WITH VEGETABLES

Vegetables add a special quality to whole grain breads. Ingredients such as potatoes, carrots, beans, squash, tomatoes, and pumpkin add color and delicate textures to breads as well as flavors and aromas. When added to yeast-risen breads, these vegetables do not produce the same qualities or flavor that they bring to quick breads, which are really more familiar to us.

Over the years I have incorporated almost every vegetable you can think of into a bread. If I have leftover cooked vegetables or vegetable soup, I simple purée it, then incorporate it into a bread dough, adding it as a liquid ingredient. Almost always, I have found that adding a vegetable to a whole grain bread gives the bread a lovely and moist texture. I always use a whole grain flour rather than white flour because most vegetables have some color, and they could turn a white flour bread into a "dirty" gray, whereas a whole grain bread is only enriched in color.

Use your imagination with leftover vegetables. Try cooked purée tomatoes (or tomato juice) with rye flour and caraway seeds in a French bread loaf; brush the top of the loaf with water and egg white and sprinkle with more seeds and coarse salt. This makes a great snack bread.

A purée of leftover carrots in a whole wheat bread with black walnuts and raisins is especially delicious toasted and buttered for breakfast. Or try mashed potatoes: add them to a rye bread seasoned with instant minced onion and made into pull-apart rolls; serve these hot with butter and a softened cheese spread.

HUNGARIAN POTATO CARAWAY LANGOSH

To make the interesting pattern on this bread, let it rise in a well-floured bread basket with a pronounced design. After rising and before baking, invert the risen dough from basket onto a greased baking sheet.

MAKES 1 LOAF

2 packages active dry yeast	2 teaspoons salt
½ cup warm water, 105° F.–115° F.	2 medium potatoes, boiled and put through ricer or
1 teaspoon sugar	mashed

> 2 tablespoons caraway seeds
> 1 cup milk, scalded and cooled
>   to 105° F.–115° F.
>
> 1 cup light or dark rye flour
> 3 to 4 cups bread flour or
>   all-purpose flour

In large mixing bowl, dissolve yeast in warm water; add sugar and let stand until yeast foams, about 5 minutes. Stir in salt, potatoes, caraway seeds, and milk. Add rye flour and beat until smooth. Slowly stir in the bread flour until stiff dough forms. Turn out onto lightly floured surface and let stand 15 minutes. Knead for 10 minutes, until dough is smooth and satiny. Wash bowl, grease it, add dough, and turn over to grease top. Cover and let rise until doubled, about 1 hour. Shape dough into a smooth round ball. Select a large, shallow basket with a definite strong weave and lightly spray it with vegetable oil. Dust heavily with flour. Place dough with smooth side down into the basket. Let rise in a warm place until doubled, about 1 hour. Preheat oven to 375° F. Before baking, invert dough from basket onto lightly greased baking sheet. Brush with water. Bake for 45 minutes or until golden. Brush once while baking with water. Cool on rack.

BEAN-POT BREAD

This bread is excellent baked in a straight-sided pottery dish, either round or oblong. The beans give the whole wheat bread a wonderful flavor and texture.

MAKES 1 LARGE OR 2 MEDIUM LOAVES

> 1 cup warm water,
>   105° F.–115° F.
> 2 tablespoons light or dark
>   molasses
> 1 package active dry yeast
> 1 can (8 ounces) baked beans,
>   puréed
>
> 2 tablespoons vegetable oil
> 1 teaspoon salt
> 2 cups whole wheat flour
> 1½ to 2 cups bread flour or
>   unbleached all-purpose
>   flour

In large mixing bowl, combine the water, molasses, and yeast. Stir and let stand for 5 minutes until yeast foams. Add bean purée, oil, salt, and whole wheat flour; beat until smooth. Add the bread flour, ½ cup at a time, stirring to keep mixture smooth. When dough is stiff, cover and let stand 15 minutes. Turn out onto lightly floured board and knead until smooth and springy, about 10 minutes. Wash bowl, grease it, add dough ball, turn over, and cover; let rise until doubled, about 1½ hours. Grease a round or oblong 1½-quart pottery casserole dish with straight sides, or grease two 8½ x 4½-inch loaf pans. Shape dough to fit dish or pans, then place with smooth side up. Let rise until doubled, about 45 minutes to 1 hour. Preheat oven to 350° F. Bake 35 to 40 minutes, until browned and crusty. Remove from dish or pans and cool on rack.

FRESH POTATO WHEAT BREAD

Grated fresh potatoes and wheat germ add 2 interesting flavors to this moist bread.

MAKES 2 LOAVES

2 medium potatoes, pared
1 cup water
2 packages active dry yeast
¼ teaspoon ground ginger
1 cup warm water,
    105° F.–115° F.
⅓ cup nonfat dry milk
2 tablespoons sugar
1 tablespoon salt

¼ cup vegetable oil
½ cup wheat germ
3 cups whole wheat flour
3 to 3½ cups bread flour or
    unbleached all-purpose
    flour
2 tablespoons butter, melted
2 tablespoons additional flour

Grate potatoes into the 1 cup water; reserve. Potato and water together will measure 2 cups. In large mixing bowl, add the yeast and ginger to warm water; stir and let stand 5 minutes until foamy. Add the dry milk, sugar, salt, vegetable oil, wheat germ, and potatoes with liquid; stir until blended. Add the whole wheat flour and beat well. Add bread flour gradually, beating first to keep mixture smooth, then when dough is stiff, cover and let rest 15 minutes. Sprinkle board with remaining flour, turn dough onto board, and knead until smooth and elastic, about 10 minutes. Wash bowl, grease it, and add dough to bowl; turn over to grease top. Cover, and let rise in a warm place until doubled, about 1 to 1½ hours. Punch dough down. Divide in half. Shape each into a round ball. Cover baking sheets with parchment paper or lightly grease. Place dough, smooth side up, onto baking sheets and press down to flatten slightly. Let rise until doubled, about 1 hour. Brush with melted butter and sprinkle with flour. With sharp edge of knife or razor, make a ¼-inch cut across the center of each loaf. Preheat oven to 375° F. Bake 30 to 35 minutes or until golden brown. Remove from pans and cool on wire racks.

PEPPERED FRESH VEGETABLE HOAGIE BUNS

Try these buns for spicy sausages hot off the barbecue, or for sandwiches made with a variety of sliced cheeses, tomatoes, lettuce, and marinated cucumbers. The buns are made with all kinds of fresh garden vegetables: cabbage, carrots, celery, parsley. Make miniature buns as appetizers and serve with cream cheese and red pepper jelly.

MAKES 12 LARGE OVAL BUNS OR 36 MINIATURE BUNS

1 package active dry yeast
¼ cup warm water,
    105° F.–115° F.
2 tablespoons honey
1 teaspoon salt
1 tablespoon coarsely cracked
    black pepper
½ cup nonfat dry milk
¼ cup lard or vegetable oil
1 egg

1 cup water
¾ cup coarsely chopped
    cabbage
1 carrot, cut into chunks
¼ cup sliced celery
¼ cup minced parsley
3 cups whole wheat flour
1 to 1½ cups bread flour or
    unbleached all-purpose
    flour

In large mixing bowl, dissolve yeast in warm water. Add honey, salt, pepper, dry milk, lard, and egg; let stand 5 minutes until yeast bubbles up through the top of the ingredients in the bowl. Combine the 1 cup water, cabbage, carrot, and celery in blender or food processor with steel blade in place. Process or blend until smooth; add to yeast mixture. With a spoon, stir in the minced parsley with the whole wheat flour and bread flour to make a stiff dough. Let rest 15 minutes. Turn out onto lightly floured surface and knead for 10 minutes or until smooth and elastic. Shape into a ball. Wash bowl, grease it, add dough to bowl, and turn over. Cover; let rise in a warm place until doubled, about 1½ hours. Punch down; divide in half and divide each half into 6 parts for hoagie buns; shape each into an oval with pointed ends. For miniature buns, divide dough into 36 parts and shape each into a smooth round ball. Place on greased cookie sheets and let rise until doubled, about 45 minutes. Preheat oven to 375° F. Bake 15 to 20 minutes for large buns or 10 to 15 minutes for miniatures.

SPICED ZUCCHINI WHOLE WHEAT BREAD

When zucchini is plentiful, you can freeze it, freshly shredded, in amounts just right for this bread. This is a really good-tasting bread with a chewy crust and a moist, full flavor.

MAKES 2 LOAVES

1 package active dry yeast	1 teaspoon grated orange rind
⅓ cup warm water, 105° F.–115° F.	1½ cups shredded fresh zucchini
2 tablespoons well-packed brown sugar	½ cup whole wheat flour
¼ cup nonfat dry milk	⅓ cup wheat germ
1 egg	2¾ to 3 cups bread flour or unbleached all-purpose flour
2 tablespoons butter, melted	
2 teaspoons ground coriander	⅔ cup dark raisins
1 teaspoon salt	

In large mixing bowl, dissolve yeast in warm water; add brown sugar and let stand 5 minutes until yeast foams. Stir in the dry milk, egg, butter, coriander, salt, orange rind, and zucchini. Add the whole wheat flour and wheat germ and beat well. Stir in 1 cup of the bread flour; beat 50 strokes, then add the remaining flour slowly just until dough is stiff. Let rest 15 minutes. Turn out onto floured board and knead until smooth, about 5 minutes. Wash bowl, grease it lightly, and add dough to the bowl. Cover and let rise until doubled, about 45 minutes. Turn out onto board again and knead in the raisins. Divide dough in half. Shape each half into a smooth ball and place on greased or parchment-covered baking sheet. Or, divide in half and shape into loaves; place into two 8½ x 4½-inch loaf pans. Let rise until doubled, about 45 minutes. Slash loaves on sheets with 1-inch diagonals and brush with water. Preheat oven to 375° F. Bake 25 to 30 minutes or until loaves sound hollow when tapped. Remove from pans and cool on wire rack.

ONION-STUFFED BRAID

Even though this is a no-knead bread, it has enough firmness to be able to stuff and braid the dough.

MAKES 1 LARGE LOAF

WHEAT DOUGH:

1 package active dry yeast
1¼ cups warm water,
    105° F.–115° F.
1 cup light or medium rye
    flour
3 cups bread flour or
    unbleached all-purpose
    flour

1 cup nonfat dry milk
¼ cup butter, at room
    temperature
¼ cup sugar
1 egg
1½ teaspoons salt

ONION FILLING:

¼ cup butter
3 large onions, minced
¼ cup grated Parmesan cheese

¼ cup chopped parsley
1 tablespoon caraway seeds
½ teaspoon salt

GLAZE:

1 egg   *Caraway seeds for top*
2 tablespoons milk

Prepare yeast dough. In large mixer bowl, dissolve the yeast in warm water. Add the rye flour, 1 cup of the bread flour, and the dry milk, butter, sugar, egg, and salt. Beat with mixer at medium speed until smooth. Stir in remaining flour to make a stiff dough, moistening all of the flour. Scrape down sides of bowl. Cover and let rise in a warm place until doubled, about 1 hour.

To prepare filling, heat butter in skillet and add onions; sauté over low heat until soft but not browned (20 to 25 minutes), stirring occasionally. Remove from heat and add Parmesan, parsley, caraway seeds, and salt. Set aside.

When dough has risen, stir down and turn out onto floured surface. Roll or pat out to make a 12 x 18-inch rectangle. Cut into 3 equal strips along the 18-inch length of the dough. Spread filling over the length of each dough strip. Roll each into a rope, pinching to seal in the filling.

Braid strips loosely. Cover a baking sheet with parchment paper or lightly grease it. Place braid on baking sheet. Let rise in a warm place until doubled, about 1 hour. Beat egg and milk together to make glaze and brush top of loaf. Sprinkle with caraway seeds. Preheat oven to 350° F. Bake 35 to 40 minutes or until golden. Let cool in pan 5 minutes, then remove onto rack.

CARROT WHOLE WHEAT BREAD

Carrots, prunes, honey, and whole wheat flour add the character that gives this bread distinction. I like to shape it into standard loaves so that I can slice and toast it for breakfast.

MAKES 3 LARGE LOAVES

1½ cups warm water,   *1 teaspoon sugar*
105° F.–115° F.   *¼ teaspoon ground ginger*

2 packages active dry yeast	2 teaspoons salt
½ cup honey	¼ cup butter or shortening,
2 cups whole wheat flour	softened or melted
½ cup nonfat dry milk	4 to 4½ cups bread flour or
2 cups chopped cooked prunes	unbleached all-purpose
2 cups shredded raw carrots	flour

In large bowl, combine ½ cup warm water, sugar, ginger, and yeast; stir and let stand 5 minutes until yeast foams. Add the remaining warm water, honey, whole wheat flour, dry milk, prunes, carrots, salt, and butter; beat well. Add bread flour gradually, beating after each addition until a stiff dough is formed. Let rest 15 minutes. Turn out onto lightly floured board and knead for 10 minutes until dough is smooth and elastic. Wash bowl, grease it, and add dough to bowl. Turn over. Cover. Let rise in a warm place until doubled, 1 to 1½ hours. Punch down. Divide into 3 parts. Shape each into a loaf. Grease three 8½ x 4½-inch loaf pans. Place loaves into pans. Let rise until doubled, 45 minutes to 1 hour. Preheat oven to 375° F. Bake 30 to 35 minutes or until loaves sound hollow when tapped. Remove from pans and let cool on wire racks.

SPICED TOMATO-CELERY RYE BREAD

Split these long, narrow loaves with a sharp knife and stuff the halves with cheese and cold cuts, lettuce, and crispy vegetables.

MAKES 2 LONG NARROW LOAVES OR 12 INDIVIDUAL BUNS

½ cup warm water,	2 cups light rye flour
105° F.–115° F.	¼ cup butter or shortening,
1 teaspoon sugar	softened or melted
¼ teaspoon ground ginger	2 teaspoons celery salt
2 packages active dry yeast	2 teaspoons caraway seeds
1½ cups tomato juice, warmed	3½ to 4 cups bread flour or
to 105° F.–115° F.	unbleached all-purpose
¼ cup well-packed light or	flour
dark brown sugar	

In a small bowl, combine warm water, sugar, ginger, and yeast; stir and let stand until yeast foams, about 5 minutes. In a large bowl combine the tomato juice, brown sugar, and rye flour. Add the yeast mixture and beat well. Add butter, celery salt, and 2 cups of the bread flour; beat until smooth. Add enough of the remaining flour to make a stiff dough. Let rest 15 minutes. Turn out onto floured surface and knead for 10 minutes or until smooth and satiny. Wash bowl, grease it lightly, and add dough to the bowl. Turn over to grease top. Cover and let rise in a warm place until doubled. Turn dough out onto lightly oiled surface and divide in half. Shape each half into a long, narrow French bread loaf. Place on lightly greased baking sheets. Let rise until about doubled, 45 minutes to 1 hour. Slash either lengthwise or crosswise about ⅓ inch deep. Brush with water. Preheat oven to 375° F. Bake 30 to 35 minutes, or until browned and loaves sound hollow when tapped. Or, divide dough into 12 parts and shape into 12 oval loaves. Place on lightly greased baking sheets; let rise until doubled, slash lengthwise, brush with water, and bake at 375° F. for 15 to 20 minutes or until crusty and browned. Cool on rack.

GOLDEN PUMPKIN BREAD

You may substitute squash or sweet potatoes for the pumpkin in this bread. Bake them in their shells or skins, then purée the flesh before using.

MAKES 2 COILED BREADS

½ cup warm water,
    105° F.–115° F.
1 teaspoon sugar
¼ teaspoon ground ginger
2 packages active dry yeast
¾ cup milk, scalded
    and cooled to
    105° F.–115° F.
½ cup brown sugar
1 cup whole wheat flour
1 cup unprocessed bran

½ cup butter or shortening,
    softened or melted
1½ teaspoons salt
1 teaspoon ground cinnamon
1 cup cooked, puréed pumpkin
3½ to 4 cups bread flour or
    unbleached all-purpose
    flour
Evaporated milk to brush
    loaves

In small bowl, combine warm water, sugar, ginger, and yeast; let stand in a warm place until yeast foams, about 5 minutes. In large bowl, combine the milk, brown sugar, whole wheat flour, and bran, then add yeast mixture; beat well. Add softened butter, salt, cinnamon, and pumpkin. Stir in 2 cups of the flour, beating well. Stir in enough remaining flour to make a stiff dough. Let stand 15 minutes. Turn out onto lightly floured surface and knead until smooth and satiny, about 10 minutes. Wash bowl, grease it, and add dough to bowl; turn over, cover, and let rise in a warm place until dough has doubled, about 1 to 1½ hours. Turn out onto lightly oiled surface and divide in half. Pat one part at a time to make a strip of dough ⅓ inch thick and 6 inches wide and as long as the portion of dough will reach. Fold each strip in half lengthwise, then, with folded edge of strip up, roll tightly into a coil. Place in greased 8- or 9-inch round cake pans. Brush tops of loaves generously with melted butter so that it trickles into the folds of the coils. Let rise until doubled in bulk. Preheat oven to 350° F. Bake 40 to 45 minutes. About 10 minutes before bread is done baking, brush tops of loaves with evaporated milk so that they will brown to a beautiful russet hue.

CHEESE BREADS

Bread and cheese has been a time-honored combination as far back as historical records go. So it isn't surprising the idea of adding the cheese to the bread dough also appears in breads around the world. The two seem made for each other.

Cheese mixed into bread dough adds richness and flavor. Shredded cheese will tend to make the bread more dense as the cheese melts into the crumb of the bread. Cube cheese or chunked cheese must be no larger than in about ½-inch pieces, but when used, creates an interesting texture in a loaf of bread. In my Cheesy Picnic Loaf, the cheese melts and makes lined "holes" in a mosaic pattern in each slice.

Cheese rolled into the bread so that it is identifiable turns a loaf of bread itself into a snack, if not a meal. Cheese can also be folded in, rolled in, and used to top bread, adding flavor, chewiness, interest, and a more satisfying quality to the loaf.

CHEESES THAT WORK BEST

Select cheeses that are firm in texture, with a rather high melting point if you want to add it as chunks or work it into the dough after shredding. There are lots of choices on the cheese counter; here are some examples of cheeses I have found successful:

CHEDDAR CHEESE: Works because it will not melt and run out of the loaf during baking. Cheddar cheese has a natural affinity to rye breads and molasses-flavored breads.

SWISS CHEESE: In chunks or shredded and rolled into a loaf, this stays inside the bread, creating interesting texture and flavor.

PROVOLONE: Shedded or in chunks, this gives bread flavor and does not melt and run out as easily as a softer cheese. Provolone is excellent for rolling into bread.

MONTEREY JACK: This cheese is soft and will melt out of a loaf but is excellent as a topping for bread—pizzalike.

PARMESAN CHEESE: Works well as a cheese that is rolled into a loaf along with herbs and perhaps pepperoni.

MUNSTER CHEESE: Soft, but can be contained as a filling for bread; it has a great affinity for rye breads.

COTTAGE CHEESE: Makes a rich addition to a yeast dough. See recipes in the chapter on No-Knead Casserole Breads—the Potter's Onion Wheat Bread and the Caraway-Rye Loaf.

CHEESY PICNIC LOAF

This is a version of the classic Anadama Bread with chunks of aged sharp Cheddar cheese interspersed throughout the loaf, which creates mosaiclike slices. Perfect for a picnic!

MAKES 1 LOAF

¼ cup yellow cornmeal
½ cup boiling water
1 package active dry yeast
½ cup warm water,
　　105° F.–115° F.
¼ cup dark molasses
2 tablespoons butter or
　　margarine, softened
1 teaspoon salt

2½ to 3 cups bread flour or
　　unbleached all-purpose
　　flour
½ pound sharp Cheddar
　　cheese, cut into ½ inch
　　dice
Butter or margarine to brush
　　top of loaf

In small bowl, mix cornmeal and boiling water; stir and let stand until cool. In large mixing bowl, dissolve yeast in warm water; let stand 5 minutes until yeast foams. Add molasses, butter, salt, and the cornmeal mixture. Stir in bread flour slowly, keeping batter smooth, until stiff dough forms. Let rest 15 minutes. Turn out onto lightly floured board and knead for 5 to 8 minutes or until dough is smooth and elastic. Wash bowl, grease it, and add dough to bowl; turn over to grease top. Cover and let rise until doubled, about 1 hour. Punch dough down and knead in the cheese cubes until they are dispersed throughout the dough. Grease a 9-inch pie pan generously. Shape dough into a ball and place dough, smooth side up, into greased pan. Let rise until doubled, about 1 hour. Preheat oven to 375° F. Bake until loaf is golden and sounds hollow when tapped, 30 to 35 minutes. Remove from pan immediately, brush with butter, and cool on rack.

SWISS HERB CROWN

This bread is baked in a ring mold, and when you snip the top of the cheese-stuffed roll, it is transformed into a beautiful "crown."

MAKES 1 LARGE RING

⅓ cup butter, melted
2 teaspoons olive oil
½ teaspoon each dried basil, savory, chervil, and tarragon
½ teaspoon freshly ground black pepper
¼ teaspoon dried thyme
1 package active dry yeast
¼ cup warm water, 105° F.–115° F.
1¾ cups milk, scalded and cooled to 105° F.–115° F.

2 tablespoons sugar
2 teaspoons salt
2 cups whole wheat flour
2 to 2½ cups bread flour or unbleached all-purpose flour
1½ cups shredded Swiss cheese
1 egg white, lightly beaten

Brush an 11- or 12-cup ring mold generously with the melted butter; place mold in freezer for 5 minutes; brush again with remaining butter. Chill again.

In small bowl, combine oil, basil, savory, chervil, tarragon, pepper, and thyme. Set aside.

In large bowl, dissolve yeast in warm water; add milk and sugar. Let stand for 5 minutes until yeast foams. Add salt and herb mixture. Stir in the whole wheat flour and beat until smooth. Slowly add the bread flour until a stiff dough forms. Let rest 15 minutes. Turn out onto lightly floured surface and knead, adding just enough flour to keep from sticking, until dough is satiny and smooth, about 10 minutes. Shape into a ball. Wash bowl, grease it, and add dough to

bowl. Turn over to grease top. Cover and let rise in a warm place for 1 to 1½ hours or until doubled.

Punch dough down, roll on lightly oiled surface into a 10-inch circle. Sprinkle with the cheese. Fold edges toward center to form a ball. Let rest, covered, for 10 minutes. Roll out to make a 10 x 24-inch rectangle; roll up tightly, starting at a long edge. Pinch seam to seal. Join open ends to make a circle. Pinch to seal. Place into butter-coated mold. Let rise in a warm place until doubled, about 1 to 1½ hours.

Preheat oven to 375° F. Brush loaf wtih egg white. With scissors at a 45-degree angle, snip surface of dough at 2-inch intervals about ½ inch deep. Bake for 40 to 50 minutes, or until loaf sounds hollow when tapped. Cool in pan for 5 minutes, then turn out onto rack and finish cooling.

CHEESE AND ONION-FILLED CARAWAY WHEAT BREAD

This rich caraway and wheat-flavored bread has a swirl of cheese and onion filling in the center.

MAKES 1 LOAF

½ cup warm water,
    105° F.–115° F.
1 package active dry yeast
½ teaspoon salt
1 tablespoon sugar
3 eggs, at room temperature

1 tablespoon caraway seeds
½ cup butter, softened
1 cup whole wheat flour
2 to 2½ cups bread flour or
    unbleached all-purpose
    flour

FILLING:

¼ cup grated Parmesan cheese

½ cup freshly chopped onion

In large mixer bowl, mix warm water and yeast. Let stand 5 minutes until yeast is foamy. Add salt, sugar, eggs, caraway seeds, butter, and whole wheat flour. Beat until smooth using electric mixer or wooden spoon. Stir in enough bread flour to make a stiff dough. Turn out onto floured board and knead until smooth and satiny, about 5 minutes. Wash bowl, grease, and add bread dough to bowl; turn over to grease top. Cover and let rise in a warm place until doubled, about 1 hour.

Turn dough out onto lightly oiled surface. Roll out to make a rectangle 8 x 16 inches. Sprinkle with the Parmesan cheese and onion. Roll up tightly. Grease a 9 x 5-inch loaf pan and place loaf into pan, seam side down. Let rise in warm place until doubled. Preheat oven to 375° F. Bake loaf for 30 to 35 minutes, or until it sounds hollow when tapped.

PEPPERONI CHEESE BREAD

This is an excellent bread for appetizers. Bake it in a tall tin can, enclosing one end firmly with foil, or bake it in a special mold called a valtrompia, available in specialty cookware stores. Or use enclosed, hinged molds, in which the loaves are uniform, sometimes in whimsical shapes like scalloped rounds, hearts, or stars. If you do not have the fancy molds or do not wish to use cans, this bread is excellent when shaped into long, skinny baguettes. After baking and cooling, slice the loaves crosswise into thin slices and spread with butter or a spicy cheese or pâté.

MAKES 2 LOAVES

1 package active dry yeast
½ cup warm water,
　　105° F.–115° F.
1 teaspoon sugar
1 cup milk, scalded and cooled
　　to 105° F.–115° F.
1 tablespoon dried basil leaves
1 teaspoon salt
½ teaspoon dried red pepper
　　flakes

1 cup dark rye flour or
　　whole-wheat flour
2 to 2¼ cups bread flour or
　　unbleached all-purpose
　　flour
1 cup shredded sharp Cheddar
　　cheese
1 cup finely diced pepperoni
Cornmeal for dusting sheets

In large mixing bowl, dissolve the yeast in warm water; add the sugar and let stand 5 minutes until yeast foams. Stir in the milk, basil, salt, red pepper flakes, and rye or whole wheat flour; beat until very smooth. Add enough bread flour to make a stiff dough. Let dough rest 15 minutes. Add the cheese and pepperoni. Turn out onto floured board and knead for 8 to 10 minutes or until dough is elastic and its surface looks satiny. Wash bowl, grease it, add dough to bowl, turn

over to grease top, cover, and let rise in warm place for 1 hour or until doubled. Punch down. Divide dough in half. Fill greased tin cans or molds ⅔ full. Follow manufacturer's directions for rising and baking. Or shape into long, narrow loaves. Sprinkle a baking sheet with cornmeal and place loaves on top. Let rise until almost doubled, 45 minutes. Slash lengthwise and brush with water. Preheat oven to 400° F. Bake 35 to 40 minutes or until crusty. Brush twice with water during baking. Remove from oven and cool on wire racks.

WHEAT AND COTTAGE CHEESE HAMBURGER BUNS

Make these into miniature buns for a party, or larger for a teenage hamburger barbecue.

MAKES 12 LARGE OR 24 MINIATURE BUNS

2 packages active dry yeast
½ cup warm water,
*   105° F.–115° F.*
¼ cup well-packed light or
*   dark brown sugar*
2 teaspoons salt
2 tablespoons butter, melted
1 cup small-curd creamed
*   cottage cheese*

2 eggs
2 cups whole wheat flour
2 to 2½ cups unbleached
*   all-purpose flour*
Melted butter to brush baked
*   buns*

In large mixer bowl, dissolve yeast in warm water; add the brown sugar and let stand 5 minutes until yeast foams. Add salt, butter, cottage cheese, eggs, and whole wheat flour; beat at low speed until mixture is blended, then on high speed for 3 minutes. With spoon, stir in enough all-purpose flour to make a stiff dough. Let rest 15 minutes. Turn out onto floured surface and knead until smooth and elastic, 5 to 8 minutes. Wash bowl and grease it, place dough in greased bowl, turn to grease top. Cover and let rise in a warm place until doubled, about 1 hour. Punch dough down. Divide into quarters. For large hamburger buns, divide each quarter into thirds. For miniature hamburger buns, divide each of these in half to make 24 pieces. Shape into smooth, round balls and place on greased or parchment-covered baking sheet, smooth side up. Flatten slightly, and let rise before baking, about 45 minutes or until doubled. Preheat oven to 375° F. Bake 15 to 20 minutes or until golden. Brush with butter.

LITTLE BREADS

WHOLE WHEAT HONEY CROISSANTS

Wait till you taste these delectable treats! These are easier to make than the classic croissants, which require rolling in layers of butter, but they are remarkably good.

MAKES 36 CROISSANTS

2 packages active dry yeast
1¼ cups warm water,
   105° F.–115° F.
½ cup nonfat dry milk
4 tablespoons honey
2 cups unbleached all-purpose
   flour

2 cups whole wheat flour,
   preferably stone-ground
2 teaspoons salt
3 sticks butter, cut into ½-inch
   pieces
1 egg, beaten with 1
   tablespoon milk

In small bowl, dissolve yeast in warm water; add milk and honey; set aside until yeast is foamy. In large mixing bowl, combine all-purpose flour, whole wheat flour, and salt. Cut in butter until butter pieces are the size of kidney beans. Add yeast mixture to flour mixture and, with spatula, carefully fold mixtures together just until flour is moistened. Press dough into a ball. Wrap and refrigerate 4 to 24 hours. On lightly floured board, pound dough with side of rolling pin to flatten to about 8 inches square. Roll out to about 12 inches square. Fold in thirds. Pound with side of rolling pin again to double the width of the dough, and roll out to make a rectangle about 8 x 14; fold in the opposite di-

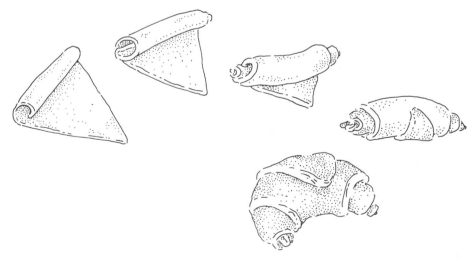

rection. At this point, the dough should have rather even edges. Roll out again and repeat the folding and rolling process 6 times. If necessary, refrigerate between "turns." Refrigerate dough for 30 minutes after last rolling. Divide in half. Place one part into refrigerator and roll second part out to make a rectangle 16 inches square. Cut into thirds, making 3 strips 16 inches long. Cut into triangles, making the cuts about 5 inches wide at the base; you will end up with 5 perfect triangles and two "halves." Piece the halves together to make the sixth triangle. Roll up each triangle, beginning with the 5-inch edge toward the tip. Cover baking sheets with parchment paper and arrange rolls in a crescent shape, at least 3 inches apart, on prepared pans. Repeat to make 6 croissants from each strip. Repeat for second half of dough. Let rise until about doubled, 30 to 45 minutes when the kitchen is warm, 1 to 2 hours when it is cold. Preheat oven to 450° F. and bake for 10 to 12 minutes or until golden. Remove from pans and cool on wire racks.

WHOLE WHEAT HAMBURGER BUNS

This basic dough is also excellent for dinner rolls or cinnamon rolls.

MAKES 12 LARGE HAMBURGER BUNS OR 24 DINNER ROLLS

1 package active dry yeast
½ cup warm water,
    105° F.–115° F.
½ cup milk, scalded
    and cooled to
    105° F.–115° F.
⅓ cup butter, softened

1 egg
1 cup whole wheat flour
¼ cup light or dark brown
    sugar
1 teaspoon salt
2 to 2½ cups unbleached
    all-purpose flour

In large mixing bowl, dissolve yeast in warm water; let stand 5 minutes until yeast foams. Add the milk, butter, egg, whole wheat flour, brown sugar, and salt; blend well. Add all-purpose flour to make a stiff dough. Turn out onto lightly floured board and knead until smooth, about 5 minutes. Wash bowl, grease it, and add dough; turn over to grease top of dough and cover. Let rise until doubled, about 1 to 1½ hours. Punch down and shape as directed below. Cover and let rise. For hamburger buns, divide dough into 12 pieces. Shape each into a round bun. Place 3 inches apart on greased baking sheet and flatten slightly. Cover; let rise until doubled, about 1 hour. Preheat oven to 400° F. Bake 12 to 15 minutes. Cool on racks.

DINNER ROLLS: Divide dough into 24 pieces. Shape into balls. Place in well-buttered 9 x 13-inch baking pan or into two 8- or 9-inch round pans. Let rise until doubled, about 45 minutes to 1 hour. Preheat oven to 375° F. Bake 20 to 25 minutes or until golden. Cool on racks.

CINNAMON ROLLS: Roll dough out to make an 12 x 18-inch rectangle. Brush with ¼ cup softened butter and sprinkle with a mixture of ½ cup sugar, ⅓ cup brown sugar, ½ cup raisins, and 1 teaspoon cinnamon. Roll up, starting with an 18-inch side. Cut into 18 slices. Place cut side down in a buttered 9 x 13-inch pan. Let rise about 1 hour or until doubled. Preheat oven to 375 ° F. Bake at 375° F. for 25 to 30 minutes. Frost if desired with Powdered Sugar Icing (page 28).

WHOLE WHEAT BREADSTICKS

Super easy, excellent eating, these are grainy breadsticks that you'll love with any salad or soup.

MAKES 4 DOZEN BATONS

2½ to 3 cups whole wheat flour, preferably stone-ground	1 cup butter, melted
	1 egg
	½ cup water
1 cup unprocessed bran	1 teaspoon baking powder

GLAZE:

1 egg, beaten with 2 tablespoons water	½ to ¾ cup sesame seeds

In large mixing bowl, combine 2 cups of the flour with the bran. Make a well in the center and pour in the butter, egg, water, and baking powder and mix, adding more flour as necessary to make a soft, unsticky dough. Mix glaze in pie pan and have ready. Put ½ cup sesame seeds into another pie pan. Cover baking sheets with parchment paper or grease well. Divide dough into 4 parts. Divide each part again into 4, and then each of the resulting parts into 3. Between palms of hands and work surface, roll each part into a thin breadstick about 6 inches long. Roll first in the egg mixture, then in sesame seeds, and place on prepared sheets. Preheat oven to 350° F. Bake 20 to 30 minutes until golden and crispy.

YEASTED BRAN STICKS

Chewy and wonderful, these crispy sticks have both yeast and baking powder in them as leavening agents. They are great to serve with a vegetarian soup or a salad with lots of greens and fresh vegetables.

MAKES 64 STICKS

2 packages active dry yeast
⅓ cup warm water,
    105° F.–115° F.
1 tablespoon honey
2 eggs
4 cups whole wheat flour,
    preferably stone-ground

1 cup unprocessed bran
1 cup sunflower seeds
1 cup butter, melted
1 cup milk, scalded and cooled
    to 105° F.–115° F.

GLAZE:

1 egg white mixed with
    2 tablespoons water

In a small bowl, dissolve the yeast in warm water; add the honey and set aside until mixture foams. Mix in the eggs. In large mixing bowl, combine 2 cups of the whole wheat flour, bran, sunflower seeds, butter, milk, and yeast mixture. Gradually add the remaining flour to make a soft dough. On lightly floured board, knead well, about 10 minutes, until smooth and elastic, adding remaining flour if needed to keep from sticking. Cover baking sheets with parchment paper or grease them. Divide dough into 4 parts. Divide each part again into 4 parts, then divide each resulting part into 4 parts. You should have 64 pieces of dough. Roll each out between palms of hands and board to make sitcks about 8 or 9 inches long; place on prepared sheets and brush with the mixture of egg white and water. Preheat oven to 350° F. Bake 15 to 20 minutes until golden and crisp.

WHEAT GERM ENGLISH MUFFINS

These grainy and flavorful muffins are great split and toasted, served with jam and cream cheese. Or use them as a base for poached eggs, creamed seafood or chicken, or just melted cheese.

MAKES 12 STANDARD MUFFINS

1 package active dry yeast
½ cup warm water,
     105° F.–115° F.
½ cup milk
½ cup cold water
1 tablespoon honey
2 cups whole wheat flour

1 to 1¼ cups unbleached
    all-purpose flour
½ cup wheat germ
1 teaspoon salt
½ teaspoon baking soda
Yellow cornmeal, preferably
    stone-ground

In large bowl, dissolve yeast in warm water; set aside for 5 minutes or until yeast foams. Scald milk and add cold water; pour into bowl, add honey, and cool to lukewarm. Add to yeast mixture along with whole wheat flour. Cover and let stand in warm place until mixture has risen to about double its volume, about 1 hour. Stir down. Stir in 1 cup of the all-purpose flour, wheat germ, salt, and soda to make a stiff mixture. Turn out onto lightly floured board and knead until dough is smooth and springy, about 10 minutes. Wash bowl, lightly grease it, add dough, and turn over. Cover and let rise for 30 minutes or until

mixture has not quite doubled. Grease 12 English muffin rings (tuna cans with both ends removed are ideal). Roll dough out to ⅓ inch thickness. Cut into circles using the rings and leave dough inside the can. Transfer to a flat surface, and let rise until doubled, about 1 hour. Dust both sides with cornmeal. Heat an ungreased griddle to 350° F. Toast muffins on both sides until browned, about 6 to 8 minutes per side, removing ring after first side is browned. Let muffins cool on rack. Separate halves with fork. Wrap and refrigerate. Toast before serving.

HERBED WHOLE WHEAT PINWHEELS

Shaped the same as cinnamon rolls, these delicious, savory pinwheels are great for a buffet dinner.

MAKES 16 PINWHEELS

1 package active dry yeast
¼ cup warm water,
*   105° F.–115° F.*
1 tablespoon sugar
1⅓ cups milk, scalded
*   and cooled to*
*   105° F.–115° F.*
¼ cup butter, melted

¼ cup well-packed light or
*   dark brown sugar*
1 teaspoon salt
1 cup whole wheat flour
2 to 2½ cups bread flour or
*   unbleached all-purpose*
*   flour*
Sesame seeds

HERB FILLING:

3 green onions, chopped   2 teaspoons dill weed
4 tablespoons butter

GLAZE:

1 egg, beaten with
  2 tablespoons milk

In large mixing bowl, dissolve yeast in warm water; add sugar and let stand 5 minutes until yeast foams. Stir in the milk, butter, brown sugar, salt, and whole wheat flour. Add bread flour gradually to make a stiff dough; turn out onto lightly floured board and knead in remaining flour until dough is smooth and satiny, about 10 minutes. Wash bowl, grease it, add dough to bowl, turn over to grease top, cover, and let rise in warm place until doubled, about 1½ hours.

Meanwhile, prepare filling. Sauté green onions in butter over low heat until soft but not browned, about 10 minutes. Punch dough down and, on a lightly oiled surface, roll out a 12 x 16-inch rectangle. Sprinkle evenly with the onion and then with the dill weed. Roll lengthwise jellyroll fashion. Slice into 1-inch pieces and arrange on a lightly greased baking sheet, slightly apart. Let rise until doubled, about 1 hour. Brush with glaze and sprinkle with sesame seeds. Preheat oven to 375° F.; bake rolls until golden, 15 to 20 minutes.

HERBED SWIRL BREAD: (One 10-inch Bundt loaf.) Prepare Herbed Whole Wheat Pinwheels as directed but cut the slices into 2-inch pieces and place into well-greased Bundt pan with cut ends down. Push slices as close together as possible. Cover and let rise until doubled, about 1 hour. Brush with glaze and sprinkle with sesame seeds. Preheat oven to 375° F. Bake 30 to 40 minutes or until golden.

RAISIN RYE BAGELS

Bagels look like doughnuts, but that's where the similarity ends. They are chewy breads, delicious freshly baked. Bagels are first cooked in water, then baked. That's what gives them their characteristic chewiness.

MAKES 12 BAGELS

1½ cups light rye flour
¼ cup sugar
1 tablespoon salt
2 packages active dry yeast
1½ cups water

2 tablespoons butter
2 cups unbleached all-purpose
  flour
2 cups golden or dark raisins

POACHING LIQUID:

Water
1 tablespoon sugar

2 teaspoons salt

GLAZE:

1 egg white mixed with 1
  tablespoon water

Poppy, caraway, or sesame
  seeds
Coarse salt

In large mixing bowl, stir together the rye flour, sugar, salt, and yeast. Heat the water and butter to 120° F.–130° F. and add to the dry ingredients; beat 2 minutes until very smooth. Add all-purpose flour, ½ cup at a time, and beat until very smooth, then add enough to make a stiff dough; stir in the raisins. Turn out onto floured board and knead for 10 minutes until dough is very smooth. Set in clean, greased bowl and turn to grease top of dough. Cover; let rise in a warm, draft-free place until doubled, about 1 hour. Punch dough down. Divide into 4 parts. To poach, heat 1 inch of water in a large skillet until simmering and add the sugar and salt. Divide dough into 12 pieces; shape 3 at a time into smooth balls. Poke a hole into each piece and stretch and smooth it out to make a doughnut shape. Put 3 to 6 bagels at a time into simmering water. (The number you can poach at once depends on how wide your pan is, but beware, they do rise and get bigger!) Simmer 3 minutes, turn over, and simmer 2 minutes. Turn again and simmer 1 minute more. Drain well. Place on baking pan lined with parchment paper. Mix glaze and brush tops of bagels with mixture; sprinkle with seeds or salt as desired. Preheat oven to 375° F. Bake 25 to 30 minutes or until golden.

RYE-WHEAT BREADSTICKS

For snacks, appetizers, or with an Italian-style dinner, these breadsticks—crunchy with sesame seed and hearty with whole grain flavor—are perfect. They are quick to make, too, because you do not have to wait for the dough to rise before you shape them.

MAKES 32 BREADSTICKS

2 packages active dry yeast
1 cup warm water,
   105° F.–115° F.
1 tablespoon dark molasses
¼ cup vegetable oil
1½ teaspoons salt
½ cup wheat germ
¾ cup dark rye flour

¾ cup whole wheat flour
1½ cups unbleached
   all-purpose flour
1 egg white beaten with
   1 tablespoon water
Kosher salt
Sesame or poppy seeds

In mixing bowl, dissolve yeast in warm water; add molasses and let stand 5 minutes until yeast foams. Stir in oil, salt, wheat germ, rye flour, whole wheat flour, and all-purpose flour until dough is stiff. Let rest 15 minutes. Shape into a ball. Turn out onto floured work surface and divide into quarters. Divide each quarter into quarters to make 16 pieces. Divide each piece in half. Shape into a long, ropelike strand by rolling between palms of hands and breadboard. Fill a baking sheet with sides to about ¼ inch depth of oil. Dip strands in oil on both sides and place on another baking sheet. Brush tops with egg white mixture and sprinkle with salt and either sesame or poppy seeds. Preheat oven to 350° F. Bake 30 to 45 minutes, or until sticks are crisp and golden.

HERBED OATMEAL BUTTERHORNS

A well-chosen bread can stand alone as the food served for tea or a simple brunch. Herbed and buttered, these fragrant crescent rolls are excellent with green pepper jelly and cream cheese as the only accompaniments.

MAKES 32 BUTTERHORNS

2 packages active dry yeast
¼ cup warm water,
    105° F.–115° F.
½ cup sugar
1 cup milk, scalded
    and cooled to
    105° F.–115° F.

½ cup butter, melted
1 teaspoon salt
4 eggs, beaten
1 cup rolled oats
3½ to 4 cups unbleached
    all-purpose flour
½ cup herb butter (recipe
    follows)

In large mixing bowl, dissolve yeast in warm water; add 1 tablespoon of the sugar and let stand 5 minutes until yeast foams. Stir in remaining sugar, milk, butter, salt, eggs, and rolled oats and beat until blended. Slowly add the flour to make a smooth but still sticky dough. Cover and let rise until doubled, about 1 hour. Punch down, and divide dough into quarters. On lightly oiled board, roll out one piece at a time to make a circle 10 inches in diameter. Brush each circle with ¼ of the herb butter. Cut each circle into 8 pie-shaped wedges. Cover 4 baking sheets with parchment paper or lightly grease them. Roll wedges from wide side toward tips and shape into crescents; place

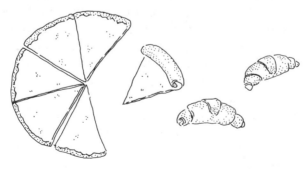

them on the prepared baking sheets with the points under. Let rise until puffy, about 45 minutes. Preheat oven ot 375° F. and bake rolls about 15 minutes or until golden.

HERB BUTTER: Blend ½ cup softened butter with 1 tablespoon mixed herbs (tarragon, chervil, parsley, basil).

CORNMEAL-OAT ENGLISH MUFFINS

These English muffins are really easy to make—basically a no-knead bread. The dough is ready for cutting out, rising, and baking after just a good beating with a spoon.

MAKES ABOUT 18 MUFFINS

2 packages active dry yeast
2 cups warm water,
    105° F.–115° F.
½ cup shortening or lard,
    softened
1 tablespoon sugar
2 teaspoons salt
½ cup yellow cornmeal

1 cup quick or old-fashioned
    rolled oats
5 to 5½ cups bread flour or
    unbleached all-purpose
    flour
Cornmeal for dusting baking
    sheets

In a large bowl, dissolve yeast in water; let stand 5 minutes until yeast foams. Add shortening, sugar, salt, cornmeal, oats, and 1 cup of the bread flour; beat until smooth. Gradually add remaining flour to make a stiff dough, beating well after each addition. On floured surface, roll out to ¼- to ⅜-inch thickness. Cut into rounds with floured 4-inch cutter. Place on ungreased baking sheets sprinkled with cornmeal. Sprinkle with additional cornmeal. Let rise in warm place for 30 minutes or until light. With pancake turner, remove muffins from baking sheets and gently ease onto a preheated griddle, about 360° F. Bake for 7 minutes on each side until light golden brown. Cool. Split, toast, and butter. Serve hot with marmalade or jelly.

WHOLE WHEAT PITA BREAD

Pita or "pocket" bread originated in the Middle East and has become popular in the United States in the past several years. As it bakes, the bread puffs up to make a balloon-like loaf. After baking you simply compress the loaf and stack them so that they can be stored. Be sure not to bake the loaf so long that the bread is crispy, or it will crumble when you compress it. Stacked and stored in a sealing plastic bag, they keep several days refrigerated or they may be frozen indefinitely. To serve, either cut across the middle and make 2 "shells," or slit around the edge of the pocket about halfway and load with sandwich filling.

MAKES 16 PITA BREADS

> 1 package active dry yeast
> 2½ cups warm water,
>   105° F.–115° F.
> 1 tablespoon sugar
>
> 2 teaspoons salt
> 2 tablespoons salad oil
> 5½ to 6 cups whole wheat
>   flour

In large mixing bowl, dissolve the yeast in warm water; add the sugar and let stand 5 minutes until yeast foams. Add the salt, oil, and half the whole wheat flour, beating well. Gradually add enough of the remaining flour to make a stiff dough. Let stand 15 minutes. Turn out onto lightly floured board and knead until smooth and elastic, about 10 minutes. Cover with plastic wrap and a towel. Let rest 20 minutes. Punch dough down and divide into 4 parts. Divide each into 4. Shape each piece into a smooth ball. On lightly floured surface, roll out each ball to make a 6-inch circle. Cover; let rise 30 minutes. Place 6 rounds of dough at a time on a large wire rack. Place rack in oven on oven rack. Preheat oven to 500° F. Bake 4 to 5 minutes or until rounds are puffed and tops begin to brown. Remove from rack; cool. Or, if you have a pizza stone or baking tile, place into oven as you preheat the oven. Slide risen round of dough onto heated stone and bake 4 to 5 minutes or until puffed.

FRUITED BATH BUNS

A classic from Bath, England. We once enjoyed the white flour version of these buns hot for breakfast with a pot of steaming tea. I have since learned to make them with whole wheat flour and enjoy them even more!

MAKES 12 BUNS

2 cups whole wheat flour
1 to 1½ cups bread flour or
    unbleached all-purpose
    flour
¼ cup light or dark brown
    sugar
¼ cup butter, softened
1 package active dry yeast
½ teaspoon salt
½ cup milk

1 egg, beaten
½ teaspoon almond extract
½ cup finely chopped mixed
    candied fruit
1 egg white
1 tablespoon cold milk
Sugar, preferably coarse pearl
    sugar or crushed sugar
    cubes

In large mixer bowl, measure 1 cup of the whole-wheat flour, the brown sugar, butter, yeast, and salt. With electric mixer, mix until blended, about 1 minute. Heat milk in saucepan to 120° F.–130° F.; blend egg and almond extract into milk. With mixer going, add milk to flour mixture and beat until smooth, about 3 minutes on high speed. Add remaining flour gradually until dough becomes very stiff. When mixer can no longer handle the dough, stir with spoon. Let stand 15 minutes. On lightly floured board, knead until smooth and satiny, about 5 minutes. Let rest 15 minutes, then knead the candied fruit into the dough. Shape into a ball and place in lightly greased bowl; turn to grease top. Cover and refrigerate 4 to 24 hours, or let rise until doubled. Uncover dough and let stand at room temperature (if refrigerated) for 20 minutes. Divide into 12 equal parts. Shape each into a smooth ball and place on greased or parchment-covered baking sheet; flatten dough with palm of hand. Beat egg white slightly and brush top of each bun with it. Sprinkle with the sugar. Let rise about 30 minutes. Preheat oven to 350° F. Bake 15 to 20 minutes, until golden. Remove from pan and cool on wire rack.

SIMPLE SAVORY PAN ROLLS

Flavored with onion and herbs, these are perfect with a poultry menu. Try these pan rolls for Thanksgiving dinner.

MAKES 16 ROLLS

2 packages active dry yeast
½ cup water, 105° F.–115° F.
2 tablespoons sugar
2 teaspoons salt
1 tablespoon instant minced
    onion
1 teaspoon poultry seasoning
3 eggs

½ cup wheat germ
1 cup whole wheat flour
2 to 2½ cups bread flour or
    unbleached all-purpose
    flour
2 tablespoons butter, melted
2 tablespoons sesame seeds

In large bowl, dissolve the yeast in warm water; add the sugar and let stand 5 minutes until yeast foams. Stir in salt, onion, poultry seasoning, eggs, wheat germ, and whole wheat flour; beat vigorously until very smooth. Add the bread flour to make a stiff dough. Let rest 15 minutes. Turn out onto lightly floured surface and knead 5 minutes or until satiny and smooth. Wash bowl, grease it, and place dough into bowl; turn to grease top. Cover; let rise in warm place until light and doubled, about 1 hour. Punch down dough and divide into quarters. Divide each quarter into quarters. Shape each into a smooth ball. Dip tops into melted buter and then into sesame seeds. Place in greased 9-inch square baking pan. Cover and let rise in a warm place until doubled, about 30 minutes. Preheat oven to 375° F. Bake 20 to 25 minutes or until golden brown. Remove from pan, and cool on wire racks.

SOFT WHEAT PRETZELS

A pretzel party is lots of fun! Have the dough ready to roll into strands and then shape, simmer, and bake. When the freshly baked pretzels are baked, serve them warm from the oven with mustard or butter, and with bowls of hot soup. Soft pretzels are always best served the same day they are baked.

MAKES 12 PRETZELS

1 package active dry yeast	6 cups water
1 cup warm water, 105° F.–115° F.	2 tablespoons baking soda
1 tablespoon sugar	1 egg white
1 teaspoon salt	Coarse salt
2½ to 3 cups whole wheat flour	Caraway seeds

In large bowl, dissolve the yeast in warm water; add sugar and let stand 5 minutes until yeast foams. Add salt and 2 cups of whole wheat flour; beat well. Beat in enough additional flour to make a stiff dough. Let rest 15 minutes. Turn dough out onto lightly floured board and knead 5 minutes or until very smooth and satiny. Clean the board and lightly rub it with oil. Cover dough and let rest 10 minutes. Divide into 12 equal parts. Shape each part into a strand about 20 inches long. Shape each strand into a pretzel and place on parchment-covered baking sheet. Let pretzels rise for 30 minutes, until almost doubled. In large, shallow, nonaluminum saucepan or frying pan, bring the water to a boil; add the soda. Carefully lift pretzels one at a time off baking sheet, using a large pancake turner, and lower them into boiling water. Cook until pretzels are puffy, about 15 seconds. Remove pretzels from water using a slotted spoon and place ½ inch apart on parchment-covered baking sheet. Brush with egg white and sprinkle with salt and caraway seeds. Bake in preheated 400° F. oven for 20 minutes or until golden.

SOFT RYE PRETZELS

Soft pretzels are simple to prepare. I have taught kids as young as six years old to make them. The only difficult part is lifting the pretzels in and out of the boiling water bath before baking. They can easily lose their shape.

MAKES 12 PRETZELS

1 package active dry yeast
1 cup warm water,
    105° F.–115° F.
1 tablespoon sugar
1 teaspoon salt
½ cup light or medium rye
    flour

1½ to 2 cups unbleached
    all-purpose flour
6 cups water
2 tablespoons baking soda
1 egg white
Coarse salt
Caraway seeds

In large bowl, dissolve the yeast in warm water; add sugar and let stand 5 minutes until yeast foams. Add salt, rye flour, and 1 cup of the all-purpose flour; beat well. Beat in enough additional flour to make a stiff dough. Let rest 15 minutes. Proceed as in previous recipe for Soft Wheat Pretzels.

CRISPY CARAWAY WHEAT PRETZELS

Light, crunchy, and golden brown—and flavored with whole wheat, honey, and caraway seeds—these make a great snack. Bake the pretzels until they are golden brown and crispy at a low oven temperature.

MAKES 24 PRETZELS

1 package active dry yeast
1 cup warm water,
   105° F.–115° F.
1 tablespoon dark brown
   sugar
1 tablespoon caraway seeds
1 teaspoon salt
¼ cup vegetable oil

2½ to 3 cups whole wheat
   flour
Additional oil to dip strands
   of dough
1 egg white, beaten
Coarse salt
Caraway seeds

In large bowl, dissolve the yeast in warm water; add brown sugar and let stand 5 minutes until yeast foams. Add caraway seeds, salt, oil, and 2 cups of the flour; beat well. Add enough flour to make a stiff dough. Let rest 15 minutes. Turn dough out onto lightly floured board and knead 5 minutes or until very smooth and satiny. Clean the board and lightly rub it with oil. Cover dough and let rest 10 minutes. Divide into quarters. Divide each quarter into thirds, then divide each piece in half. You should have 24 equal pieces. Shape each part into a strand about 12 inches long. Dip each strand into oil and shape into a pretzel; place on greased or oiled baking sheet. Let pretzels rise for 30 minutes, until puffy looking. Brush with egg white and sprinkle with salt and caraway seeds. Bake in preheated 300° F. oven for 30 to 45 minutes or until pretzels are crisp.

CORNMEAL DINNER ROLLS

This refrigerator yeast dough requires no kneading and is easy to roll out and shape.

MAKES 4 DOZEN ROLLS

1 package active dry yeast
½ cup warm water,
    105° F.–115° F.
⅓ cup yellow cornmeal
½ cup sugar
1 teaspoon salt
½ cup butter or shortening,
    melted

2 cups milk
2 eggs
3½ to 4½ cups bread flour or
    unbleached all-purpose
    flour
Melted butter

In large mixing bowl, dissolve yeast in warm water. In small saucepan, combine cornmeal, sugar, salt, shortening, and milk. Heat to a boil, stirring, and cook until thickened. Cool to lukewarm. Add eggs, then stir into yeast mixture. Add enough flour to make a soft dough, about 3½ cups. Cover and let rise until doubled, about 1 hour. Stir down. Cover with plastic wrap and refrigerate overnight. Turn dough out onto lightly floured board and roll out to ¼-inch thickness, about 24 inches square. Spread with melted butter and roll up jellyroll fashion. Use additional flour as necessary to prevent stickiness. Cut into ½-inch slices and place into buttered muffin cups, cut side up. Let rise until doubled in bulk, about 1 hour. Preheat oven to 400° F. Bake at 400° F. for 12 to 15 minutes or until golden.

CORNBREAD BANANA CARAMEL ROLLS

Use half the Cornmeal Dinner Roll dough and make these wonderful sticky buns!

MAKES 24 ROLLS

1½ cups light or dark brown
    sugar
¾ cup butter, softened
¼ cup dark corn syrup or
    maple syrup

1 cup chopped walnuts
½ recipe Cornmeal Dinner
    Roll dough
1⅓ cups (about 3 large)
    mashed ripe bananas

In saucepan, combine 1 cup of the brown sugar, ½ cup of the butter, the corn syrup, and walnuts. Heat, stirring until mixture comes to a boil. Spread in a 9 x 13-inch buttered baking dish.

Roll out Cornmeal Dinner Roll dough to make a 16-inch rectangle. Spread with remaining butter. Combine the mashed bananas with the remaining ½ cup brown sugar. Spread over the dough evenly. Roll up and seal roll by pinching edges of dough into the roll. Cut into 16 slices and place slices in the prepared baking dish. Let rise until doubled in bulk, about 45 minutes. Preheat oven to 375° F. Bake 25 to 35 minutes.

WHOLE WHEAT STEAMED BUNS

Steaming gives yeast buns a special flavor and texture. All you need is a big soup kettle or canning kettle with a cover. Set a wide can with both ends cut off (such as a tuna can) in the bottom to keep the pan of dough out of the water and fill the pot with a few inches of water. Set heat just high enough to make a small head of steam, cover, and steam until the bread is done. This is a handy no-knead refrigerator dough.

MAKES 24 STEAM BUNS

2 packages active dry yeast
1 cup warm water,
    105° F.–115° F.
½ cup sugar

½ cup butter, melted
3 eggs, beaten
1 teaspoon salt
5 cups whole wheat flour

In large mixing bowl, dissolve yeast in warm water; add sugar, stir, and let stand 5 minutes until yeast foams. Add butter, eggs, salt, and 2 cups of flour. Beat until mixture is smooth, using electric mixer if desired. Add remaining flour and beat until smooth. Cover and refrigerate 2 to 24 hours. Turn dough out onto lightly floured board and knead into a ball. Divide into 24 pieces. Shape each into a round ball. Place on a wide plate that will fit into the steamer. Cover and let rise until doubled, about 1 hour. Place in steamer and steam for 20 minutes. Serve warm with a stir-fried main dish, or a soup, a salad, or tea.

WHOLE GRAIN FLATBREADS

Flatbreads made with whole grains may have been the first breads ever made by man. A simple mixture of flour and water that is pounded and flattened, cooked perhaps on hot stones next to a fire or on a flat stone just above the heat to crackerlike crispness or to a soft and pliable chewiness, is familiar to cultures around the world. I've often pondered the coincidence of flatbreads. How is it that the Mexican *tortilla* is so similar to Norwegian *lefse?* Or that American Indian frybread is so similar to the *poori* of India? Similar breads, made by similar methods in very dissimilar locations in the world, indicate just one thing—that flat breads are as basic to human culture as playing pat-a-cake is to children all over the world.

There is not much technique to be learned when making flatbread, except for one important thing. The thickness or thinness of each bread is critical—that is, if it is to be authentic. After rolling out the dough to the required thinness, all these breads are either baked on a griddle (usually dry) or in an oven.

Because of their thinness and simplistic formula, flatbreads made with whole grains have an earthy, satisfying flavor. Sometimes I savor them with no spread or topping. Sometimes I spread them thickly with butter, or cheese, or pâtés, or all three.

In my repertoire are a number of favorites. These are the flatbreads that are prepared with whole grain flours, either entirely or in part; wheat, rye, oats, and corn are dominant. Some of the breads are thin and crisp. some are crackerlike, and some are soft and pliable. All are delicious.

WHOLE WHEAT CRACKERS

To save time and frustration, I have discovered that it is simplest to roll out the cracker dough right *onto* a baking sheet, then cut it into squares and trim the edges. The crackers are extra attractive if you use a "crinkle" pastry wheel or cutter.

MAKES ABOUT 100 CRACKERS

1½ cups whole wheat flour	¼ cup sugar
1½ cups unbleached	1 teaspoon salt
all-purpose flour	½ teaspoon baking soda

½ cup shortening, butter, or
   lard

¾ cup buttermilk
Wheat germ to dust baking
   sheets

In large mixing bowl, combine flours, sugar, salt, and soda. Cut short-ening into small pieces, then blend into flour mixture until mixture resembles coarse crumbs. Stir in buttermilk to make a stiff dough. Chill 30 minutes (or as long as 24 hours). Cut dough into 2 parts. Lightly grease and sprinkle two 14 x 17-inch baking sheets with wheat germ. Flatten each portion of dough and place on the prepared baking sheets. Roll out until dough covers sheet, or until it is very thin; add more wheat germ if necessary to keep dough from sticking to rolling pin. With pastry wheel or straight, long knife, score dough into 2-inch squares. Bake in a preheated 350° F. oven until golden brown and crisp. If dry, these will store very well. Store in airtight container.

WHOLE WHEAT SESAME CRACKERS

These are made like cookies, but are not sweet. Once you've tasted homemade crackers, you may never reach for a box in the supermar-ket! Roll this dough out right onto the baking sheet; to stabilize the sheet while rolling, place a damp cloth under it.

MAKES ABOUT **100** CRACKERS

1 cup whole wheat flour
1 cup unbleached all-purpose
   flour
1 teaspoon salt
1½ teaspoons baking powder

¼ cup buttermilk or plain
   yogurt
1 tablespoon butter
2 tablespoons sesame seeds
About ⅔ cup ice water

In mixing bowl, stir together the flours, salt, and baking powder. Stir in the buttermilk. Heat butter in fying pan and add sesame seeds; toast until golden. Add sesame seeds to flour mixture. Toss in the ice water; mix until dough forms, then knead slightly to make dough hold together. Lightly grease 2 baking sheets. Divide dough in half. Flatten each slightly, then place each on a baking sheet. Roll out right on the sheets to ⅛ inch thickness. Cut into 2-inch squares. Preheat oven to 350° F. Bake 10 minutes or until lightly brown. Cool on rack; they get crisper as they cool.

VORTERKAKER

Norwegian *vorterkaker* is a crisp rye bread that is made by the old-timers. Although we love it with butter and cheese when it is fresh from the oven, as a crisp bread it keeps well too, stored in airtight tins or in the freezer.

MAKES TWO 12-INCH ROUNDS

1 package active dry yeast	¼ cup dark corn syrup
¼ cup warm water,	2 teaspoons salt
105° F.–115° F.	1½ teaspoons each fennel and
1 teaspoon sugar	aniseed
½ cup lard or butter, melted	3 cups light rye flour
1 cup milk, scalded and cooled	¾ to 1 cup bread flour or
to 105° F.–115° F.	all-purpose flour

In a small bowl, dissolve the yeast in warm water; add the sugar and set aside for 5 minutes or until yeast is foamy. In large mixing bowl, combine the lard, milk, corn syrup, salt, fennel and anise seeds, and half the rye flour; beat well. Add the yeast mixture, the remaining rye flour, and ¾ cup of the bread flour. Beat until smooth and stiff dough forms that pulls away from sides of the bowl. Cover and let rise in a warm place for 1 hour or until almost doubled. Turn dough out onto surface sprinkled with additional bread flour and knead 5 to 10 minutes until smooth and satiny. Halve the dough, form each half into a ball, and roll each ball into a 12-inch round. Put the rounds on buttered or parchment-covered baking sheets. Using a 2-inch cookie cutter, cut a circle of dough from the center of each round. Pierce all over with a fork and let rise, covered, in a warm place for 45 minutes or until almost doubled in bulk. Preheat oven to 425° F. Bake 15 to 20 minutes or until loaves are browned. Transfer loaves to racks. Brush with warm water and let cool.

GRANDMOTHER MAKI'S RIESKA

This favorite Finnish flatbread varies in content and thickness from one part of Finland to another. One cook insists it be made of oats, another of rye, and still another of cooked potatoes and barley. The only similarity is the name, the fact that it is a flatbread, and that it is delicious!

MAKES FOUR 10- TO 12-INCH ROUND FLAT LOAVES

1 cup buttermilk
1 cup mashed potatoes
½ cup butter, melted
1 teaspoon salt
1 teaspoon baking soda
1 cup barley flour

2 cups rolled oats
2 cups unbleached all-purpose
    flour
Melted butter to brush on hot
    loaves

In large mixing bowl, combine buttermilk, potatoes, butter, salt, soda, barley flour, rolled oats, and all-purpose flour to make a smooth dough. Turn out onto a barley-floured board and divide the dough into 4 parts. Roll each part out to make a circle 10 to 12 inches in diameter. Place on heavily greased baking sheets and pierce all over with a fork. Preheat oven to 450° F. Bake *rieska* for 10 to 15 minutes or until golden. Brush with melted butter; serve hot cut into wedges.

INDIAN CHAPATI

This Indian bread is usually made with a special chapati flour. According to one source, it is impossible to make a good *chapati* with whole wheat flour; however other authentic Indian and Southeast Asian cooks acknowledge the use of it. The original *chapati*, an unleavened bread, is baked like a tortilla on a hot, ungreased griddle. If you press lightly around the edges of the *chapati* as it cooks you will encourage bubbles to form and make the *chapati* light. As they cook, wrap them in a clean tea towel until all are ready. *Chapati* are served immediately with butter or a vegetable dish. They may be stuffed with a dry curry, then rolled up if you make large, flat breads. If you roll them out to only 3½ inches, the thickness stays at about ⅛ inch and, placed on a hot griddle, they puff up to make balloonlike breads which can be stuffed.

MAKES 8 CHAPATIS

2 cups whole wheat flour
½ cup unbleached all-purpose
    flour
1 teaspoon salt

½ cup butter, melted
6 tablespoons warm water
Additional melted butter

Combine whole wheat flour, all-purpose flour, and salt in a large bowl. Stir in butter and warm water to make a smooth dough. Turn out onto lightly floured surface and knead 3 or 4 times, until smooth ball forms. Cover dough with towel and let rest for 1 hour. Divide dough into 8 balls. Roll out each to make an 8-inch round. Dust with flour, stack, and cover with towel or plastic wrap. Heat electric griddle to 450° F. (or heat griddle or skillet over high heat until drop of water bounces off surface). Cook *chapatis,* 1 at a time, until flecked with brown spots, about 2 minutes on each side. Brush with melted butter and stack as you remove them from the griddle. Wrap to keep warm and pliable. Serve immediately. Or, wrap and freeze.

POORI: Heat 1 inch of vegetable oil in large skillet to 375° F. Fry chapati dough rounds one at a time until puffed, bubbly, and brown, about 2 minutes for each side. Serve immediately.

SCOTS WHEAT CRUMPETS

Unlike English crumpets, these contain no yeast, and are more like crêpes. They can be spread with butter and jam, then rolled up before serving.

MAKES ABOUT 16 CRUMPETS

2 eggs, separated
2 cups whole wheat flour
¼ teaspoon salt

2 tablespoons sugar
2 tablespoons butter, melted
2 cups milk

In mixing bowl, beat egg yolks, then blend in the flour, salt, sugar, butter, and milk to make a smooth batter the consistency of thin cream. Whisk egg whites until they hold soft peaks. Fold into the batter. Heat a 10- or 12-inch frying pan or crêpe pan and coat with a light film of oil. Drop in 2 tablespoons of the batter and spread around pan with a spatula to make a thin cake. Cook until browned on one side, then turn over to cook other side. As the crumpets are cooked, stack them. When cool, spead with butter and honey or jam and roll up.

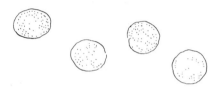

WILD RICE FRYBREAD

Wild rice adds texture to this classic American Indian frybread that is fried quickly in a shallow pan of hot oil.

MAKES 4 BREADS

1 cup whole wheat flour
1 cup unbleached all-purpose
    flour
1 tablespoon baking powder
¾ teaspoon salt

½ cup yellow cornmeal
1 cup cooked wild rice
1 cup milk
Oil for frying pan

In large bowl, blend whole wheat and all-purpose flour, baking powder, salt, ¼ cup of the cornmeal, and the wild rice. Stir in milk until dough is stiff. Divide dough into 4 parts. Knead slightly to make smooth balls of dough. Sprinkle board with remaining cornmeal. On cornmeal-sprinkled board roll each part out to about 10-inch diameter (the diameter of the frying pan). Heat oil in pan to smoking hot temperature (about 400° F.). Pick up bread and lower into the oil. Fry about 45 seconds to 1 minute on each side, or just until golden and center is cooked inside. Remove onto paper toweling. Repeat for each remaining bread. Best served hot. Serve dusted with powdered sugar if desired; these can be torn apart or cut into wedges.

BESS METSA'S ALFALFA SPROUT FLATBREAD

Wonderfully chewy and grainy, the alfalfa sprouts add not only moistness but nutrition and flavor to this bread. Delicious with cheese or served with a salad for lunch; pack it in the lunchbox, too! This dough may seem sticky to handle, so use the "oiled fingers" trick to pat the dough out flat.

MAKES 16 PIECES ABOUT 3½ TO 4 INCHES SQUARE

1 cup dark rye flour
1 cup whole wheat flour
¾ cup nonfat dry milk
½ cup sesame seeds
½ cup sunflower seeds, plain
or salted
½ to 1 teaspoon salt
(depending on whether
sunflower seeds are
salted)

½ cup well-packed alfalfa
sprouts, chopped
1 cup water
3 tablespoons vegetable oil
1 egg, beaten

In bowl, mix flours, milk, sesame seeds, sunflower seeds, and salt. Add sprouts, water, and oil, blending well. Fold in the beaten egg. Grease and flour a baking sheet and spread mixture to ¼-inch thickness over the baking sheet. If you have trouble, oil your fingers generously and pat out thin. Pierce all over with a fork. Preheat oven to 450° F. Bake 10 to 12 minutes until top feels dry, then brown under the broiler. When cooled, this becomes crisp. Break or cut into pieces. To store, wrap and freeze or put into airtight container.

FINNISH RYE HARDTACK

This bread is not "hard" until after it has had a chance to dry. It is shaped into a 12-inch flat, round loaf with a hole in the center. Delicious with butter, topped with cheese. Also brings back memories of a winter lunch with creamy potato soup!

MAKES ONE 12-INCH ROUND

1 package active dry yeast
1 cup warm water,
    105° F.–115° F.
1 teaspoon salt
1½ cups dark rye flour
1 cup bread flour or
    unbleached all-purpose
    flour

Extra dark rye flour for
    baking pan
Water to brush top

In large mixing bowl, dissolve yeast in warm water; let stand 5 minutes until yeast foams. Stir in the salt and rye flour; beat until smooth. Add the bread flour gradually, working it into the mixture with a spoon until it is no longer visible. Scrape down sides of bowl. Cover and let rise in a warm place for 1 hour or until about doubled. Butter a large baking sheet, preparing it for a 12-inch round of bread. Sprinkle with exra rye flour. Shape risen dough into a smooth, round ball, then place onto prepared baking sheet and flatten out as far as you can with your hands. With rolling pin, roll out to make a 12-inch circle. With finger, poke a hole in the center, then stretch the hole to about 2 inches in diameter, smoothing the inside of the round and flattening the bread out evenly. Let rise for 30 minutes. Pierce all over with a fork. Brush generously with water and bake in a preheated oven at 450° F. for 15 minutes. Remove onto rack. Let cool and dry until stiff (in the winter it takes just a short time). To serve, break into wedges.

SULTSINA

This rye flatbread from eastern Finland is filled with a cooked farina mixture. It is traditionally served as a snack with coffee, tea, or milk.

MAKES 4

FILLING:

½ cup milk
¼ teaspoon salt
2 tablespoons farina
1 tablespoon butter, at room
    temperature

3 to 4 tablespoons heavy
cream

RYE DOUGH:

½ cup warm water
1 tablespoon butter, melted
¼ teaspoon salt
½ cup unbleached all-purpose
    flour

½ cup dark rye flour
Additional all-purpose flour

Melted butter
Cinnamon sugar

To prepare filling, bring milk to a boil in small saucepan over medium heat. Add salt and slowly stir in farina until smooth. Return to boil and cook 1 minute, stirring constantly. Remove from heat. Cover and let stand 3 minutes. Stir in butter and enough cream to make mixture spreadable. Cover to keep warm while preparing dough.

For dough, combine warm water, butter, and salt in bowl. Beat in all-purpose flour until smooth, then mix in the rye flour. Turn dough out onto floured surface and knead until smooth, about 2 minutes, adding more all-purpose flour if dough is sticky. Shape into cylinder; cut into 4 pieces. Dust with flour. Reflour surface lightly. Pat each piece into small round cake. Roll into 8-inch rounds. Flour tops of rounds lightly. Stack; cover rounds with plastic wrap.

Heat electric griddle to 450° F. (or heat griddle or skillet over high heat until a drop of water bounces off surface). Cook 1 round of dough, turning once, until dry and spotted with brown, but still pliable, about 30 seconds on each side. Transfer to warm platter. Repeat with remaining dough. Spread 2 tablespoons filling down the center of each *sultsina*. Fold 2 opposite edges over filling, just meeting in the center, then fold in half again lengthwise. Cut into 2-inch pieces, if desired. Serve immediately with melted butter and cinnamon sugar for dipping.

APPLE WALNUT PANCAKES

Serve these with cinnamon sugar and melted butter.

MAKES TWELVE 4-INCH PANCAKES

1 cup whole wheat flour
1 cup unbleached all-purpose
*   flour*
1 teaspoon salt
2 teaspoons baking powder
1 tablespoon brown sugar,
*   light or dark*

2 cups milk
2 eggs, well beaten
2 tablespoons vegetable oil
1 cup pared and diced apple
½ cup chopped walnuts

In large bowl, combine whole wheat flour, all-purpose flour, salt, baking powder, and brown sugar. In smaller bowl, combine milk, eggs, and oil. Pour liquid ingredients into dry ingredients and stir just until mixed. Add the apples and walnuts. Preheat griddle to 375° F. Spoon 4 to 5 tablespoons of batter at a time to make pancakes. Grease griddle lightly if necessary. Bake 1 to 2 minutes on each side until golden. Serve hot.

SWEDISH RYE TACK

The surface of this chewy, fennel-flavored bread is classically textured with a square-cut knobbed rolling pin. Rye tack is delicious just buttered and eaten as bread with soup, or topped with cheese and cold cuts and eaten open-faced but out of hand. Swedish children and workers often take sandwiches such as this with them to school or work.

MAKES TWO 13-INCH ROUNDS

¼ cup warm water,
    105° F.–115° F.
1 package active dry yeast
4 tablespoons light
    (unsulphured) molasses
    or dark corn syrup
1 cup milk, scalded and cooled
    to 105° F.–115° F.
½ cup butter, melted and
    cooled

1½ teaspoons crushed fennel
    seed
¾ teaspoon salt
3 cups dark rye flour
1¼ cups bread flour or
    unbleached all-purpose
    flour

Pour water into large bowl. Stir in yeast and 1 tablespoon molasses. Let stand until yeast foams, about 5 minutes. Add remaining molasses, milk, butter, fennel seed, and salt. Mix in rye flour with wooden spoon until smooth. Stir in enough bread flour to make a stiff dough. Turn out onto floured surface. Cover and let rest 1 hour.

Grease 2 baking sheets. Knead dough until smooth and satiny, about 10 minutes. Divide dough into 2 pieces. Form 1 into a ball. Roll out directly on 1 prepared sheet to make a 13-inch round, preferably using a hardtack or knobbed rolling pin. If you do not have a hardtack rolling pin, use a plain one and prick entire surface with a fork. Cut out a 2-inch hole in the center of the round. Repeat with remaining dough. Cover and let rise in a warm area until puffy, about 45 minutes. Preheat oven to 425° F. Bake until brown around edges and firm,

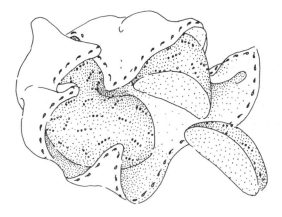

15 to 20 minutes. Transfer to kitchen towels. Brush with warm water and cover with towels. Store airtight. Cut in wedges to serve.

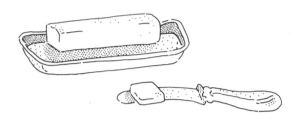

GRAHAM FLATBREAD CIGARS

After baking, these flatbreads are rolled up into cigar shapes. Serve whole or slice diagonally. Great as accompaniments for soups or salads.

MAKES 8

1½ cups whole wheat flour
1 cup unbleached all-purpose
  flour
¼ cup plus 1 tablespoon
  butter, melted

1 teaspoon sugar
1 teaspoon salt
1½ cups boiling water
Additional all-purpose flour
  for dusting

Combine whole wheat flour, all-purpose flour, 1 tablespoon butter, sugar, and salt in large bowl. Stir in enough boiling water to make a stiff dough. Cover dough and let cool, about 1 hour. Lightly flour work surface. Divide dough into 8 balls. Roll each out into a round about 12 inches in diameter, flouring surface as necessary. Lightly sprinkle with flour, stack, and cover. Heat electric griddle to 450° F., or heat a heavy skillet over high heat until a drop of water bounces off the surface. Add 1 round and cook, turning once, until leathery—30 seconds to 1 minute on each side. Remove from griddle. Immediately brush with remaining melted butter and roll up tightly into cigar shape. Repeat with remaining pieces of dough. Serve warm or at room temperature.

CINNAMON GRAHAMS

These are crispy and spicy; serve with tea or coffe.

MAKES ABOUT 5 DOZEN

1½ cups whole wheat flour
1 cup unbleached all-purpose
  flour
½ cup vegetable shortening, at
  room temperature
⅓ cup well-packed light or
  dark brown sugar
¼ cup honey

¼ cup vegetable oil
3 tablespoons cold water
1 teaspoon baking soda
1 teaspoon ground cinnamon
½ teaspoon salt
Additional all-purpose flour
  for dusting

Mix all ingredients except additional flour in large bowl until smooth, using wooden spoon. Cover with plastic wrap and refrigerate 20 minutes. Preheat oven to 425° F. Remove half the dough from refrigerator and place on ungreased baking sheet. Pat into a smooth 4- to 5-inch square. Dust with additional all-purpose flour and roll out on baking sheet to 10 x 12-inch rectangle. Cut into 2-inch squares, leaving dough in place on baking sheet. Prick entire surface with a fork. Bake until golden, 7 to 10 minutes. Repeat with remaining dough. Recut while hot if necessary. Cool on baking sheet. Crackers crisp as they cool. Store crackers in airtight containers.

WHOLE WHEAT TORTILLAS

Use these whenever flour tortillas are called for. Try them sprinkled with shredded Monterey Jack cheese, dotted with green chilies, folded in half, and browned in ¼ inch of hot oil.

MAKES 12 TORTILLAS

1 cup whole wheat flour
1 cup unbleached all-purpose
  flour
2 teaspoons baking powder

1 teaspoon salt
1 tablespoon vegetable oil
¾ to 1 cup warm water

Combine whole wheat flour, all-purpose flour, baking powder, and salt in mixing bowl. Stir in oil and enough water to make smooth dough. Turn out onto floured surface and knead several times until easy to handle. Divide into 12 balls. Roll each ball out on well-floured surface into a 9- to 10-inch round. Sprinkle lightly with flour, stack, and cover with towel or plastic. Heat electric griddle to 450° F. or heat griddle or heavy skillet over high heat until drop of water bounces off surface. Cook tortillas until lightly browned, about 2 minutes on first side and 1 minute on second. Stack tortillas as finished to keep warm and pliable.

CECILE'S OATMEAL HARDTACK

This is a Scandinavian favorite. Use the traditional Swedish hob-nailed rolling pin to get a pebbly texture. You can, however, simply roll it out with a regular pin and prick it all over with a fork.

MAKES ABOUT 5 DOZEN

¼ cup vegetable shortening, at
    room temperature
¼ cup sugar
2 tablespoons butter, at room
    temperature
1¾ cups unbleached
    all-purpose flour

1 cup rolled oats,
    old-fashioned or
    quick-cooking
½ teaspoon salt
½ teaspoon baking soda
¾ cup buttermilk
Additional oats for dusting

Cream shortening, sugar, and butter in bowl until smooth. Combine flour, oats, salt, and soda in small bowl. Add dry ingredients to creamed mixture alternately with buttermilk, blending to form stiff dough. Cover and refrigerate 30 minutes. Preheat oven to 370° F. Grease two 14 x 17-inch baking sheets. Sprinkle with oats. Remove half of the dough from the refrigerator. Shape into a smooth square on generously floured board. Transfer to the prepared baking sheet. Pat and press dough to flatten as much as possible, then roll out to edges of pan with rolling pin; trim edges. To give pebbly texture, roll over entire surface with hardtack rolling pin, or prick with fork evenly. Cut into 2 x 3-inch pieces using pastry wheel or knife, leaving in place on baking sheet. Bake until crisp and golden, 15 to 20 minutes. Repeat with remaining dough. Recut crackers while warm if necessary. Cool on racks. Store in airtight containers.

QUICK BREADS

It was 1856 when a Harvard University professor received a patent on the first baking powder, an agent which would produce the carbon dioxide necessary to leaven dough. The first leavening powders combined sodium bicarbonate with an acid and cornstarch, which served as a stable vehicle for other ingredients. When water or milk combined with the acid in the mixture, carbon dioxide was produced from the sodium bicarbonate.

But before this in England and early America cooks had been making their own "baking powder." They would take fluffy wood ashes from the hearth, add water to make a lye solution in a pot, and boil the water away leaving a dry powder in the pot. This powder was potash, or "pot" and "ash," which was refined to a form called "pearl ash." Its chemical name is potassium carbonate or potassium bicarbonate. It was used to bleach cloth and make soap, but in the presence of moisture, pearl ash releases carbon dioxide and—either by accident or intent—it was discovered that a very small pinch of pearl ash in dough caused the batter to rise as it was leavened by the carbon dioxide.

Whole grain quick breads can be moist and with a tender crumb, or can be dry and crumbly. The difference is in the balance of ingredients. It is difficult to simply substitute a whole grain flour for white flour in your favorite recipe. Whole grain quick breads sometimes require more moisture, need less sugar, and, because of the flavor of the grain, sometimes are better without a lot of extra spices. Most quick breads and muffins must be stirred gingerly—just until the dry ingredients are moistened. Not so with whole grain mixtures. It does not detract from the quality of breads and muffins to stir or even knead them. Whole grain flours have less gluten than white flours, therefore they can be stirred more. It is not a problem to stir too little, either.

What makes some whole grain breads dry? Simply a lack of moisture. Some mixtures, which may seem stiff and dry when being mixed but then have fruits (such as dates and apples) added, will turn out moist and delicious. Other mixtures without fruit may seem very liquid. Do not worry about this as whole grains tend to absorb more liquid as they bake, producing desirable results. Also, a lack of sufficient shortening sometimes makes a whole grain quick bread dry. For example, the Rice Flour Banana Bread is moist and delicious because it has ⅓ cup butter in it; the bananas also help to moisten that mixture.

Whole grain baking-powder biscuits are best with a little white flour added—up to half white flour. Without the texture of all-purpose flour, these biscuits are dry and grainy. Whole grain biscuits have a wonderful grainy, nutty flavor that just soaks up butter and homemade jams!

Whole grain muffins, on the other hand, can be made with all whole wheat flour. This is because there are other moistening ingredients in the batter that help the texture, flavor, and baking qualities of the muffin. I do not prefer the flavor of all-rye muffins; rye is best mixed with other grains to avoid a flavor that is too pronounced. Many people prefer cornmeal muffins made with the wonderful, freshly ground, moist, fine, stone-ground cornmeal. I still prefer to mix cornmeal with white flour to get a finer crumb and moister texture.

Once you get started on whole grain quick breads, you may never return to regular quick breads made with plain white flour!

CRISTABEL'S IRISH BROWN SODA BREAD

This recipe comes from a Dublin-born friend who serves it with hearty soups and stews. It slices best on the second day, but is excellent eating even while hot.

MAKES ONE 6-INCH ROUND LOAF

4 cups whole wheat flour
2 cups unbleached all-purpose
   flour
1½ teaspoons salt
1½ teaspoons baking soda
2¼ cups buttermilk or sour
   milk

In large mixing bowl, blend whole wheat flour, all-purpose flour, salt, and soda. Make a well in the center and pour in the buttermilk; mix until dough is stiff. Shape into a ball. Place on lightly greased baking sheet and flatten into a round 2 inches thick. Score a cross through from edge to edge with a sharp knife. Preheat oven to 400° F. Bake 35 to 40 minutes until golden. Cool on rack. Slice the next day.

SCOTTISH SODA BREAD

In Scotland this bread is usually cooled before it is served so that it will slice without crumbling. But it is so delicious hot from the oven that you may just give in to temptation and cut yourself a crusty, crumbly slice. Serve it at breakfast, brunch, or for tea on a Sunday afternoon with jam or honey. Or treat yourself to a memorable snack of slices of this bread, thin slices of Stilton, and a glass of port.

MAKES 1 LOAF

2 cups whole wheat flour
1 cup bread flour or
    unbleached all-purpose
    flour
½ cup rolled oats
1 teaspoon baking powder

1 teaspoon baking soda
½ teaspoon salt
3 tablespoons butter, melted
1½ cups buttermilk
Additional melted butter for
    top of hot loaf

In large mixing bowl, combine whole wheat flour, bread flour, and ¼ cup of the rolled oats. Blend in the baking powder, soda, salt, and butter. Make a hole in the center of the mixture and add the buttermilk. Stir until stiff dough forms. Sprinkle remaining oats on bread board. Turn dough out onto board and knead for just 1 minute, shaping it as you go into a perfect round loaf. There should be a rather thick coating of the extra oats on the outside of the loaf. Cover baking sheet with parchment paper or lightly grease it. Place loaf seam side down on top of baking sheet. With sharp knife, make a cross slash in the top of the loaf about ½ inch deep. Preheat oven to 375° F. Bake for 35 to 40 minutes or until loaf sounds hollow when tapped. Transfer to rack and brush generously with melted butter. For good slicing, cool for at last 4 hours.

MAPLE-RAISIN WHEAT BREAD

The simplest of breads to make, this recipe requires you to just mix these ingredients in the order given. It has been made for about a hundred years in Vermont!

MAKES 1 LARGE LOAF OR 3 SMALL LOAVES

1½ cups buttermilk
2 tablespoons butter, melted
⅔ cup maple syrup
2 teaspoons baking soda
½ teaspoon salt

1⅓ cups whole wheat flour
1⅓ cups unbleached
  all-purpose flour
1 cup dark raisins (optional)

In large mixing bowl, combine ingredients in the order given. Stir just until flour is moistened. Grease one 9 x 5-inch loaf pan or 3 smaller 5½ x 3-inch loaf pans. Preheat oven to 350° F. Bake 45 to 50 minutes for large loaf, 35 to 40 minutes for small loaves, or until a toothpick inserted in the center comes out clean. Remove from pans and cool on rack.

WHOLE WHEAT RAISIN-NUT BREAD

Serve this bread spread with cream cheese, along with a fruit salad or in place of sweets for coffee or tea.

MAKES 1 LARGE LOAF OR 3 SMALL LOAVES

3 cups whole wheat flour
3 teaspoons baking powder
1 cup honey
1¼ cups milk
2 tablespoons butter, melted

1 tablespoon ground cinnamon
¼ teaspoon ground nutmeg
1 cup dark raisins
1 cup chopped walnuts or
  pecans

In large mixing bowl, combine wheat flour, baking powder, honey, milk, butter, cinnamon, and nutmeg. Stir until well blended. Add the raisins and nuts, mixing just until they are evenly dispersed. Grease one 9 x 5-inch loaf pan, or 3 smaller 5½ x 3-inch pans. Turn dough into pans. Preheat oven to 325° F. Bake 1 hour for the large loaf, 35 to 40 minutes for small loaves, or until a skewer inserted in the center comes out clean. Remove from pans and cool on wire rack.

HONEY-MOLASSES WHEAT BREAD

Honestly a quick bread, this recipe goes together in a few minutes. If you have any left, cut it into slices and toast it for breakfast.

MAKES 1 LOAF

2 cups whole wheat flour
½ cup bread flour or
    unbleached all-purpose
    flour
1 teaspoon baking powder
1 teaspoon baking soda

½ teaspoon salt
1½ cups buttermilk
¼ cup vegetable oil
¼ cup honey
¼ cup light or dark molasses

In large bowl, combine all the ingredients, adding them in the order given. Stir 75 strokes until dry ingredients are moistened. Pour into greased 9 x 5-inch loaf pan. Preheat oven to 350° F. Bake 40 to 50 minutes or until a skewer or toothpick inserted in the center comes out clean. Serve with butter or cream cheese.

APPLE-NUT BREAD

The moistness of apples and graininess of whole wheat make this quick bread just great with a smooth, aged, sharp Cheddar cheese.

MAKES 1 LARGE LOAF OR 3 SMALL LOAVES

3 cups whole wheat flour
3 teaspoons baking powder
2 tablespoons ground
    cinnamon
1 teaspoon ground ginger
1 teaspoon ground allspice
1 cup honey

1 cup milk
2 eggs
⅓ cup butter, melted
1 cup chopped nuts
3 cups chopped fresh pared
    apple

In large mixing bowl, combine flour, baking powder, cinnamon, ginger, and allspice. In another bowl, combine honey, milk, eggs, and butter, blending well. Pour liquid ingredients over dry ingredients and blend just until dry ingredients are moistened. Stir in the nuts and apple. Grease 3 small, 5½ x 3-inch loaf pans. Preheat oven to 350° F. Turn batter into pans and bake for 35 to 40 minutes, or until a skewer inserted in the center comes out clean. Remove from pans and cool on wire rack.

PUMPKIN WHEAT BREAD

In addition to the rich spicy taste of pumpkin, this quick-to-make bread contains chopped nuts and dates which add more good taste and texture.

MAKES 1 LARGE OR 3 SMALL LOAVES

1½ cups unbleached
   all-purpose flour
½ cup whole wheat flour
1 cup well-packed brown sugar
1½ teaspoons pumpkin pie
   spice
1 teaspoon baking soda
¾ teaspoon salt

½ teaspoon baking powder
1 cup canned pumpkin
½ cup butter, melted
2 eggs
½ cup chopped pitted dates
½ cup chopped walnuts and
   pecans

In large mixing bowl, blend the flours, brown sugar, pie spice, soda, salt, and baking powder. In smaller bowl, blend the pumpkin, butter, and eggs. Pour liquid ingredients over dry ingredients and stir just until dry ingredients are moistened. Add dates and nuts. Grease one 9 x 5-inch baking pan or three 5½ x 3-inch loaf pans. Turn batter into pans. Preheat oven to 350° F. Bake until tester inserted in the center comes out clean—about 1 hour for large loaf or 30 to 35 minutes for smaller loaves. Cool 15 minutes in pan, remove from pan, and cool on wire rack.

FIG-BANANA WHEAT BREAD

The addition of dried figs and the use of whole wheat flour make this banana bread exceptional.

MAKES 1 LARGE LOAF OR 4 SMALL LOAVES

1 cup sugar
½ cup butter, at room
    temperature
2 eggs
1½ cups (3 to 4 medium)
    mashed ripe bananas

1 tablespoon fresh lemon juice
2 cups whole wheat flour
2 teaspoons baking powder
1 teaspoon baking soda
½ teaspoon salt
1 cup chopped dried figs

In large mixing bowl, cream sugar with butter until blended and smooth; add eggs and beat until light; stir in bananas and lemon juice. Stir flour, baking powder, soda, and salt together. Add to creamed mixture. Stir in figs.

Grease one 9 x 5-inch loaf pan or 4 small, 5½ x 3-inch loaf pans. Turn mixture ino pans. Preheat oven to 350° F. Bake large loaf about 1 hour or until toothpick inserted in the center comes out clean; bake smaller loaves for 30 minutes. Remove from pan or pans and cool on rack.

RICE FLOUR BANANA BREAD

Use brown or white rice flour in this bread. It is a good bread for people who cannot tolerate wheat flour.

MAKES 2 SMALL LOAVES

⅓ cup butter, softened
⅔ cup sugar
2 eggs
3 tablespoons buttermilk
1 teaspoon lemon extract
2 cups brown or white rice
    flour

1 teaspoon baking powder
½ teaspoon baking soda
½ teaspoon salt
1 cup mashed ripe bananas
1 cup toasted flaked coconut

In large mixing bowl, cream butter and sugar; beat in eggs, one at a time. Stir in the buttermilk and lemon extract. Stir rice flour, baking powder, soda, and salt together and add to the mixture along with the bananas; beat until well blended. Fold in the coconut. Turn into 2 greased 5½ x 3-inch loaf pans. Preheat oven to 350° F. Bake 50 to 55 minutes or until a toothpick inserted in the center comes out clean. Remove from pans and cool on wire racks.

SHAKER BROWN BREAD

Steamed breads have always been a fascination for me, but in Shaker communities they were made twice weekly, as many as 20 loaves at a time. Although they made large breads in molds about 2-quart size, I prefer smaller breads such as those that result from steaming the bread in 16-ounce cans.

MAKES 1 LARGE 2-QUART LOAF

1 cup whole wheat flour
1 cup medium rye flour
1 cup cornmeal, preferably
*   stone-ground yellow*
1½ teaspoons baking soda
1½ teaspoons salt

¾ cup molasses, light
*   (unsulphured) or dark*
2 cups buttermilk
2 tablespoons butter, melted
1 cup dark raisins

In large bowl, stir together the whole wheat flour, rye flour, cornmeal, baking soda, and salt. Combine molasses, buttermilk, and melted butter; blend into the dry ingredients. Stir in raisins. Grease one 2-quart mold or five 10-ounce cans, or nine to ten 8-ounce cans, or 4 cans that are 2-cup (16 ounce) capacity. Fill two-thirds full. Cover tops of cans tightly with foil. Set molds or cans on rack in large kettle. Pour in boiling water to half the depth of the mold or molds. Cover tightly and steam for 3½ hours for large single mold or 1 hour for small molds, keeping the water at a slow boil all the time. Let cool in cans 5 minutes, remove, and cool on racks; serve warm.

THREE-GRAIN BROWN BREAD

Easy to make ahead, this steamed bread is a natural for buffets, gifts, or just delicious eating. Multiple-grained and flavored with the addition of sunflower seeds and raisins, this bread has a wonderful flavor and texture. For molds, you can use almost any straight-sided cans you may have on hand—soup, tomato sauce, or 1-pound coffee cans work well. You may also use wide-mouthed canning jars (one-pint size); ones that have straight sides and no neck are ideal because you can use the 2-part rings and lids for covering the bread for steaming. A large canning kettle is ideal for steaming the bread.

MAKES THREE 1-POUND-CAN LOAVES

1 cup dark rye flour
1 cup whole wheat flour,
  preferably stone-ground
1 cup cornmeal, preferably
  stone-ground yellow
4 teaspoons baking powder
1 teaspoon salt

½ teaspoon baking soda
1¾ cups milk
¾ cup dark molasses
1 cup dark raisins
1 cup sunflower seeds or
  chopped walnuts

In mixing bowl combine rye flour, whole wheat flour, cornmeal, baking powder, salt, and soda. In another bowl, mix milk and molasses until blended; stir into the dry ingredients until smooth. Add raisins and nuts.

Grease well three 1-pound coffee cans, 6 soup cans, or four 1-pint wide-mouthed canning jars. Fill molds ⅔ full. Cover tightly; for cans or jars without their own lids, waxed paper fastened with a rubber band works well.

Place batter-filled molds into a large pot of boiling water; water should come to ⅔ the height of the molds. Steam 1-pound coffee can molds for 3 hours, keeping water at a steady boil. It will take 1½ hours for soup-can breads or 1-pint canning jars. Breads are done when top feels firm to the touch when tested by pressing finger onto top of waxed-paper-covered mold. If using 2-part canning lids, you may test one by removing from the water, opening, and touching the bread. If it is not done, simply re-cover and replace in boiling water. When breads are done, remove from water and cool a few minutes. Remove cover and slide bread out of mold onto rack. Breads may be returned to the mold, if desired, to give as gifts.

WHOLE WHEAT BAKING-POWDER BISCUITS

This is a quick fresh bread when you are pinched for time. Great for lunch with a salad or soup. Try them for tea with honey and butter.

MAKES 10 TO 12 BISCUITS

1 cup whole wheat flour
1 cup unbleached all-purpose
    flour
1 tablespoon baking powder

½ teaspoon salt
¼ cup shortening, lard, or
    butter
¾ cup milk

Measure flours, baking powder, and salt into mixing bowl. Cut in shortening until particles are fine. Stir in milk just until mixture is moistened and dough forms. Knead lightly on floured surface about 10 times. Roll out to ½-inch thickness. Cut into rounds with 2-inch cutter. Place on ungreased baking sheet. Preheat oven to 450° F., then bake for 12 to 15 minutes or until golden brown. Serve hot.

HUNGARIAN WHOLE GRAIN POTATO BISCUITS

These wonderfully flavored multiple grain biscuits are buttery and tender, great with a hearty vegetable soup for lunch or supper.

MAKES TWENTY-FOUR 2-INCH BISCUITS

1 cup whole wheat flour
1 cup unbleached all-purpose
    flour
¾ cup dark rye flour
1 tablespoon baking powder
1 teaspoon salt

1 cup butter, cold
¼ cup sour cream
1 cup cold mashed potatoes
3 whole eggs, 1 separated
2 tablespoons caraway seeds

In large mixing bowl, combine flours, baking powder, and salt. Cut in butter until about the size of kidney beans. Mix the sour cream, potatoes, and 2 whole eggs and 1 yolk together and stir into dry ingredients. Stir, then knead together. Roll out to a 16-inch square. Cut into

2-inch rounds; place on ungreased baking sheet. Brush with reserved egg white; sprinkle with caraway seeds. Preheat oven to 400° F. Bake 15 minutes or until lightly browned.

WHEAT GERM BISCUITS

Use your little round cookie cutter for these biscuits. Each biscuit "sandwiches" a layer of toasted wheat germ for extra goodness. Serve these dainty biscuits with a chilled vegetable soup.

MAKES 12 BISCUITS, 1½ TO 2 INCHES IN DIAMETER

1 cup toasted wheat germ
½ cup unbleached all-purpose
    flour
2 teaspoons baking powder

1 teaspoon salt
1 teaspoon sugar
2 tablespoons butter, firm
¼ cup ice water

In mixing bowl, combine ½ cup of the wheat germ with the flour, baking powder, salt, and sugar. Cut in butter until mixture resembles coarse crumbs. Add water and toss with fork or spatula until dough holds together in a firm ball. Roll or pat out on lightly floured surface to a ½-inch thickness. Cut in rounds and place on greased or parchment-covered baking sheet. You should have 24 rounds. Sprinkle 12 of them with remaining ½ cup wheat germ. Top each with another round to make a "sandwich." Press firmly to seal edges. Preheat oven to 350° F. and bake about 15 minutes until browned. Serve hot.

WHOLE WHEAT SCONES

These are excellent served warm with butter, better yet served with a well-aged Cheddar cheese.

MAKES 8 SCONES

1½ cups whole wheat flour
½ cup unbleached all-purpose
    flour
3 teaspoons baking powder
2 tablespoons sugar
½ teaspoon salt
⅓ cup butter, at room
    temperature

2 eggs, slightly beaten
⅓ cup heavy (whipping)
    cream
Additional whole wheat flour
    to sprinkle over tops
3 tablespoons melted butter for
    tops

In large mixing bowl, stir together whole wheat flour, all-purpose flour, baking powder, sugar, and salt. With fork, blend in the butter until mixture resembles coarse crumbs. Stir eggs and cream together and add to flour mixture to make a stiff but slightly dry dough. Turn out onto lightly floured board and knead a few turns to make a smooth ball. Grease a baking sheet lightly, and place ball of dough onto baking sheet. Dust top with additional whole wheat flour and press down to make an evenly thick round 8 inches in diameter. With straight-edged knife, cut into 8 wedges, but leave wedges in place. Drizzle melted butter over. Preheat oven to 425° F. and bake for 13 to 15 minutes, until golden. Serve warm. Or, split and toast if any are left for another meal.

RYE-WHEAT SCONES

Delicious with butter and wild strawberry jam, these quick-to-make scones are also delicious with a crisp vegetable salad in the summer or vegetable chowder in the winter.

MAKES 8 SCONES

½ cup quick or old-fashioned
    oats
½ cup whole wheat flour
½ cup dark rye flour
3 teaspoons baking powder
2 tablespoons sugar

½ teaspoon salt
½ cup butter
2 eggs, beaten
⅓ cup milk
Rolled oats for the tops
Caraway seeds for tops

In large mixing bowl, combine oats, wheat, rye flour, baking powder, sugar, and salt. Cut in butter until mixture resembles coarse crumbs. Beat eggs and milk together. Fold egg-milk mixture into the dry ingredients until a stiff baking-powder biscuit type of dough forms. Sprinkle work surface with rolled oats and caraway seeds and turn dough out onto it. Pat and shape into a cake about 9 inches in diameter, pressing the oatmeal and caraway seeds into the top of the dough. Cover a baking sheet with parchment paper and place dough onto it. With long, straight knife, score, cutting completely through dough, into 8 wedges; leave wedges in place. Preheat oven to 425° F. Bake 13 to 15 minutes or until golden. Serve hot.

BARLEY SCONES WITH HONEY GLAZE

These scones are baked in butter in a heavy skillet and glazed with brandy-flavored honey after baking.

MAKES 8 SCONES

1 cup unbleached all-purpose
flour
1 cup barley flour
4 teaspoons baking powder
¼ teaspoon salt

1 cup butter, cold
⅔ cup buttermilk
¼ cup honey
2 tablespoons brandy

In large mixing bowl, combine flours, baking powder, and salt. Cut in ½ cup cold butter until mixture resembles coarse meal. Gradually add buttermilk; toss lightly with fork to make a soft dough. If dough seems too dry, toss in 1 to 2 tablespoons more buttermilk. Knead gently on floured surface for 1 minute or until dough holds together and seems to be evenly mixed. Divide dough into 2 parts. Roll out to make a 9-inch circle. Cut into 8 wedges. Melt ¼ cup of the remaining butter in a heavy skillet. Preheat oven to 400° F. When foam subsides, place wedges in skillet; bake in oven 5 minutes, then turn over carefully using a pancake turner. Bake an additional 5 minutes. Meanwhile, combine honey, remaining butter, and brandy in small saucepan. Heat until bubbly. Reduce heat and simmer, stirring frequently, for 4 minutes. Remove from heat; whisk until thickened and blended. Brush glaze over baked scones. Serve immediately.

OATMEAL PECAN SCONES

Pecans are not a traditional ingredient of scones, but they add so much to the flavor! These are baked on a hot griddle over low heat.

MAKES 8 SCONES

1 cup quick or old-fashioned rolled oats	½ cup butter, cold
	½ cup chopped pecans
1¾ cups whole wheat flour	¾ to 1 cup buttermilk
1 teaspoon baking soda	2 tablespoons honey

In large mixing bowl, combine oats, wheat flour, and soda. Cut in butter until the mixture resembles coarse crumbs. Mix in the pecans. Mix buttermilk with honey and add to dry ingredients, tossing just until dry ingredients are moistened. Turn out onto lightly floured board and knead 5 to 10 times until dough forms a ball. Divide dough into 8 parts. Shape each into a round cake by rolling or patting out until ¼ inch thick. Bake on a hot greased griddle over low heat (or set fry pan to 325° F.) for 10 minutes or until scones have risen. Increase heat to medium (350° F.–375° F.) and brown underside about 6 minutes. Turn over and brown other side, about 5 minutes. Serve hot with homemade preserves or honey.

WHOLE WHEAT AND CURRANT SCONES

These are best hot from the oven, but if you have any left over, split the wedges horizontally and toast them for breakfast.

MAKES 8 SERVINGS

1½ cups whole wheat flour
½ cup unbleached all-purpose
    flour
3 teaspoons baking powder
3 tablespoons sugar
½ teaspoon salt
½ cup butter, at room
    temperature

1 cup dried currants
2 eggs, slightly beaten
⅓ cup heavy (whipping)
    cream
Additional whole wheat flour
    to sprinkle over top
3 tablespoons melted butter for
    top

In large mixing bowl, stir together whole wheat flour, all-purpose flour, baking powder, sugar, and salt. With fork, blend in the butter until mixture resembles coarse crumbs. Add currants and fold to mix them in evenly. Beat eggs and cream together and add to flour mixture to make a stiff, but slightly dry dough. Turn out onto lightly floured board and knead a few turns to make a smooth ball. Grease a baking sheet lightly, and place ball of dough onto baking sheet. Dust top with additional whole wheat flour and press down to make an evenly thick round 8 inches in diameter. With straight-edged knife, cut into 8 wedges but leave wedges in place. Drizzle melted butter over. Preheat oven to 425° F. and bake for 13 to 15 minutes, or until golden. Serve warm. Or split and toast, if any are left, for another meal.

HONEY WHEAT MUFFINS

A good, basic, whole grain muffin, these have a not-too-sweet, healthy taste and are excellent served with a fruit salad or with an omelet for breakfast or brunch.

MAKES 12 MUFFINS

¾ cup unbleached all-purpose
    flour
¾ cup whole wheat flour
2 teaspoons baking powder
½ teaspoon salt

½ cup honey
½ cup milk
¼ cup butter or margarine,
    melted
1 egg, lightly beaten

In large mixing bowl, combine all-purpose flour, whole wheat flour, baking powder, and salt. In small bowl, mix together honey, milk, butter, and egg. Pour liquid ingredients over dry ingredients and with spatula fold together until dry ingredients are just moistened. Turn mixture into greased muffin tins. Preheat oven to 400° F. Bake 15 to 25 minutes or until golden. Serve hot with butter.

MOLASSES GRAHAM GEMS

I found this recipe in an old cookbook in which muffin recipes were referred to as "gems." Quick to stir up, these muffins are rich with the grainy taste of whole wheat flour.

MAKES 12 MUFFINS

½ teaspoon baking soda
1 cup buttermilk
1 egg, beaten
2 tablespoons molasses, light
    or dark

2 tablespoons butter, melted
½ teaspoon salt
2 cups whole wheat flour

Stir soda into buttermilk; combine with egg, molasses, and butter; add salt and whole wheat flour. Blend just enough to moisten flour. Preheat oven to 400° F. Fill buttered muffin tins ⅔ full and bake 15 to 20 minutes or until golden.

BLUEBERRY WHEAT MUFFINS

Bursting with fresh blueberries and with a rich grainy taste, these muffins are for any meal of the day. For an unusual shape, bake these in small individual pie tins.

MAKES 12 MUFFINS OR ONE 9-INCH COFFEECAKE

¾ cup unbleached flour
¾ cup whole wheat flour
1 tablespoon baking powder
½ teaspoon salt
½ cup well-packed brown
    sugar, light or dark

1½ to 2 cups fresh blueberries,
    or frozen unsugared
    blueberries
½ cup milk
½ cup butter or margarine,
    melted
1 egg, lightly beaten

In large mixing bowl, combine all-purpose flour, whole wheat flour, baking powder, salt, and brown sugar. Add the blueberries and stir just until they are coated, being careful not to break them. If you are using frozen blueberries, do not thaw them completely before adding them to the dry ingredients. In small bowl, mix together milk, melted butter, and egg. Pour liquid ingredients over dry ingredients and carefully fold together until dry ingredients are just moistened. Preheat oven to 400° F. Turn mixture into greased muffin tins. Bake 15 to 25 minutes or until golden. Remove from pans and cool on rack.

HONEY FRUIT-NUT MUFFINS

Grainy and wonderful, these muffins have the flavor and perfume of honey. For a special treatment, roll these muffins in melted butter, then in cinnamon-spiced sugar while they are still hot.

MAKES 12 MUFFINS

2 cups whole wheat flour
½ cup chopped dates or dark
    raisins
½ cup chopped walnuts or
    pecans
2 tablespoons light or dark
    brown sugar
1 tablespoon baking powder

½ teaspoon salt
⅔ cup milk
⅓ cup honey
⅓ cup butter, melted, or
    vegetable oil
2 eggs, beaten
Melted butter (optional)
Cinnamon sugar (optional)

Combine flour, dates, nuts, brown sugar, baking powder, and salt in bowl. In another bowl, combine milk, honey, butter, and eggs. Pour liquids over dry ingredients and stir just until dry ingredients are moistened. Fill greased muffin cups ⅔ full. Preheat oven to 400° F. Bake 15 to 20 minutes. If desired, roll hot muffins first in melted butter, then in cinnamon sugar, and serve immediately.

CINNAMON SUGAR: Mix ½ cup sugar with 1 tablespoon ground cinnamon.

HONEY BRAN MUFFINS

Fragrant with honey, these muffins are excellent served with butter and orange marmalade for breakfast, brunch, or lunch.

MAKES 12 MUFFINS

1½ cups 100-percent bran
   cereal
1¼ cups milk
1 egg, beaten
⅓ cup butter, melted
½ cup honey
1¼ cups unbleached
   all-purpose flour

1 tablespoon baking powder
½ teaspoon salt
1 cup chopped dates or dark
   raisins
¼ cup toasted wheat germ

In large mixing bowl, mix bran cereal and milk; let stand 5 minutes. Stir in egg, butter, and honey. Combine flour, baking powder, salt, and dates or raisins. Sprinkle flour mixture over bran mixture and fold together just until flour is moistened. Turn muffin mixture into greased pans. Preheat oven to 400° F. Bake 15 to 20 minutes or until golden. Remove from tins and cool on wire rack.

RAISIN RYE MUFFINS

The molasses and flavorings give these muffins a color and taste similar to Swedish rye bread.

MAKES 12 MUFFINS

1 cup light rye flour
1 cup unbleached all-purpose
    flour
2 teaspoons baking powder
1 teaspoon baking soda
½ cup dark or light raisins
1 tablespoon grated orange
    rind
1 teaspoon each caraway seeds
    and fennel seeds

½ teaspoon salt
⅔ cup buttermilk
⅓ cup dark molasses
⅓ cup butter, melted, or
    vegetable oil
2 eggs, beaten

In large mixing bowl, combine rye flour, all-purpose flour, baking powder, soda, raisins, orange rind, caraway and fennel seeds, and salt. In another bowl, combine buttermilk, molasses, butter, and eggs. Pour liquid ingredients over dry ingredients and stir just until dry ingredients are moistened. Fill greased muffin cups ⅔ full. Preheat oven to 400° F. Bake 15 to 20 minutes or until muffins are golden and done in the center. Serve warm with butter.

REFRIGERATOR THREE-GRAIN MUFFINS

Keep a batch of this muffin dough on hand to bake in short order. In fact, you can bake up just 1 or 2 muffins at a time in the microwave oven if you sometimes are alone. Simple double-line a Pyrex custard cup with cupcake papers, fill about ½ full with the muffin dough, and microwave on HIGH for about 30 seconds for each muffin; 6 muffins will take about 2½ minutes. Refrigerated, this dough will keep up to 4 weeks.

MAKES 5 TO 6 DOZEN MUFFINS

2 cups boiling water
6 cups 100-percent bran cereal
1 cup shortening
1 cup dark or light brown
    sugar
1 cup sugar
1 cup honey
4 eggs
1 quart buttermilk

1 cup dark or light rye flour
1½ cups quick or
    old-fashioned rolled oats
1 cup whole wheat flour
2 cups unbleached all-purpose
    flour
5 teaspoons baking soda
2 teaspoons salt

In large mixing bowl, pour boiling water over 2 cups bran cereal. Cool. In another mixing bowl, blend shortening, sugars, and honey. Add eggs, buttermilk, rye flour, rolled oats, whole wheat flour, all-purpose flour, soda, and salt; mix well. Stir in soaked bran cereal and remaining dry cereal. Store in covered container in refrigerator and bake as needed. To bake, fill well-greased muffin cups ⅔ full. Preheat oven to 400° F. Bake 15 to 20 minutes.

THREE-GRAIN NUT MUFFINS: After filling greased muffin cups with muffin dough, spoon 1 tablespoon chopped walnuts over the top of each muffin.

THREE-GRAIN SPICE MUFFINS: After filling greased muffin cups with muffin dough, sprinkle tops of muffins with cinnamon sugar.

THREE-GRAIN DATE-NUT MUFFINS: After filling greased muffin cups with muffin dough, press chopped dates and nuts into center of each muffin with a spoon.

CATHY'S OATMEAL GEMS

These muffins are an excellent accompaniment to a meal—not too sweet, and grainy with lots of oatmeal in them.

MAKES 12 LITTLE MUFFINS

2 cups rolled oats, quick or
    old-fashioned
1½ cups buttermilk
1 teaspoon baking soda
¼ cup dark molasses

⅛ teaspoon salt
1 egg, beaten
1 cup unbleached all-purpose
    flour

Mix rolled oats and buttermilk and let stand 8 hours or overnight. Add soda, molasses, salt, egg, and flour. Blend, but do not beat. Bake in well-buttered muffin tins in a preheated 400° F. oven for 15 to 20 minutes or until golden. Serve hot with butter and homemade jam.

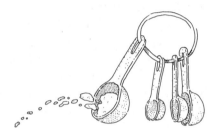

OAT-CRANBERRY MUFFINS WITH CINNAMON CRUST

Cinnamon and oatmeal give character to the "Dutchy crust" topping on these muffins. If you do not have fresh or frozen cranberries, either leave out the fruit or substitute blueberries, fresh pitted cherries, or fresh chopped apple.

MAKES 12 MUFFINS

¾ cup whole wheat flour
¾ cup unbleached all-purpose
    flour
½ cup rolled oats, quick or
    old-fashioned
2 teaspoons baking powder
1 teaspoon baking soda
½ cup well-packed brown
    sugar, dark or light

1 cup fresh or frozen whole
    cranberries
½ cup buttermilk
2 eggs
½ cup butter or margarine,
    melted

CRUST:

¼ cup butter or margarine,
    softened
¼ cup well-packed brown
    sugar, dark or light
¼ cup rolled oats, quick or
    old-fashioned

¼ cup unbleached all-purpose
    flour
1 teaspoon ground cinnamon

In large mixing bowl, combine whole wheat flour, all-purpose flour, rolled oats, baking powder, baking soda, and brown sugar. Add cranberries and stir until coated. In small bowl, beat together buttermilk, eggs, and butter. Pour over dry ingredients and fold together just until moistened. In small bowl, for topping combine the softened butter, brown sugar, rolled oats, flour, and cinnamon to make a crumbly mixture. Turn batter into greased muffin tins filling pans ⅔ full. Top each with the crumbly mixture. Preheat oven to 400° F. Bake 15 to 25 minutes or until golden. Remove from pans and cool on rack.

GOLDEN SWEET CORN MUFFINS

Whole kernel corn in these cornbread muffins adds an interesting texture. Try them with a hearty vegetable soup.

MAKES 12 MUFFINS

1 cup unbleached all-purpose
    flour
½ cup yellow cornmeal
½ cup sugar
1 tablespoon baking powder
½ teaspoon salt
1 cup fresh, drained, canned
    or frozen whole kernel
    corn

½ cup milk
2 eggs
½ cup butter or margarine,
    melted

In large mixing bowl, combine flour, cornmeal, sugar, baking powder, and salt. Add corn, tossing until kernels are coated. In small bowl, combine milk, eggs, and melted butter. Pour liquid ingredients over dry ingredients. Carefully fold together just until dry ingredients are moistened. Batter will be slightly thinner than for other muffin mixtures. Turn into greased muffin tins, filling pans ⅔ full. Preheat oven to 400° F. Bake 15 to 25 minutes or until golden. Remove from pans and cool on rack.

WHEAT GERM POPOVERS

Popovers "pop" because of the high ratio of liquid in the mixture which creates steam inside the little breads during baking. Popovers are always the quickest of quick breads to make.

MAKES 6 JUMBO OR 12 REGULAR POPOVERS

¾ cup unbleached all-purpose
    flour
¼ cup wheat germ
1 cup milk

1 tablespoon butter, melted
½ teaspoon salt
3 eggs

Combine all ingredients in container of blender or food processor with steel blade in place. Process or blend for 2½ minutes continuously. Grease and flour 12 muffin cups or 6 large (6-ounce) popover pans or custard cups. Pour batter into prepared pans. Fill each about ¾ full. Preheat over 375° F. Bake 35 to 40 minutes or until dark brown and crispy. Serve immediately.

RYE POPOVERS

Some old-time cooks like to start popovers in a cold oven and set the temperature at 450° F. for 30 minutes, then reduce the heat to 350° F., baking for 10 to 15 minutes longer. This works well if your oven does not have a speed-preheat setting.

MAKES 8 LARGE POPOVERS

¾ cup light or medium rye
    flour
¼ cup unbleached all-purpose
    flour
¼ teaspoon salt

2 eggs
1 tablespoon butter, melted
1 cup milk

In mixing bowl, stir rye flour, all-purpose flour, and salt together. Break eggs into the dry mixture; add butter and milk. Beat until smooth, using a whisk. Fill well-greased muffin or popover pans ⅔ full. Bake in a hot 450° F. oven for 20 minutes, then reduce temperature to 350° F. and bake 15 to 20 minutes longer.

HEALTHY OATMEAL-NUT WAFFLES

Just throw all the ingredients but the rolled oats and nuts into the blender or food processor, and you're ready for waffles!

MAKES 4 TO 6 SERVINGS

2 cups milk
2 eggs
1½ cups whole wheat pastry
    flour or regular whole
    wheat flour
⅓ cup butter melted, or oil

2 teaspoons baking powder
2 tablespoons dark or light
    brown sugar
1 cup old-fashioned rolled oats
1 cup chopped walnuts or
    pecans

Put milk, eggs, flour, butter, baking powder, and brown sugar into blender or food processor with plastic or steel blade in place. Process until blended. Add the oats and nuts. Stir to blend. Bake in preheated waffle iron until waffle stops steaming and is golden (approximately 5 minutes). Excellent with homemade jam, honey, or fruit syrups.

BREADS
THAT MAKE A MEAL

Everyone knows that breads can make a sandwich, which can make a meal. The natural extension of that idea is a bread that has a topping or filling baked right in, such as a pizza or the lamb-topped lahmajoun of the Middle East. This is one of my favorite categories of baking. They're great for a party!

Besides being delicious, these breads have the great advantage of also being economical and unusually nutritious. These combinations are ideal meat and cheese extenders. Because breads, especially whole grain breads, are high in protein, B vitamins, and fiber so essential for health, they add nutritional benefits to the meat, cheese, and egg fillings. And since you use less of the filling ingredients, you reduce fat content. This chapter contains a variety of delightful pizzas and stuffed breads, but you'll also find an interesting selection of breads that make a meal in the chapter on Stir-and-Pour Breads.

ONION-RYE KUCHEN

Filled with a custardy mixture of butter-sautéed onions, eggs, sour cream, and ham, this pie is delicious served hot for brunch, lunch, or supper. Cold, it makes good snacking.

MAKES 6 TO 8 SERVINGS

1 package active dry yeast	1 teaspoon salt
1 cup warm water,	1 cup light rye flour
105° F.–115° F.	¾ to 1 cup unbleached
½ cup nonfat dry milk	all-purpose flour
1 teaspoon sugar	

FILLING:

2 large onions	2 tablespoons unbleached
4 tablespoons butter or	all-purpose flour
margarine	1 tablespoon caraway seeds
2 eggs	1 teaspoon salt
¼ cup sour cream	1 cup diced cooked ham

In large bowl, dissolve yeast in warm water; add dry milk and sugar and let stand 5 minutes until yeast foams. Stir in salt, rye flour, and part of the all-purpose flour; beat until smooth. Slowly add the remaining all-purpose flour to make a soft dough. Turn out onto lightly floured board and knead until smooth, about 5 minutes. Wash bowl, grease, and add dough to bowl; cover and let rise for 1 hour or until doubled. Meanwhile, chop onions and sauté in butter over low to medium heat until cooked through and soft, but not browned. Combine in bowl with the eggs, sour cream, all-purpose flour, caraway seeds, salt, and ham. Punch dough down. Grease a 9-inch square baking pan or an 11-inch tart pan with a removable bottom. Press dough into pan to fit bottom and build up the sides. Let rest for 20 to 30 minutes or until puffy. Spoon onion filling into pan. Heat oven to 375° F. and bake 30 minutes until filling is set. Cool 5 minutes, then remove onto wire rack. Serve hot or cold.

WHOLE WHEAT SAUSAGE AND EGG PIZZA

Try this for brunch. Kids love it, and can lend a "helping" hand in making it, too!

MAKES 6 SERVINGS

CRUST:

1½ cups whole wheat flour
¾ teaspoon salt
½ cup shortening

4 to 6 tablespoons ice-cold
water

FILLING:

1 pound pork sausage meat

1 cup shredded fresh potato (1
 medium), or equivalent
 frozen hash-browned
 potatoes

1 tablespoon butter

1 cup (4 ounces) shredded
 Cheddar cheese

5 eggs

¼ cup milk

½ teaspoon salt

⅛ teaspoon ground pepper

2 tablespoons grated Parmesan
 cheese

To prepare crust, measure flour and salt into mixing bowl. Cut in shortening until mixture is crumbly. Add ice water, tossing mixture with a fork until dough holds together in a ball. Flatten slightly; smooth edges. Roll out onto floured pastry cloth to a circle 14 inches in diameter. Place into a 12-inch lightly greased pizza pan. Build edges up to make a rim. Preheat oven to 450° F.

Meanwhile, brown sausage in pan and drain. In another pan, brown the potatoes in the butter until soft, about 5 minutes. Prebake crust for 10 minutes, then reduce heat to 375° F. Sprinkle sausage into crust; add potato and Cheddar cheese, distributing everything evenly. In small bowl, beat eggs, milk, salt, and pepper and pour over meat, potatoes, and cheese in pan. Sprinkle with the Parmesan cheese. Bake 25 minutes until edges are golden and pizza is lightly browned. Serve hot, cut into wedges.

WHOLE WHEAT BEEF PIZZA

This pizza is quick and easy to make. There is no waiting for the moist crust to rise—just mix, spread in pan, fill, and bake!

MAKES 4 TO 6 SERVINGS

FILLING:

1 pound extra-lean ground
 beef

¼ pound fresh mushrooms,
 sliced

1 small onion, minced
1 teaspoon salt
¼ teaspoon pepper

1 teaspoon Italian herb
   seasoning
1 can (6 ounces) tomato paste

CRUST:

1½ cups whole wheat flour
1 package active dry yeast
1 teaspoon sugar
½ teaspoon salt

½ cup sour cream
½ cup water
¼ cup shortening
1 egg

TOPPING:

¼ cup sliced green or black
   olives
½ teaspoon fennel seeds

1 cup (4 ounces) shredded
   Mozzarella cheese
¼ cup Parmesan cheese

To prepare filling, put beef, mushrooms, and onion into heavy skillet and cook over medium heat until meat loses its pinkness and moisture has evaporated from the pan. Add salt, pepper, herb seasoning, and tomato paste. Cool.

To prepare crust, combine flour, yeast, sugar, and salt; mix well. In saucepan, heat sour cream, water, and shortening until warm (120° F.–130° F.); add to flour mixture. Add egg. Stir by hand until smooth. Spread in greased 12-inch pizza pan. Spoon filling evenly onto crust. Sprinkle with olives, fennel seeds, Mozzarella, and Parmesan cheeses. Bake at 375° F. for 30 to 35 minutes until light golden brown. Serve immediately.

LAHMAJOUN

At first glance this meat-topped flatbread appears to be a pizza, but the flavor is decidedly Middle Eastern. Here the whole wheat dough is an ideal foil for the spicy lamb filling. For convenience, you can make these, freeze them, and serve at a party several weeks later. I like to serve these lamb pies with a topping of chopped tomatoes, green peppers, and a dab of sour cream.

MAKES 12 SERVINGS

CRUST:

1 package active dry yeast
1¼ cups warm water,
        105° F.–115° F.
1 teaspoon sugar
1 teaspoon salt

¼ cup butter, melted
1 cup unprocessed bran
2 to 2½ cups whole wheat
    flour

LAHMAJOUN MEAT FILLING:

1 pound ground lamb
1½ cups minced fresh onion
1 large green bell pepper,
    minced
1 large red bell pepper, minced
1 large clove garlic, minced
1 teaspoon salt
2 tablespoons fresh lemon juice
2 tablespoons chopped fresh
    mint or 1 tablespoon
    dried mint

2 tablespoons chopped fresh
    parsley
½ teaspoon freshly ground
    black pepper
¼ to 1 teaspoon crushed hot
    red pepper
4 small fresh tomatoes, cored,
    seeded, and puréed in
    blender

In mixing bowl, dissolve yeast in warm water and add the sugar; let stand 5 minutes until yeast foams. Stir in the salt, butter, bran, and whole wheat flour until soft dough forms. Turn out onto lightly floured board and knead until dough is soft, smooth, and unsticky, about 5 to 8 minutes. Wash bowl, grease it, add dough to bowl, turn over to grease top. Cover with a towel. Let rise in a warm place until doubled, about 1 hour. While dough rises, prepare meat filling. In bowl, mix all the filling ingredients together. Punch dough down and divide into 12 egg-sized balls. Let stand a few minutes, then roll out each into an 8-inch flat round. Divide filling equally among dough rounds and spread smoothly. Place on parchment-covered or greased baking sheets. Cover rounds with the meat mixture. Bake in a preheated 450° F. oven for 15 to 20 minutes.

CALZONE

These delicious turnovers are reminiscent in flavor of pizza, but they have a special appeal of their own. Use whole wheat pastry flour for these to achieve the right tender dough. Serve these in winter with minestone and in summer with a big green salad enriched with slices of sweet red pepper, sweet onion, and artichoke hearts.

MAKES 2 CALZONE—4 SERVINGS

CALZONE DOUGH:

2 packages active dry yeast
1½ cups warm water,
    105° F.–115° F.
2 tablespoons honey
2 tablespoons olive oil

½ teaspoon salt
2 cups unbleached all-purpose
    flour
3 to 3½ cups whole wheat
    pastry flour

FILLING:

1 can (8 ounces) tomato sauce
    with mushrooms and
    onion
1 teaspoon basil
1 teaspoon oregano
¾ pound fresh Italian
    sausages, mild, medium,
    or hot

2 cups shredded Mozzarella
    cheese
1 cup grated Parmesan cheese
¾ cup grated Romano cheese
Olive oil for dough

In large mixing bowl, dissolve the yeast in warm water; add the molasses and let stand 5 minutes until yeast foams. Add the oil, salt, and all-purpose flour; beat well. Stir in enough of the whole wheat pastry flour to make a very stiff dough. Cover and let rise until doubled, about 1 hour. During this time the dough will become soft.

Meanwhile prepare the filling. Heat tomato sauce with basil and oregano; reserve. Simmer the sausages in water to cover for 20 minutes. Drain, cool, and remove casings. Slice thinly. Combine the cheeses; reserve.

Divide risen dough in half. Roll out on floured board to make

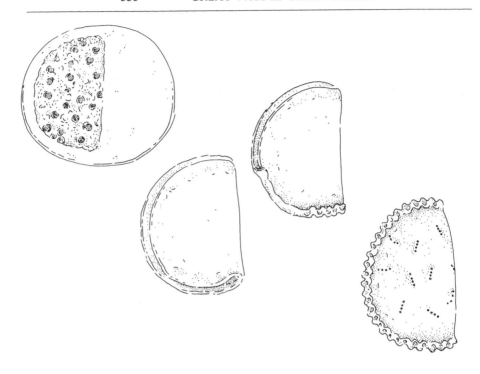

an 11-inch circle. Brush lightly with olive oil and spread half the to-mato sauce over half the dough circle to within ½ inch of the edges. Top sauce with half the sausage and sprinkle each with half the cheese mixture. Fold plain half over filling to within ¼ inch of opposite edge. Roll bottom edge up over top edge and pinch or crimp together to seal. Brush with olive oil. Transfer to baking sheet that has been covered with parchment paper or that is lightly greased. Repeat for other half of dough, using remaining sauce and cheese. Pierce tops with a fork. Preheat oven to 375° F. Bake 20 to 25 minutes or until golden brown.

STUFFED INDIAN PARATHA

The vegetable-stuffed breads of India are ideal for vegetarian menus or simply to be served as a snack, appetizer, or an accompaniment with soups or salads. The fillings are spicy and flavorful. The basic bread is an Indian *paratha*, which is filled, flattened, and fried.

MAKES 16 BREADS

BREAD:

1 cup whole wheat flour	1 teaspoon salt
2½ cups bread flour or	1 cup clarified butter (ghee)*
unbleached all-purpose	¼ cup plain yogurt
flour	1 cup water

In large bowl, combine whole wheat flour, bread flour, salt, and ¼ cup of the melted butter. Mix thoroughly. Add yogurt and enough water to make a stiff dough; turn out onto lightly floured board and knead for 6 to 8 minutes or until smooth. Cover with bowl and set aside for 30 to 40 minutes.

Divide dough into 16 equal portions. Divide each of the 16 into 2 portions. Roll portions into thin, flat circles, 5 to 6 inches in diameter, on lightly floured board. Place 2 tablespoons of one of the following fillings on one of the 32 dough circles, spreading it evenly to within ½ inch of the edges; then cover it with one of the remaining circles. Brush edges with water and seal. Flatten each *paratha* with your hands and roll out gently, being careful that stuffing does not ooze out. Heat an ungreased heavy skillet or griddle and place 1 filled paratha in the pan. Cook about 1 minute, until browned in spots. With a wide spatula, turn over and add 1 tablespoon *ghee* or melted butter. Cook slowly for 2 minutes; turn over again. Add more butter and fry until golden and crisp, and browned on both sides. Fill and fry remaining breads the same way. Serve with chutney.

CAULIFLOWER FILLING: This classic filling has a hot tang to it, which you can control by the amount of green chili and *garam masala* you add to the mixture. If you are not able to get a ready-blended *garam masala* (an Indian spice blend) you can blend your own.

---

* To clarify butter, melt 2 sticks unsalted butter over low heat. Milk solids will fall to bottom. Pour clarified butter (it will be clear) into a cup or jar and discard milky residue.

MAKES FILLING FOR 16 BREADS (ABOUT 2 CUPS)

*2 to 4 tablespoons clarified
    butter or oil*
*1 medium yellow onion, finely
    chopped*
1 large clove garlic, minced
*2½ teaspoons freshly minced
    gingerroot*
Pinch of cumin seeds
*1 green chili, seeded and
    chopped*

*1 small cauliflower, trimmed
    and chopped (about 4
    cups)*
1¼ teaspoons salt
1¼ teaspoons ground cumin
*½ to 1 teaspoon garam
    masala,* or to taste*
¼ teaspoon ground turmeric

Heat butter in skillet; add onion, garlic, gingerroot, cumin seeds, and chili and fry until onion is soft. Add cauliflower, salt, ground cumin, *garam masala* to taste, and turmeric. Fry 2 minutes more; cover and cook until cauliflower is tender but not mushy, about 6 to 8 minutes. Uncover and cook until moisture evaporates. Makes enough filling for one batch of 16 stuffed breads.

POTATO FILLING:

MAKES FILLING FOR 16 STUFFED BREADS (ABOUT 2 CUPS)

*3 to 4 tablespoons butter or
    vegetable oil*
*1 medium yellow onion,
    chopped*
1 to 2 cloves garlic, minced
*½-inch piece gingerroot, finely
    minced*
*3 large potatoes, peeled, boiled,
    and mashed*
2 green chilies, seeded and

*finely chopped, or 1 can
    (3 ounces) chopped green
    chilies*
1¼ teaspoons salt
1¼ teaspoons ground cumin
*1¼ teaspoons chopped fresh
    coriander leaves*
½ teaspoon turmeric
*½ teaspoon garam masala or
    to taste*

* *Garam masala* is a blend of toasted ground spices that varies from cook to cook in India but that usually consists of cardamom, coriander, cinnamon, cloves, black pepper, and cumin. You can buy it in Indian or specialty food shops or you can prepare it at home. Proportions of spices vary but you might want to start with 2 tablespoons of each spice. Toast the whole spices in a low oven for approximately 20 minutes and then, after discarding cardamom pods, grind the spices in a blender until finely pulverized.

Heat butter or oil in frying pan. Add onion, garlic, and gingerroot, and fry until onion is soft. Add mashed potatoes, chilies, salt, cumin, coriander leaves, turmeric, and *garam masala* and fry for 8 minutes or until moisture evaporates. Use filling immediately or cool to room temperature, cover, and hold up to 2 hours before using. If made the day before, cover and refrigerate.

SOUTHWESTERN CORNBREAD

The cornbread in this recipe is really just the crust for a filling of meat, green chilies, and onion. The topping is Monterey Jack cheese; and the end result is a meal in itself. Serve it with pinto or red beans and a tossed green salad. Use fresh, stone-ground cornmeal from an organic or natural food store for the very best results.

MAKES 4 SERVINGS

1 tablespoon butter
1 cup chopped onions
¼ pound lean ground meat
1 can (4 ounces) chopped
    green chilies, drained
¼ cup yellow cornmeal,
    preferably stone-ground
1 egg, beaten

½ cup milk
¾ teaspoon baking soda
½ teaspoon salt
¼ cup diced slab bacon, rind
    removed
1½ cups shredded Monterey
    Jack cheese

In 10-inch frying pan, heat the butter; add the onions and cook over medium heat until onions are soft, about 10 minutes. Add meat and cook until pinkness is gone. Drain off fat. Add the green chilies. In mixing bowl, combine cornmeal, egg, milk, soda, salt, and corn. In another cast-iron skillet, brown the bacon until crisp, about 5 minutes over medium-high heat. Pour half of the cornmeal batter into the skillet. Preheat oven to 375° F. Top with the meat mixture, then add the remaining batter. Sprinkle with cheese and bake 25 to 30 minutes or until bread is lightly browned.

KIELBASA IN RYE

This is excellent as an appetizer, first course, or luncheon main dish. Tasty rye bread encloses a spicy kielbasa sausage, which dramatically appears in each slice of bread, right in the center. Select a sausage that is perfectly straight, since one that is curved might pop out the side of the bread. You can make this bread ahead and freeze it if desired for a party.

MAKES 6 FIRST-COURSE SERVINGS OR 18 COCKTAIL SLICES

RICH RYE BREAD:

1 package active dry yeast
⅓ cup warm water,
    105° F.–115° F.
½ tablespoon sugar
1 teaspoon salt
2 eggs

½ cup butter at room
    temperature
1 cup light or dark rye flour
1½ to 2 cups unbleached
    all-purpose flour

FILLING:

12-inch fully cooked kielbasa
    or garlic sausage,
    skinned

GLAZE:

1 egg

2 tablespoons milk

To prepare bread, in large bowl dissolve yeast in warm water; add sugar, and stir. Let stand 5 minutes until yeast foams. Add salt and eggs; beat well. Cut butter into small pieces and add to liquid. Beat in the rye flour until blended and add all-purpose flour, ½ cup at a time, until flour is evenly moistened and dough holds together in an irregular mass. Shape into a ball and place on floured board. Pick dough up and slap down onto board 100 times until smooth and satiny, or knead for 10 minutes. Wash bowl, grease it, and add dough to bowl;

turn over to grease top and cover. Let rise in a warm place until doubled, 1 to 2 hours. Punch down, knead briefly. On lightly floured board roll dough out to make an oval about 12 inches across and 15 inches long. Place skinned sausage on one narrow end of the dough and roll up, pressing out all the air bubbles as you go. Pinch ends together to seal. Place roll with seam side down onto lightly greased baking sheet. Let rise in a warm place until loaf looks puffy, 45 min to 1 hour. Whisk egg and milk together to make a glaze, then brush loaf with the glaze. Preheat oven to 375° F. Bake 30 to 35 minutes or until golden. Remove from pan and cool on wire rack; serve warm, cut into slices.

INDEX

Beatrice Ojakangas is the author of more than twenty cookbooks, including *The Great Holiday Baking Book, The Great Scandinavian Baking Book,* and *Scandinavian Feasts,* all published by the University of Minnesota Press. Her articles and recipes have appeared in *Bon Appétit, Gourmet, Cooking Light, Cuisine,* and *Redbook,* and she has been a guest on television's *Baking with Julia Child* and *Martha Stewart's Living.* She lives in Duluth, Minnesota.